Men's Friendships

RESEARCH ON MEN AND MASCULINITIES SERIES

Series Editor:
MICHAEL S. KIMMEL, SUNY Stony Brook

Contemporary research on men and masculinity, informed by recent feminist thought and intellectual breakthroughs of women's studies and the women's movement, treats masculinity not as a normative referent but as a problematic gender construct. This series of interdisciplinary, edited volumes attempts to understand men and masculinity through this lens, providing a comprehensive understanding of gender and gender relationships in the contemporary world.

EDITORIAL ADVISORY BOARD

Volumes in this Series

Men's Friendships

Edited by Peter M. Nardi

SAGE PUBLICATIONS
International Educational and Professional Publisher
Newbury Park   London   New Delhi

For information address:

SAGE Publications, Inc.
2455 Teller Road
Newbury Park, California 91320

SAGE Publications Ltd.
6 Bonhill Street
London EC2A 4PU
United Kingdom

SAGE Publications India Pvt. Ltd.
M-32 Market
Greater Kailash I
New Delhi 110 048 India

Printed in the United States of America

Library of Congress Cataloging-in-Publication Data

Men's friendships / edited by Peter M. Nardi.
      p.   cm. — (research on men and masculinities; 2)
    Includes bibliographical references and index.
    ISBN 0-8039-3773-3. — ISBN 0-8039-3774-1 (pbk.)
    1. Men —Psychology. 2. Masculinity (Psychology) 3. Friendship—
Sociological aspects. 4. Men—Family relationships. 5. Men—
Social networks. 6. Homosexuality, Male—Psychological aspects.
I. Nardi, Peter M. II. Series.
HQ1090.M47 1992
302.3'4'081—dc20   91-45060
                                             CIP

93 94 95 96 10 9 8 7 6 5 4 3 2

Sage Production Editor: Judith L. Hunter

Contents

Foreword

This volume is the second volume in the Sage Series on Research on Men and Masculinity. The purpose of the series is to gather together the finest empirical research in the social sciences that focuses on the experiences of men in contemporary society.

Following the pioneering research of feminist scholars over the past two decades, social scientists have come to recognize gender as one of the primary axes around which social life is organized. Gender is now seen as equally central as class and race, both at the macro, structural level of the allocation and distribution of rewards in a hierarchical society, and at the micro, psychological level of individual identity formation and interpersonal interaction.

Social scientists distinguish gender from sex. Sex refers to biology, the biological dimorphic division of male and female; gender refers to the cultural meanings that are attributed to those biological differences. While biological sex varies little, the cultural meanings of gender vary enormously. Thus we speak of gender as socially constructed, the definitions of masculinity and femininity as the products of the interplay among a variety of social forces. In particular, we understand gender to vary spatially (from one culture to another); temporally (within any one culture over historical time); and longitudinally (through any individual's life course). Finally, we understand that different groups within any culture may define masculinity and femininity differently, according to subcultural definitions; race, ethnicity, age, class, sexuality, and region of the country all affect our different gender definitions. Thus it is more accurate to speak of "masculinities" and "femininities" than to posit a monolithic gender construct. It is the goal of this series to explore the varieties of men's experiences, remaining mindful of specific differences among men, and also aware of the mechanisms of power that inform both men's relations with women and men's relations with other men.

Men's friendships are a recurrent theme in discussions of men's lives. How are men's friendships different from women's friendships? What are the obstacles to intimacy between men? What are the key features of men's friendships? How do men's friendships vary among different groups of men? Why does friendship seem so difficult for men to sustain?

These are the questions that inform Peter Nardi's collection, *Men's Friendships*. The authors in the collection use a variety of methods—historical inquiry, psychoanalysis, network analysis, feminist theory—to explore the dynamics and meanings of friendship in men's lives. Several authors detail the ways in which different groups of men, such as black men, gay men, and athletes, manifest different patterns of friendships, and how some of these might be useful to other men in expanding their own friendships.

Several of these articles also shed some light on the recent popular interest in "male bonding," a more temporally limited experience of male-male intimacy in the context of retrieving a mythic "deep" masculinity. In this regard, Spain's article serves as a valuable cautionary tale. In her survey of the anthropological literature, she finds that those cultures in which male bonding rituals are most evident and ritually important are also the cultures in which women's status is lowest. Thus any consideration of male friendships must remain aware that such relationships take place not in the seemingly neutral zone of homosocial intimacy, but are simultaneously played out against a broader canvas of male-female relationships. Even in our most emotionally vulnerable revelations, our experiences with other men are still structured by power and privilege.

MICHAEL S. KIMMEL
Series Editor

1

"Seamless Souls"

An Introduction to Men's Friendships

PETER M. NARDI

When Montaigne described friendship as "souls that mingle and blend with each other so completely that they efface the seam that joined them," he was talking about his friendship with another man. The images of friendships in both myth and everyday life were historically male-dominated. They were characterized in terms of bravery, loyalty, duty, and heroism (see Hammond & Jablow, 1987). This explains why women were often seen as not capable of having "true" friendships. But today the images of ideal friendship are often expressed in terms of women's traits: intimacy, trust, caring, and nurturing, thereby excluding the more traditional men from true friendship (see Sapadin, 1988).

Attempts to alter how men construct their friendships on a wider cultural level involve major shifts in the way men's roles are structured and organized. For one, friendships between men in terms of intimacy and emotional support inevitably introduce—in ways they never had done before—questions about homosexuality. As Rubin (1985, p. 103) found in her interviews with men: "The association of friendship with homosexuality is so common among men." For women, there is a much longer history of close connections with other women, so that the separation of the emotional from the erotic is more easily made.

Lehne (1989) has argued that homophobia has limited the discussion of loving male relationships and has led to the denial by men of the real importance of their friendships with other men. In addition, "the open expression of emotion and affection by men is limited by homophobia. . . . The expression of more tender emotions among men is thought to be characteristic only of homosexuals" (p. 426). So men are raised in a culture with a mixed message: Strive for healthy, emotionally intimate friendships, but be careful—if you appear too intimate with another man you might be negatively labeled homosexual. Part of this has to do with what Herek (1987) calls "heterosexual masculinity," an idea that includes such personal characteristics as independence, dominance, toughness, and success. It also is defined by what it is not—not feminine and not homosexual. Thus, to be masculine in today's culture requires a distancing from any behavior that may indicate homosexuality, including emotionally close friendships with other men.

This certainly wasn't always the case. As a good illustration of the social construction of masculinity, friendship, and sexuality, one need only look to the changing definitions and concepts surrounding same-sex friendship during the nineteenth century (Rotundo, 1989; Smith-Rosenberg, 1975). Romantic friendships could be erotic but not sexual, since sex was linked to reproduction. Because reproduction was not possible between two men, the close relationship was not interpreted as being a sexual one: "Until the 1880s, most romantic friendships were thought to be devoid of sexual content. Thus a woman or man could write of affectionate desire for a loved one of the same gender without causing an eyebrow to be raised" (D'Emilio & Freedman, 1988, p. 121).

However, as same-sex relationships became medicalized and stigmatized in the late nineteenth-century literature, "the labels 'congenital inversion' and 'perversion' were applied not only to male sexual acts, but to sexual or romantic unions between women, as well as those between men" (D'Emilio & Freedman, 1988, p. 122). Thus, the twentieth century is an anomaly in its promotion of female equality, the encouragement of male-female friendships, and its suspicion of intense emotional friendships between men (Richards, 1987). Yet, in ancient Greece and medieval Europe, chivalry, comradeship, virtue, patriotism, and heroism were all associated with close male friendship. Manly love, as it was often called, was a central part of the definition of masculinity (Richards, 1987).

Same-sex friendship between men was highly revered in ancient Greece and during the European Renaissance. Sherrod (1987, p. 231) writes: "Based on literary sources, we can assume that educated Europeans 500 years ago, like educated Greeks 2500 years ago, held a high regard for intimate friendships." Historical evidence also suggests a high level of intimacy and romantic friendships between young men during the nineteenth century. Rotundo (1989, p. 1) quotes Daniel Webster in 1800 calling his best male friend "the partner of my joys, griefs, and affections, the only participator of my most secret thoughts." He argues that such phrases were typical of middle-class men during their youth. Friendship, beyond the companionship of boyhood, evolved into one "based on intimacy, on a sharing of innermost thoughts and secret emotions . . . a friend was a partner in sentiment as well as action" (Rotundo, p. 1).

The romantic nature of male friendships in middle-class nineteenth-century America can in part be explained by the absence of words and concepts for homosexuality. Physically affectionate relationships between men and even the sharing of beds were not uncommon between young men. Since the desire to engage in sexual acts between two men was seen as something beyond human nature, a sexual connection was not made with physical touch or sleeping together. Furthermore, when homosexuality was thought about, it was almost always in terms of a particular sexual act, not an identity or personal characteristic. Rotundo concludes:

> [A] man who wished to kiss or embrace an intimate male friend in bed did not have to worry about giving way to homosexual impulses because he would not assume that he had them. In the Victorian language of touch, a kiss or an embrace was a gesture of strong affection at least as much as it was an act of sexual expression. (p. 10)

However, as distinctions began to be made between homosexuality and heterosexuality in the late nineteenth century—a distinction that was now seen to be rooted in a person's biological and psychological urges, not something that was an external unnatural impulse—the stigma attached to same-sex touch and intimacy grew. By the turn of the century, a form of male relationships was gone: "Romantic male friendship is an artifact of the nineteenth century" (Rotundo, p. 21).

In contrast, contemporary society holds a set of social meanings and prohibitions about homosexuality to such a degree that ordinary touches, and certainly the act of "sleeping together," often are interpreted in homosexual terms when they occur between two men. Thus, studies of friendship today consistently argue that close friendship is rarely experienced by men in our culture.

Bell (1981) believes that gender images, identities, and roles significantly limit the display of certain emotions, especially those viewed as feminine. This leads, then, to restrictions in how friendships are socially constructed. As Allan (1989, p. 73) says, "Given the dominant images there are of what being masculine entails, it is not surprising that ties of friendship between males are based around sociability rather than intimacy."

The changing nature of and imagery associated with male friendships over time and across culture signify the close interaction that exists between the social structure at various historical moments and the articulation of gender roles and sexuality in terms of friendship. Some of the change can be traced to the nature of the socioeconomic and political order, especially as expressed in the world of work. Hegemonic masculinity closely involved defining labor as either "men's work" or "women's work," thus resulting in a tension between the gender order and the class order (Carrigan, Connell, & Lee, 1987).

Some of the change in definitions about masculinity and intimacy can also be linked to the relationship between men and women in different historical periods. As Kimmel (1987, p. 14) stated it: "Although both masculinity and femininity are socially constructed within a historical context of gender relations, definitions of masculinity are historically reactive to changing definitions of femininity." Thus, when changes occurred in how work was organized and how the family was structured, women's roles entered the public sphere and femininity was redefined. Given the relational nature of gender, masculinity in turn began to be reconstructed.

The emergence of sexual political movements, such as gay liberation and the women's movement, in the mid- to late twentieth century was a result of these structural changes and gender redefinitions in the nineteenth century. And these movements further threatened the traditional power relationship not only between men and women but also between men and men, leading to additional questioning of the hegemonic masculinity.

But whatever the actual forces are that have created alterations in men's roles historically, they illustrate one important thesis, namely that as definitions about masculinity change, how friendships are organized by men also is affected. Not only can this be seen historically, but it also points out the importance of looking at men's friendships as equally variable today. If the argument holds that certain social structural elements have contributed to how friendship and gender are constructed over time, then that must also apply within any one time period as well. Variations within gender, based on location within the social structure, should be evident. Allan (1989, p. 71) reasons that "men's position within the social structure tends in the main to encourage the formation of sociable relationships with others, but, at the same time, to restrict the extent to which the self is revealed in them."

The failure of most of the literature on friendship to consider the diversity within gender has led to the global differences traditionally presented in the literature. Women's friends are seen as expressive and men's as instrumental. "Face-to-face" characterizes women's friendship patterns, while "side by side" describes men's. Caldwell and Peplau (1982), in their study of college students' friendships, found that both men and women desired intimacy in their friendships, but differed in what that meant. Men were nearly twice as likely as women to say they preferred "doing some activity" with their best friend and sought a friend who "likes to do the same things." Women chose "just talking" with a friend and someone who "feels the same way about things" as more important aspects of their intimate friendships.

Similar findings are reported when it comes to issues related to disclosure. Davidson and Duberman (1982, p. 817) claim that women disclose more personal information about self, yet "men *perceive* that they are being open and trusting, even though they report little investment in the personal and relational levels of the friendship." But Allan (1989, p. 66) warns that we must be careful in making conclusions about global gender differences in the absence of a more complex analysis of other social structural influences:

> There is, of course, a danger here of "reifying" gender differences by underplaying the other factors which shape people's friendships. . . . [I]n order to analyse friendship satisfactorily it is necessary to examine the range of social and economic factors that pattern an individual's immediate social environment, rather than focusing solely on any particular one. . . . [F]riendship is certainly influenced by gender, but exactly in what way depends on the interaction there is with the other factors that collectively shape the personal space for sociability that people have.

What is needed, therefore, is an analysis of the differences within each of the genders and the social forces that shape the ways friendship is organized. The essays in this book are one such step in this direction. The premise here is that while variations may exist modally between men and women and how they structure their friendships, the variations within each group are greater. To illustrate this argument, this collection represents a variety of perspectives on men's friendships. While some similarities exist, what strikes the reader most clearly is the wide range men have in their friendship. Central to this understanding is the role culture and social structure play in contributing to how friendships differ. For each group discussed, we can see how the social roles of masculinity, the organization of friendship groups, and the meanings these have within the subculture are all shaped by and interact with the social structure.

Perspectives on Men's Friendships

Most of the articles in this collection reflect early stages of research on the topic of men's friendships. Despite years of work on the issue, most of what has already been published tends to focus on global and modal comparisons between men and women. Gender is typically the key variable in studies of friendship. What became clear in the search for articles on men's friendships is how few people have begun with the assumption that there may be greater variation within gender than between genders. Thus, these articles represent the beginning point of what is hoped to be a stronger focus on the diversity that exists within men and how they develop and maintain friendships with other men and women. The articles often raise more questions than they answer.

Historical and Philosophical Views

Friendship as a social concept is subject to variations in how the social order is constructed. This is especially evident when looking at the issue from a historical and philosophical perspective. The first section of the book focuses on philosophical and historical questions related to the topic of men's friendships. In Chapter 2, "Rejection, Vulnerability, and Friendship," Victor Seidler writes that Enlightenment modernity brought a stronger emphasis on privacy and individuality, thereby eliminating the civic, public responsibilities of friendship. He argues that friendship has become a private concern, our identities have been established in individual terms, and friendships no longer bear witness to our identities. Seidler develops his argument that men take friendships for granted because today they are seen as part of the private realm—the background—and not part of the more important public domain in which masculine identities are given meaning. Friendships in men's lives within a culture of modernity have been marginalized into the private realm.

As men, he argues, we learn to maintain power by sustaining an image of self-sufficiency and by denying the importance of others. Men risk rejection and vulnerability by opening up to friends and by expressing emotions and feelings publicly. The threats to self-sufficiency, self-esteem, and independence are partly a function of the changing moral culture and the ways masculinity has been defined in a more public era of modernity.

How the relationship between masculinity and friendship has changed over time is clearly presented in Karen Hansen's chapter, " 'Our Eyes Behold Each Other': Masculinity and Intimate Friendship in Antebellum New England." By looking at an exchange of letters between two young, working-class men in the nineteenth century, Hansen raises provocative questions about gender, class, intimacy, and friendship. Romantic friendships among men were not uncommon and, in many cases, were similar to the intense romantic friendships of middle-class, white women. By historically situating men and the variety of emotions available to them in a particular context of economic and social forces, Hansen shows us not what was necessarily typical of men's friendships in early nineteenth-century New England, but what was possible. Unlike today, the suppression of emotions was not essential to demonstrate manliness. Historical variations in men's experiences illustrate the construction of the boundaries of acceptable masculine behavior and masculinity.

Social Structural Variations

Much of the writing on friendship tends to emphasize a personal or individual approach, thereby underplaying the relationship between friendship and social structure (Allan, 1989). The second part of the book illustrates how strong the connection is between social structure and men's friendships. By introducing such variables as gender. family roles, marital status, dating situations, work roles, and network ties, these chapters present a strong case for getting beyond a simplistic, global description of the nature of men's friendships. In one form or another, each author makes the case that the nature of men's friendships varies depending on specific social structural characteristics.

Daphne Spain's "The Spatial Foundations of Men's Friendships and Men's Power" introduces a fascinating variable to the traditional list of age, race, gender, and class. She argues that "spatial separation" can reinforce certain social distinctions, which can affect solidarity and friendship formation. Spain hypothesizes that male friendships are strongest in societies with a high degree of gender segregation, and that men's power relative to women is reinforced when spatial separation enhances male friendships.

Spain tests her ideas by examining the presence of men's ceremonial huts in 81 nonindustrial societies, and the relationship between measures of "male solidarity" and men's formal and informal power. She speculates about this relationship in contemporary society and the implications gendered spatial arrangements have today for enhancing male solidarity and power.

The relationship between social structure and friendship is forcefully illustrated in "Men in Networks: Private Communities, Domestic Friendships" by Barry Wellman and his collaborators. He argues that men's friendships are linked to changes in the nature of community. Specifically, he feels that friendships operate in today's social world out of households rather than in public places. Wellman explores this premise by focusing on men's personal community network of active relationships, including kin, neighbors, workmates, and female friends. As men's friendships move into the house, friendships no longer are primarily about accomplishing important things (such as economic or political survival), but they become ends in themselves. To see friendship in terms of openness and companionship, rather than about the comradely virtues of skills at doing things, is a result of the growing dominance of the service sector in the economy over the manipulation of material goods, Wellman argues. In short, there is a strong relationship between structural changes in society and various forms of friendships for men.

Theodore Cohen illustrates a similar point in his chapter, "Men's Families, Men's Friends: A Structural Analysis of Constraints on Men's Social Ties." He develops the argument that when friendships compete with other social roles and relationships for men's time and loyalty, friendships frequently lose. These external, structural factors that shape men's opportunities for and maintenance of friendship include the impact of marriage, fatherhood, and work roles. Cohen explores the family and work lives of 30 married men through a series of semistructured interviews, focusing in particular on the entrance into marriage and into fatherhood. The role marriage plays and the time fatherhood entails gradually lead to a consolidation of their emotional lives in their marriages and children, away from peer relationships.

Just as changes in family and marriage roles affect the amount of time men have for developing and maintaining friendships, so too do these changes affect how and what men disclose with their friends. Helen Reid and Gary Alan Fine investigate this issue by interviewing 16 men about their cross-sex friends in "Self-Disclosure in Men's Friendships: Variations Associated with Intimate Relations." Rather than assume that all men have some essential difficulty in self-disclosing, Reid and Fine began with the sociological premise that certain structural conditions might account for variations in the way men disclose with friends. They argue that self-disclosure is partly a role phenomenon related to whether the men have an intimate other whose expectations must be met. The maintenance of intimate relationships through norms of exclusivity, Reid and Fine explain, and access to one with whom the men can focus personal disclosures directly affect the amount and quality of cross-sex friendships. In other words, men do indeed disclose to friends, both male and female, when the men are neither married nor intimately involved with someone romantically.

Clearly, the gender of one's friends is a key structural variable that defines and constrains the nature of friendship. Yet, there is relatively less research on the subject of cross-sex friendships. Scott Swain's "Men's Friendships with Women: Intimacy, Sexual Boundaries, and the Informant Role," addresses the issue and shows how this "subversive activity" can create social change in gender-based behavior. He argues that men's friendships with women tend to modify masculine-typed restrictions on ways of expressing affection and intimacy. Typically, these friendships center on problem solving and disclosing about heterosexual love relationships. Thus, friends serve as informants by sharing and sensitizing each other to their styles of intimacy. Swain feels that close cross-sex friendships present an opportunity for men to expand the limits of rigid conceptions of masculinity and to explore emotional areas and issues of dependency.

Cultural Diversity

If such structural variables as gender, marital status, spatial segregation, work roles, and community ties can affect how men's friendships are constructed and maintained, then surely subcultural and cross-cultural differences based on sexual orientation, race, and ethnicity should also mediate them (see Gilmore, 1990). The third part of the book focuses on cultural diversity in men's friendships.

Too often, research on friendship assumes a heterosexual perspective. The arguments traditionally made in the scant literature on cross-sex friendships about men's friendships with women almost always take the perspective of heterosexual attraction. My article on "Sex, Friendship, and Gender Roles Among Gay Men" introduces sexual orientation as an important variable to consider in the discussion of men's friendships. In particular, I look at the issue of sex among friends, an issue that usually is a key topic in the discussions of cross-sex friendships but is virtually left unresearched. An interesting form of this can be studied when looking at the friendships of gay men. Since people typically have friends of the same gender and since gay men are sexually attracted to people of the same gender, the topic of sex and friendship can easily be studied among a group of gay men.

In the process of studying this issue, there are further questions raised about the connections between gender roles and sexual orientation, in particular, how concepts of masculinity are shaped by and, in turn, shape cultural concepts of homosexuality and heterosexuality. By uncovering the dynamics of men's friendships and sex, much is learned about men's roles and masculinity.

Similar evidence emerges in Walter Williams' chapter, "The Relationship Between Male-Male Friendship and Male-Female Marriage: American Indian and Asian Comparisons." Challenging the notion that men are incapable of close, intimate friendships with other men, Williams first discusses cultures in which men's friendships are more intimate. He then focuses on same-sex friendships among North American Indians and shows where many men typically get their intimate needs met more by male friends than by wives.

Williams also makes the argument that in many cultures there are two types of close bonds—structured mixed-sex marriage-kinship systems and unstructured same-sex friendship networks—that work to complement and strengthen each other, rather than to compete for time, as several of the articles on marital status in Part Two of this book demonstrated. He illustrates this proposition by describing a Javanese wedding and marriage and how it relates to same-sex friendships.

Clyde Franklin's "Hey, Home—Yo, Bro: Friendship Among Black Men" discusses the meanings of masculinity among a group of working-class and upwardly mobile African-Americans and relates these to their friendship networks. Research on black men's friendships is virtually nonexistent, yet exploratory research by Franklin suggests some interesting variations based on race and class. Working-class friendships among African-American men are often self-disclosing and close, in part due to a shared political ideology. Among upwardly mobile men, however, acceptance of society's definitions of traditional masculinity result in a loss of male-male friendships both quantitatively and qualitatively, Franklin argues. For some, race is the variable that helps structure men's friendships; for others, class becomes the organizing characteristic. One subculture that provides a fascinating perspective on men's friendships is the world of athletics. One of the primary components of how masculinity is defined in our culture is the relationship to sports. How this, in turn, contributes to the way friendship is structured is the focus of Michael Messner's "Like Family: Power, Intimacy, and Sexuality in Male Athletes' Friendships." He begins by urging us to go beyond either a "feminine" standard of understanding men's friendships or a "separate but equal" approach, and to ask the feminist question about how these male friendship patterns fit into an overall system of power. He illustrates this perspective by examining both the quality of men's friendships with each other and the ways these friendships shape men's attitudes and relationships with women.

In so doing, Messner uncovers the gender dimensions of the sports subculture and how it relates to the social process of masculine gender identity construction. He also describes the development of a kind of "covert intimacy," which needs to be assessed not in masculine or feminine terms, but in the larger context of structured power relations between men and women, and between men and other men.

These chapters together present a variety of perspectives on the issue of men's friendships. They are speculative, exploratory, and suggestive of the kind of research that needs to be done. They go beyond research that uses gender or sex roles as demographic variables. These studies reorganize existing knowledge and introduce newer perspectives within a framework of men's studies that sees masculinity and men's roles as socially and historically constructed and views masculinity and femininity as relational concepts (see Kimmel, 1987).

Acknowledgments

My involvement in editing this volume began years ago when Drury Sherrod discussed his own work on men's friendships with me. His articles, his ideas, and his enthusiasm for the topic got me interested in the field and started my own thinking about it. Michael Kimmel's work in men's studies also began appearing. Conversations with him furthered my excitement about the area and resulted in his suggestion of editing this book. To both of them, my sincere thanks for introducing me to new intellectual subjects.

The actual process of reviewing and soliciting articles is not a solitary activity. Assistance and encouragement came from Lourdes Arguelles, Glenn Goodwin, Kelly Jones, Ruben Martinez, Stuart McConnell, Stephen Murray, Al Schwartz, Susan Seymour, Steven Smith, and Neil Albright.

A SONG

1

Come, I will make the continent indissoluble;
I will make the most splendid race the sun ever yer shone upon;
I will make divine magnetic lands,
        With the love of comrades,
        With the life-long love of comrades.

2

I will plant companionship thick as trees along all the rivers of
        America, and along the shores of the great lakes, and all
        over the prairies;
I will make inseparable cities, with their arms about each other's
        necks;
        By the love of comrades,
        By the manly love of comrades.

3

For you these, from me, O Democracy, to serve you, ma
        femme!
For you! for you, I am trilling these songs,
        In the love of comrades,
        In the high-towering love of comrades

WALT WHITMAN
First published in 1860

I DREAM'D IN A DREAM

I Dream'd in a dream, I saw a city invincible to the attacks of
the whole of the rest of the earth;
I dream'd that was the new City of Friends;
Nothing was greater there than the quality of robust love—it led
the rest;
It was seen every hour in the actions of the men of that city,
And in all their looks and words.

WALT WHITMAN
First published in 1860

References

Allan, G. (1989). *Friendship: Developing a sociological perspective.* Boulder, CO: Westview.

Bell, R. (1981). *Worlds of friendship.* Beverly Hills, CA: Sage.

Caldwell, M., & Peplau, L. A. (1982). Sex differences in same-sex friendships. *Sex Roles, 8*(7), 721-732.

Carrigan, T., Connell, R., & Lee, J. (1987). Hard and heavy: Toward a new sociology of masculinity. In M. Kaufman (Ed.), *Beyond patriarchy* (pp. 139-192). Toronto: Oxford University Press.

Davidson, L., & Duberman, L. (1982). Friendship: Communication and interactional patterns in same-sex dyads. *Sex Roles, 8*(8), 809-822.

D'Emilio, J., & Freedman, E. (1988). *Intimate matters: A history of sexuality in America.* New York: Harper & Row.

Gilmore, D. (1990). *Manhood in the making: Cultural concepts of masculinity.* New Haven: Yale University Press.

Hammond, D., & Jablow, A. (1987). Gilgamesh and the Sundance Kid: The myth of male friendship. In H. Brod (Ed.), *The making of masculinities: The new men's studies* (pp. 241-258). Boston: Allen & Unwin.

Herek, G. (1987). On heterosexual masculinity: Some psychical consequences of the social construction of gender and sexuality. In M. Kimmel (Ed.), *Changing men: New directions in research on men and masculinity* (pp. 68-82). Newbury Park, CA: Sage.

Kimmel, M. (1987). Rethinking "masculinity": New directions in research. In M. Kimmel (Ed.), *Changing men: New directions in research on men and masculinity* (pp. 9-24). Newbury Park, CA: Sage.

Lehne, G. (1989). Homophobia among men: Supporting and defining the male role. In M. Kimmel & M. Messner (Eds.), *Men's lives* (pp. 416-429). New York: Macmillan.

Richards, J. (1987). "Passing the love of women": Manly love and Victorian society. In J. A. Mangan & J. Walvin (Eds.), *Manliness and morality: Middle-Class masculinity in Britain and America 1800-1940)* (pp. 92-122). Manchester, England: Manchester University Press.

Rotundo, A. (1989). Romantic friendships: Male intimacy and middle-class youth in the northern United States, 1800-1900. *Journal of Social History, 23*(1), 1-25.

Rubin, L. (1985). *Just friends: The role of friendship in our lives.* New York: Harper & Row.

Sapadin, L. (1988). Friendship and gender: Perspectives of professional men and women. *Journal of Social and Personal Relationships, 5*(4), 387-403.

Sherrod, D. (1987). The bonds of men: Problems and possibilities in close male relationships. In H. Brod (Ed.), *The making of masculinities: The new men's studies* (pp. 213-239). Boston: Allen & Unwin.

Smith-Rosenberg, C. (1975). The female world of love and ritual: Relations between women in nineteenth-century America. *Signs, 1*(1), 1-29.

2

Rejection, Vulnerability, and Friendship

VICTOR J. SEIDLER

The Need for Friends

Within a liberal moral culture, acknowledging our need for friends can be difficult. As men we grow up learning to be independent and self-sufficient. Friendship grows out of shared interests and otherwise is often marginal to our identity. The meaning of our lives is given by the ends and goals that we have set for ourselves through reason. This means that we learn to do without others. We learn to do without friends. We learn to identify ourselves with the work that we do within the public realm. Much of our sense of ourselves is drawn from our achievements within this public realm of work, and we use this to help us deal with our feelings of guilt and isolation when it comes to our friendships. We learn not to acknowledge our need for friends and at some level to regard this need as a sign of weakness. Even if we would welcome friendship, we learn to live without it.

Often it can be difficult to admit our isolation and loneliness because to do so would make us seem vulnerable and can leave us feeling bad about ourselves. It is often easier for us to think that we really do not need the friendship of others and that we are surviving well without it. To acknowledge these feelings is to admit that we are not in control of our lives, and we learn to want to have this control. As Stuart Miller says in his insightful book, *Men and Friendship*:

> Most men, particularly if they think about it, if they let themselves feel their personal truth about it, will admit that they are disappointed in their friendships with other men. Men may have wives, they may even have women friends,

but their relationships with other men, which could be a true echo of their own manhood, are generally characterised by thinness, insincerity and even chronic wariness. (1983, p. xi)

I want to explore some of the sources of this wariness, and I want to connect it to an abiding fear of rejection and vulnerability.

Miller's (p. xii) method is "warmer and less systematic, more inward and intimate than those of . . . other authors." As he says, "I could find no other way to get at the truth about friendship between men." It is a strength of his book that he seeks ways of illuminating the emotional realities of friendship that are often missing in academic studies. He records how men will often glow "when one brings up the topic of friendship" and are visibly glad to contemplate the subject and to discuss it while at the same time they find it hard to talk about what friendship means to them. He reports a common exchange:

Q: Do you have friends?   *A*: A few.

Q: Tell me about them.   *A*: There's really not much to tell.

Q: Why do you like them?   *A*: Well, they're nice. We have fun together, share interests.

Q: Are they important to you?   *A*: Sure.

Miller acknowledges that there is much more to say but somehow most men find the subjects "unutterable." There is an avoidance that has to do with the difficulty of the feelings that this topic raises for men. He also shows the limits of methods within sociology that confine themselves to the language that people utter. Often what is not said is as significant as what is spoken. It will be difficult for us to develop qualitative methods within sociology until we explore ways of grasping the emotional realities within people's lives. These are too often derided and devalued as "personal" or "subjective." They fall out of the research practice. This is one reason why the issues raised by men's friendships with each other promise to throw light upon crucial questions about the development of a qualitative method within sociology.

Miller found that for men it can be difficult to talk about friendship. He thinks that this difficulty is "partly . . . a lack of poetry in most men. They do not have the words for such a subject. Partly it is a taboo against looking at something so sacred. Often it is a reluctance to look at something so painful." (p. xiii) The point is that most men do not let themselves think or feel about friendship. We learn to put away our early memories as childish things, though, as Miller discovered, "all men secretly cherish the memories." (p. xi) We remember the time when we believed in true friendship and when we thought we had got it. Miller reminds us of the cry of the four musketeers who promised "all for one and one for all." With a smile we can all remember these words but, as Miller has it:

> Over the years, the pain of men's loneliness, the weakening of their male ties, the gradually accumulating disillusionment with male friends, the guilt at their own betrayals of others, are just ignored. Partly it is a result of resignation. We lower our expectations. The older we get the more we accept our essential friendlessness with men. (p. xi)

The thinness of men's relationships with each other and the ways that they seem to be constantly undermined through competition and jealousy are distinctive features of modern society. Historically, there have been many times in which men's relationships with each other were much more passionate and involved. It is important to be both historically specific about these processes and careful about the class and ethnic background of the men that we are thinking about. At the same time, there are significant processes within modernity that have their source in the particular identification between masculinity and reason. Within modernity men have learned to see reason as their own possession. It is partly because of this that we learn to feel easy in thinking about friendship in terms of shared interests that seem to be objective. It is harder for us to focus upon the emotional dimensions of friendship. This reflects the difficulties that we have as men in dealing with the emotional aspects of our relationships and, in turn, is reflected within a social theory that has a language of relationships that is often a matter of rules within a Durkheimian tradition, or of meanings within a Weberian tradition. Both rules and meanings have traditionally been conceived within rationalist terms. It is partly because of this that we have learned to look to women to interpret our emotional experience for us.

As men, acknowledging our need for friendship can be difficult because this need mirrors our image of ourselves. Our relationships with men are often about *doing things* with them. This is not to underestimate the importance in male friendships of shared activities. It is often an important quality of men's relationships with each other that we have the ability to "hang out" with each other without apparent pressure. But we often feel uncomfortable when emotional issues emerge in our relationships with men and we will often stay silent about them. We might talk about them with our women friends more easily than we would talk about them with other men. This is partly because of the competitive character of our relationships with other men and the feeling that if we let other men know what we feel, they could easily use this knowledge against us. In our relationships with women, we can often make ourselves vulnerable in bringing up these emotional issues because we can assume to have a certain control within these relationships about how this knowledge might be used. We look toward women to provide us with an emotional understanding that we can find difficult to achieve for ourselves. But often the dependency that this leaves us in as men is something that we are quite blind to.[1]

So it can become difficult to separate our consideration of friendship between men from our sense of men's relationships with women. Perceptions may have changed under the influence of feminism, but men have been slow to learn about how to take more responsibility for their emotional lives. As heterosexual relationships have moved into a period of crisis, men have increasingly been forced to learn about drawing support and understanding from relationships with other men because women have increasingly refused to provide this emotional work.

Self-Esteem and Rejection

Why do so many men say that they are closer to women than to men? It can seem as if men do not need relationships with other men because they have relationships with women. Men often trust their relationships with women in a way that they cannot trust their relationships with other men. This point has a direct bearing upon our thinking about the *quality* of our friendships with men. The inescapability of competition seems to undermine our relationships with men. At some level it seems difficult to avoid envy of the achievements of our friends since their successes seem to reflect upon our own self-esteem and sense of self-worth. Sometimes it is as if we would prefer not to know how our friends are doing, because we end up feeling bad that we cannot in an uncomplicated way feel good for them. We would want to wish them well, but somehow we find it hard to do. This is particularly acute in middle-class friendship between men.

We can end up feeling bad about ourselves for not being able to be more generous in our feelings.

It is easy for our competitive feelings to undermine the friendships that we are developing. Possibly it would be easier if we could acknowledge these competitive feelings in our relationships, but often we deny them because these feelings reflect badly on ourselves. It is as if we want to secure our friendships as a space within which competition does not operate, though in the public world of work we recognize how significant competitive relationships are within a capitalist economy. As Max Weber illuminated in *The Protestant Ethic and the Spirit of Capitalism*, there is an important connection at a level of identity with a Protestant ethic that constantly leaves us feeling inadequate in ourselves. We only know that we are doing well if we can be convinced that we are doing *better* than others. We learn to develop a sense of self in relation to others. As men we seem to have a particularly strong connection to this Protestant ethic.[2]

Our friendships are formed partly in the context of competitive relationships. This is what makes us wary in our relationships with men, because everything we do seems to reflect back upon our sense of adequacy and self-worth. Maintaining some distance in our relationships feels safer. This seems to be a way of preventing us from the judgments that can too easily flow from the achievements of our friends. It also reflects upon the ways in which our identities as men are fixed through our work within the public realm, so that we can maintain a distance from our friendships, which are seen as part of the private realm and therefore not bearing directly upon our sense of identity and self-worth. It is partly because of this that we can do without our friendships. They are seen as additional embellishments to our lives, which can make our lives fuller than they would otherwise be. This can also help explain how it is that friendships seem to remain more marginal or secondary, particularly within middle-class men's lives. We live in contradiction between verbally acknowledging the importance of our friendships, which, within a culture of modernity, are marginalized into the private realm, and our experience of the public realm within which our identities as men are firmly fixed.[3]

Thinking about these issues more personally, I have some old friends, some of whom stretch back to when I was a teenager. But also I am not good at friendships. Friendship is something I still need to learn, though I am struck how, within a liberal moral culture, we tend to think of friendship as something that simply happens to us, as if we either have friends or we do not have any. It is not something that we ever learn about, in a similar way that we never really learn how to have relationships. As men we never learn how to *cultivate* our friendships or to recognize that our friendships need to be constantly fed and nourished. We unceasingly take them for granted, as they are part of the private realm, part of the background that we assume, and from which we move into the public realm where "important" things happen for us in relation to our identities. We never learn to pride ourselves in being good at friendship because, within the split between public and private that is so integral to modernity, we never learn to value or give meaning to these aspects of our experience, even if we pay lip service to them.

I am continually having to learn the same lesson, that if friendship is important to me then I have to give it time and attention. There seems to be a process of falling away or discontinuity in my friendships, such that I always seem to be building anew. I find it difficult to take the initiative, such as calling someone on the telephone or inviting a friend out. At some level I fear rejection. I grew up in a family of four brothers, so that there was always enough to do with them. Because I had so many brothers, I did not feel a need to have friends. Similarly, I have often found it easier to operate in the context of groups or collectives, because here again there is less need to learn to take individual initiative, which could mean rejection. The people that I lived with often became the center of my life and everyday activity and in that way often took up the energies that might otherwise have gone toward friendships.

Friendship and Discontinuity

Chodorow's (1979) work helps us think about the ways boys learn their masculinity in separating from their mothers and in learning a negative definition of masculinity. Emotions and feelings tend to be identified with the mother and so with the feminine, and we learn our masculinity in making a break with these qualities.[4] At some level we learn that to be a man means to be able to live an independent and self-sufficient life, and so to live without relationships. Where we are ready to acknowledge the importance of relationships, it becomes difficult to acknowledge the emotions and feelings that go along with them, particularly the dependency that we can feel. We can want to have these relationships without having to feel too dependent upon them, so that we can always learn to live without relationships. This relates to the question of discontinuity because we think that at any moment we might be forced to live without relationships, without the love and support that we draw from them. This is part of the image of masculinity as hero. Sometimes this form of masculinity can shape our friendships with men so that we never really risk ourselves within them. We can feel safer because we have not made ourselves vulnerable.

There are some friends that I can go without seeing for months, but when we meet we can *connect* at a deep level. We can talk and understand each other and we can share ourselves and our experience with each other. This seems to happen despite the time that has gone by when we have not seen each other at all. We can take up where we left off months back. With other friends it is harder, and contact feels more locked; there are more silences and unexpressed feelings.

Friendships between men take on many different forms that need to be explored. Sometimes it can be difficult to communicate the changes we have experienced within ourselves and our lives because we can be fixed in a particular way within a particular relationship. We can find it hard to share these new aspects of ourselves because to do so can be threatening to the form that a particular friendship has taken. Similarly we have to recognize that friendships can have a natural cycle, especially when we have outgrown a particular relationship or when communication has been blocked because both partners have grown away from each other. This can be painful to acknowledge, particularly if the friendship is long-standing and to give it up would seem a great loss. But friendships have a way of going in and out of focus. Letting them go, so as to make space for something new in our relationships to develop, is often necessary. Establishing new relationships in our late thirties and early forties can be particularly daunting, since most people seem to hang onto relationships that were formed when they were at college.

As men we tend to be self-contained so that we do not ask our friends for support, even when we need it. We may be ready to share ourselves only in desperate or extreme situations. To make ourselves vulnerable is to take a risk that we have learned to avoid. Our female friends or partners can be left feeling useless or "left out," and our men friends often feel as if there is very little that they can do for us. It is precisely because we make so few demands on our relationships that others can find it difficult to make demands upon us. One of the ways that we sustain power and control in relationships is by overtly demanding very little. Others then are likely to feel bad because of the demands they are ready to make on us. This holding back is an aspect of the way our denial of our needs serves to structure the power that, as men, we maintain in our relationships.

We maintain our power through sustaining an image of ourselves as self-sufficient. However important we say others are to us, we deny this in our behavior toward them. This can make them feel insecure in their relationship with us, because they are left feeling that they care so much more about us than we seem to care about them. Simmel was one of the few classical sociologists who was prepared to investigate the different ways that men and women invest their emotional energy in their relationships. According to Simmel, the vision of objectivity that we inherit within the human sciences has a particular relationship to masculinity.[5] As men we seem able to put our relationships aside because so much of our identity is invested in work. Women typically find it much harder to leave emotions and feelings behind when they have had an upsetting conflict in a relationship. As men we learn to separate or cut off from these emotions in order to focus upon the work before us.

This does not mean that our relationships with men are not important to us, but the ways that they are important might differ. It becomes important for men to be able to go out or do things with each other, go to the pub or go fishing together, and men can feel a strong loyalty or bonding with their mates. But this loyalty seems to have a different basis because it often does not grow out of personal and intimate knowledge of the other person. It seems more common for women to connect with each other on an everyday basis than it is for men. Often it is part of male friendship for men to be there for each other without really challenging each other emotionally. Often we want our friends to be there for us and we are ready to support them in a similar way.

Sometimes these relationships can be collusive, particularly when it is a matter of complaining or grumbling about women. We sometimes appeal to a masculine consensus that men "know what women are like," or that "you can't trust them, can you?" where what we are looking for at another level is reassurance in our relationships with men. Men learn to share with each other more emotionally, sometimes only with drink when a man, for instance, is "down in the dumps," but even here men fear rejection if they show themselves. In part, a fear of rejection goes along with the competitive institutions at work, and men often want friendship to be an area of life where they will not be rejected or even fear rejection. Men want to feel safe with each other in a way in which they perhaps cannot be with women.

Gender differences are significant because it is often in relationships with women that men have to deal with unfamiliar emotions and feelings. If a woman says "I hate my life" or "I hate the way we live," then often men will see it as their role to be reassuring or to find some kind of solution for the situation, saying "it won't be so bad." Men are less used to dealing with this emotional level because of the ways that masculinity is tied up with rationality. Thus, a woman might say, "I have a right to feel this way, to have my murderous or angry feelings." For men this often seems unreasonable or extreme, and we can feel that we have to moderate the situation. Often this is because we cannot deal with these feelings within ourselves and we never learned to acknowledge that emotions have a logic of their own.

Within modernity we learn as man that our emotions have to be rational before we can really allow ourselves to have them. We learn to protect ourselves against these feelings because they so readily bring into question our very sense of masculine identity. To have feelings is in itself threatening to our male identity. Often we have not learned to *know* ourselves in these emotional ways, and our relationships with men can often provide security against these feelings.

As men we learn to provide solutions for the feelings that our partners have. So for instance, if our partner says that she is feeling frustrated or depressed, we might see it as our task to show her that there is no "reason" for her to feel this way. But often all our partners want is to be heard and for their emotions to be recognized and validated. They can resent the fact that we are offering them solutions when they have not asked for this kind of help. But this can make us feel resentful because we have tried to help in the ways that we know. This way of relating creates difficulties in communicating in our relationships with men. We find it hard to give the kind of emotional support that men are used to getting from women. This goes some way to explaining the frustration that men can feel in their relationships with other men.

Men sometimes find it difficult to relate to each other more emotionally or to give support. Learning to *listen* to our friends can be difficult because we assume that what is being called for is a solution to a problem that they are bringing to us. Through therapy, men often learn the meaning of support and so redefine their relationships with each other. As women withdraw their support from men and expect men to give support to each other, so a new generation under the impact of feminism has learned to communicate more openly with each other. But this is still threatening for many men.

Friendship and Vulnerability

Men find it hard to be vulnerable and to ask for support in their friendships because they can feel that it is wrong to talk about emotional or personal relationships with women. We learn to treat these issues as private and as something that has to be solved in the relationship itself. It is harder for us to acknowledge that the difficulties we have in our relationships might well be shared by other men. We learn to conceal the difficulties we have out of a fear that they will reflect badly upon us and that our friends might even reject us if they knew what we were really like. So it is that we learn to treat friendship, somewhat paradoxically, as part of our public life and relationships. This seems to separate out men's relationships with each other from the relationships that women often have. As men we are often on our "best behavior" when we are with our male friends. This can help illuminate some of the tensions and contradictions in modern friendships between men, for it helps us to appreciate the difficulties men have in sharing their vulnerability. So men will typically not share the details of their intimate relationships, especially in relation to women, when they are with their men friends. They will treat this as personal and therefore as something that they have to sort out on their own. It may seem unreasonable to make demands on men friends to hear about conflicts in these areas of their lives. This is changing slowly, but men can still feel indebted in a way that can make them feel uncomfortable, as if something is owed that will have to be paid back. This discomfort connects to a fear of dependency that men have, as if friendships will be undermined or will not take the strain of such inequality.

Men's difficulty in sharing themselves is striking. Sharing seems to prove our inadequacy as men for it can show a failure to be able to deal with our lives on our own. We worry that we may not live up to our image of ourselves as independent and self-sufficient. This distance from our emotional experience is deeply embedded within modernity and explains in part the *difficulties* that men have in relationships. It also provides the larger context within which we can understand our difficulties in our relationships with our fathers. Chodorow (1979) argues that boys' relationships with their fathers are often abstract because fathers are not involved in an ongoing way with their children. Father absence creates an experience of discontinuity where boys are striving to compare themselves with their fathers. Chodorow takes this to be a source of the difficulties that boys and, later, men have in sustaining continuous relationships, including relationships men can form with each other.

As boys we often have to contend with the disappointment of our fathers not having been there for us. We have to learn to accept the necessities of their work and a sense that what really matters to them takes place outside the context of the family. We often learn to be resigned and simply to accept whatever they have to offer us. Our anger can often feel impotent, especially if it brings punishment. But this can be a way of gaining attention from our fathers, for at least it is a form of contact. We can go to great lengths to engage our fathers in more of an ongoing relationship, but often this effort fails. It is striking how few men feel that, when they were boys, they had a rich and fulfilling relationship with their fathers. Often we seek attention from our fathers when all that we really need is contact; all we want to do is spend time with them. Perhaps we spend hours silently filling the shelves of our fathers's shop, or helping him out in a workshop simply to be close. The need for contact may not be articulated or even experienced clearly.

As children we are relatively powerless, so that our anger at not being recognized or related to by our fathers simply gets us in trouble. We learn to suppress this anger, so much so that we fail to recognize it at all. We put up with what is offered to us and somehow learn to feel grateful. It is training for accepting very little in our relationships. As we grow up, we come to have few expectations in our friendships with men. We find it hard to trust these relationships out of a fear that we will be disappointed. We can find ourselves testing these relationships, as if it is hard to believe that our friends will really be there for us. Because our fathers were often not there for us, it is difficult to trust our relationships with men. We hide the pain that we carry from our childhood and learn to expect very little. We learn to cope on our own and, at some level, we expect in the end to be on our own if things get really tough.

It is hard to make ourselves vulnerable in our relationships if we feel that we might be hurt yet again. As Miller (1983) suggests, most men are so used to living without a true and genuine friendship that they do not even recognize what they miss. This loss is too painful to see, and it involves too many risks for us to initiate a new relationship. We conceal our own vulnerability and, as men, we learn to fear it because it reflects upon our very sense of male identity because it is inevitably taken as a sign of weakness. We learn to live without the support and love of our male friends. We do not expect too much from them and we learn to live without support.

Within modernity we learn to think of friendships in possessive and quantitative terms. We like to think of ourselves as "having friends" and we feel bad about thinking that we might not have good friends. But it is hard to think about relationships in *qualitative* terms, so that we think about the quality of our friendships and what needs are being met through individual relationships. Having learned to think about wants and desires in utilitarian terms, we rarely learn to think of the deeper ways that we are nourished by our friendships. This language of relationships seems out of places within a utilitarian culture, and social theory has found few ways of reinstating it. In this context Simmel's work is significant because he attempts to provide a qualitative language for social theory.

Friendship and Value

Within a tradition of Enlightenment modernity, we tend to see the ends and goals of individual life as chosen by reason alone. Through reason, we supposedly establish our values. This tradition makes it difficult to recognize our feelings as a source of meaning and value. Emotions tend to be treated as personal and subjective, and therefore not as a source of knowledge. Within a Kantian framework we learn to subordinate our inclinations, our feelings and desires, so as to be able to achieve the ends and goals that have been set by reason alone. Kant provides a secularized form of Protestantism, which means that salvation has been replaced by individualistic conceptions of achievement and success. Happiness will supposedly be achieved with the realization of these goals.

Reflecting upon our friendships with men is a potential challenge to this tradition because we can begin to see friendship as a source of meaning and value. We can reflect upon the ways we have learned to subordinate our friendships and to think that the meaning of our lives is to be given in terms of our individually defined ends and goals. This helps to explain the ways that we have grown up to either sacrifice or subordinate our friendships since, within a Kantian framework, these are treated as hindrances to our individually achieved moral worth. To rely upon our friendships is to show that we have failed as individuals to achieve on our own terms. This places friendship in a negative light, and we are led into thinking that asking others to help us is a sign of weakness and reflects badly upon ourselves. Within this ethic that informs both a Weberian and a Durkheimian tradition in sociology, our relationships with others are seen in contingent terms. Our friendships with men are incapable of providing meaning and value in our lives, since the source of these is individualistically defined.

As we learn to reevaluate our friendships and acknowledge the potential importance of our friendships to us, we begin to recognize friendship as a source of meaning and value. This process helps us to question the individualistic orientation that has been central within a capitalist culture. We can learn to conceive of our lives in different terms and to question the possessive vision of individualism, which sees the meaning of our lives in terms of infinite success and possessions. As we develop a sense of the value of being with our friends, we can come to question an emphasis upon doing. Within a Protestant moral culture we are constantly doing things in order to assuage our feeling of inadequacy and worthlessness. It is as if constant activity provides a way of filling a black hole. This leaves us with a sense of inadequacy that affects our friendships because, at some level, we are left feeling that if others "really knew" what we were like, they would not want to be our friends.

This is the fear of rejection that haunts masculine identity within a Protestant culture. We learn to conceal our negative feelings and fantasies out of a fear that others would reject us if they were to know what we were really like. It is this negative vision of human nature that is institutionalized within a Protestant culture. We experience our natures as untrustworthy, knowing them to be evil, so it also becomes hard to trust our friendships. Because our friends "do not really know who we are," we do not trust their perceptions of us. We are left feeling that they will be there for us as long as they do not really know who we are.

A focus upon activities has become central to dominant forms of masculinity. As men we are left feeling that we have to be doing things. This helps structure our friendships as a constant set of demands and activities. Simply to *be with* our friends is difficult because being in this way can make us anxious. Partly because we cannot trust that our friends really accept us, we constantly feel we have to *do things* within the relationship. There is an underlying sense of tension and insecurity because we are left feeling that it is only because of what we do for others that our friendship is sustained. At an unspoken level, we can be haunted by a feeling that our friends do not really know who we are and that if they did, they would surely reject us. This is part of a Protestant inheritance that helps create a tension and unease in our friendships by building within us a radically individualized and isolated sense of self.

A way of coping with these unspoken tensions is to be constantly active in our friendships and to see ourselves as willing to help or do things whenever we are asked. But it can be hard to trust our friends and make ourselves vulnerable to them, because within a Protestant culture, it can be difficult to trust ourselves. We have learned at an unconscious level that our natures are not to be trusted and that if we give in to our emotions and desires, they will surely lead us astray. We present ourselves within our friendships in a way that sustains a particular image of ourselves. It can be difficult for our friendships to reach past this image and touch us more deeply. It is as if we do not want to risk the friendship by showing ourselves to be more vulnerable. We become so used to accepting what is available that we do not want to risk what we have. Because we know no alternative, we are often unaware that our friendships lack depth.

We learn to present ourselves in "acceptable" ways out of an unspoken fear of rejection. Within an Enlightenment vision of modernity, we are acceptable to others to the extent that we are not really different from them. As a child it was difficult not to feel that my Jewishness was in some way shameful because it was a difference. Somehow it stood in the way of my being "like everyone else." I learned to marginalize these aspects of my experience, and so failed really to value or integrate them. My Jewishness became part of my private life at home, with no expression within the public realm. I can remember the awkwardness I used to feel, inviting non-Jewish friends back to my home on the weekend. It was very important that my mother prepared a tea that would be acceptable to them. There was a split between my friendships at school and my friendships at home. It was as if I felt that my Jewishness would somehow compromise my masculinity and so threaten the friendships that I had slowly built up.

It took me time to learn to trust these aspects of myself within my friendships. I was careful about what I would talk about, and my Jewishness was an aspect that would often be left in the dark. As with other children who had grown up within immigrant families, it was so important for me to be accepted and liked by everyone else that I was prepared to accept the terms that others provided for me. At school I felt anxious, lest my Jewishness somehow let me down. The private ways of being that I had learned in the context of the home were hard to share in school. A fear of rejection meant that I concealed these aspects of my being and conformed to externally defined standards of behavior. I could not trust the inner movements of my being because they could so easily let me down. This helped form my friendships and also made them brittle. It helped produce a split between the inner, which tended to be kept to myself, and the outer. This fragmentation is there for many within a Protestant culture because of the negative vision we inherit of our inner natures. In my schooling as an immigrant child, this tension was given a particular form and structure.

Because I had learned to treat my Jewishness as an incidental aspect of my being, of no consequence in my relationships, I felt that in keeping it to myself I was not affecting the quality of my friendships. This is part of the dream of modernity, which makes us think that as rational selves who have separated off from our class, racial, or gender identities, we can come together in the "purest" form. Supposedly it is as rational selves that we are truly ourselves. With individually defined abilities, interests, and talents, we can relate to others as equals. Supposedly those aspects of our history and culture that we have learned to marginalize are simply forms of unfreedom, for they would determine, in Kantian terms, our individuality from the outside. They should have nothing to do with the friendships that we form, for supposedly the only thing that can matter, if these relationships are to be genuine, are the individual interests and qualities out of which they develop.

But it is people who are marginalized within a dominant culture who are required to make these sacrifices of their history and culture. People from immigrant, working-class, or ethnic backgrounds often tacitly learn to subordinate these aspects of themselves as having no bearing upon their identity. I cannot help thinking that this experience of marginalization helps to undermine the quality of the friendship that can be established, because it means that so much is left suspended beyond speech and discussion. There is so much that is not shared, and these areas of our experience stand as threatening. At another level it is difficult to think that others accept us for what we are, if we are forced to subordinate these aspects of our experience.

Friendship and Identity

Within any friendship there are often unspoken relationships of power and subordination. If in our friendships we feel forced to subordinate aspects of ourselves so that we will be accepted by others, then this is a process that weakens us. The quality of our relationships is bound to be affected by the terms upon which they are established. Our denial of our own needs is reinforced within a vision of masculinity that says that men do not have needs. This helps us to suppress aspects of our identity and to keep them concealed within relationships.

It is easily said that it does not matter whether someone is Jewish or not; what matters is how people get on "as friends." Within a secularized culture, Jews have often learned to suppress or deny aspects of their history and culture as having any enduring significance or value to them. This is one of the costs of modernity. Years later, I can still feel a certain unease in sharing aspects of Jewish culture with my non-Jewish friends. I hesitate about whether to share Chanukah rituals with my friends. Often they are genuinely interested and want to share these rituals, but I can still feel unsure and tense about it because this is to share aspects of myself that I have long hidden. These feelings of embarrassment can be difficult to cope with. These rituals are all very well when carried out in private, but somehow it is difficult to bring them into the public arena of friendship. Because I have become so used to not sharing these aspects of my experience in my friendships, it is difficult to begin to do so. I can feel as if this would be a ground for rejection.

The distinction between public and private is brought into focus because often in our friendships with men we seem to operate within the public realm. If we are involved in long-term heterosexual relationships or marriages, it can be easy to hide within these relationships as the private sphere within which our emotional lives take place. It is still striking how rarely men seem to share these aspects of their intimate relationships. It is as if we constantly have to be on our "best behavior" with our male friends. Sustaining a certain image of ourselves in their presence can be difficult.

With the impact of feminism, women have learned to take their friendships with each other much more seriously and are less available to the men in their lives. Many men feel envious of the relationships that women seem able to strike up with each other. There is a continuity in women's relationships with each other and a seemingly easy intimacy that allows women to talk about both their personal lives and their work lives, which men can find difficult to achieve. Typically, a crisis in a marriage or relationship encourages men to reevaluate the importance of their relationships with men. Since the meaning of most of our lives comes from work and through intimate sexual relationships, men take their friendships for granted and fail to acknowledge how much they mean to them. Our wariness with other men can mean that, at some level, we fail to trust these relationships and take them seriously.

As men we often take an instrumental relationship toward our friendships, thinking that we need our friends for a time of difficulty. We may not be in tune with our relationships; our energies may lie elsewhere.

This tension is reflected in our understanding of responsibility. When we think about taking responsibility within a Protestant culture, we tend to think in terms of blame. We have rationalized our experience and are constantly on guard, ready to defend our actions and behavior. As long as we can justify our feelings and behavior we know that we can defend ourselves. In our friendships, it is often a matter of both knowing that we are not to blame for what is going on and being clear that we have good reasons for our emotions and our actions. We always seem to be shifting blame and responsibility. Taking responsibility is a matter of not being blamed for a situation that we have helped to create.

Our identity exists fundamentally in individualistic terms. We are on guard and ready to defend ourselves, even against our friends. As long as we are not to blame, we can feel all right about ourselves. Our focus seems to lie in the issue of guilt and responsibility, and as long as we can tell ourselves that we are not responsible for a relationship breaking down, we can feel in the clear. It is much harder for us to share responsibility for what is happening emotionally in our friendships. If I can think that a friend has let me down, then I feel clear in the ending of a relationship. This moralism is difficult to escape within a Protestant culture. Only after we have lost contact with a friend, or a friendship has broken down, can we begin to feel what we have lost. But it can still be difficult to acknowledge our own role in what happened.

Our conception of responsibility is fundamentally tied to our conception of blame, so we can be led to assume that once responsibility has been fixed upon one person, then the other is free of it. It is harder to recognize that both parties are responsible for what happens within the relationship and that blame may not be appropriate. We lack a different vision of responsibility, one that encourages both partners to accept responsibility for what happens within their friendship. This goes together with an appreciation of the importance of communicating within the relationship. As men we can find it hard to communicate how important a particular friendship is to us. This makes us more vulnerable than we would want to admit. It may be easier to pretend that the friendship is not really important to us and that we can live just as well without it. To acknowledge otherwise is to admit a dependency that can be threatening.

Within a liberal moral culture, we learn to treat our love as if it were a scarce commodity. It is something that we learn to control quite carefully. But unless we are prepared to acknowledge our feelings for others, it can be difficult to break our isolation as men. The culture prepares us to think of our identities in individualistic and exclusive terms, which works to minimize the importance of our relationships with others. We become frightened of acknowledging how much we care for our friends because this would make us vulnerable to them. We are not used to the quality of intimate feelings between two male friends. Often we do not allow ourselves such feelings, much less allow ourselves to express them.[6]

Our identities as men have often been internalized so that we rest secure in a sense of superiority to others. We learn to admire our self-control and we learn to feel superior to others who seem unable to curb and control their emotions in similar ways. Masculinity is often tied to an internalized sense of superiority, and we often learn to feel superior to other men. This is frequently a form of self-protection that allows us to remain invulnerable. At another level, it conceals low self-esteem.

Although it is important not to generalize, and many of the themes I have discussed here could, I hope, be used to open a discussion about the specificity of masculine experience in different ethnic groups or social classes, it is also important to seek to identify experiences that we share as men. Typically, men have a capacity to cut off and separate from emotional relationships. Sometimes we withdraw into ourselves and sometimes a solemn silence takes over. It is as if we refuse to let others have our emotions, and thereby we assume superiority toward them. This is a familiar pattern in men's relationships with women, but it also occurs in men's friendships with each other. It is sustained by an underlying feeling that, when the chips are down, we can survive on our own and we basically do not need others.

This individualistic vision, shaped by a Protestant moral culture, has informed different traditions of social theory. In classical times, friendship was regarded as an important virtue and something that had to be learned. It was recognized as a civic virtue. People learned to take seriously the responsibilities of friendship as part of public life. With Enlightenment modernity, friendship has become a private and individual concern. Our friendships no longer bear witness to our identities. Our identities are established in fundamentally individual terms. Social theory, which has largely been concerned with understanding the forms of inequality and injustice that take place within the public realm, has, in classical terms, given little attention to friendship. Its visions of socialization have been presented in terms of conformity to public roles, which are largely defined through the expectations of others. It is difficult to theorize the qualitative character of our relationships and illuminate what is missing in many men's lives with the absence of true friends. Feminist theory has helped bring this issue into focus because women have refused to do the emotional work that should be the responsibility of men themselves. This may help men to reconsider the quality of their relationships and friendships, and so encourage a movement within social theory toward illuminating relationships as an important source of identity.

Notes

1. See, for example, Orbach and Eichenbaum (1983). See also the interesting discussion of power and emotional work that is provided by Miller (1981).

2. Some of the connections between the Protestant ethic and dominant forms of masculinity are further explored in Seidler (1991), especially in Chapter 2, "Morality," and Chapter 3, "Self-Denial."

3. For some interesting reflections on this public/private distinction as it bears upon the experience of men, see Elshtain (1986) and Seidler (1989).

4. Chodorow (1979) rethinks some of Freud's discussions that tended to treat the masculine as the norm. Through recasting this premise she helps identify the sources of some of the difficulties that men have in sustaining continuous relationships.

5. See Wolff (1950) and the study of Simmel by Frisby (1988). Simmel was responsive to the questioning raised by the German feminist movement of his time, so that his work has a particular resonance in our own time when these issues have reemerged. It is important to wonder how it is that sociology has failed to develop an understanding of relationships and of the emotional life of individuals and groups. More recently people have attempted to deal with this void through the introduction of psychoanalytic work.

6. This discussion of the difficulties men have with mutual intimacy is clearly embedded in the homophobia of modern culture, which is a theme deserving of a full discussion in its own right. Gay men's oppression does not form a major focus of this piece, however, as I would argue that one of the major strengths of contemporary sexual politics is the understanding that different marginalized groups have an entitlement to their own voice, to articulate their own experience.

References

Chodorow, N. (1979). *The reproduction of mothering*. Berkeley: University of California Press.
Elshtain, J. B. (1989). *Public man, private woman*. Princeton: Princeton University Press.
Frisby, D. (1988). *Sociological impressionism: A reassessment of Georg Simmel*. London: Heinemann.
Miller, J. B. (1981). *Toward a new psychology of women*. Harmondsworth, England: Penguin.
Miller, S. (1983). *Men and friendship*. London: Gateway Books.
Orbach, S., & Eichenbaum, L. (1983). *What do women want?* London: Fontana.
Seidler, V. J. (1989). *Rediscovering masculinity*. London: Routledge.
Seidler, V. J. (1991). *Recreating sexual politics*. London: Routledge.

Weber, M. (1976). *The Protestant ethic and the spirit of capitalism*. London: Allen & Unwin.

Wolff, K. (1950). *The sociology of Georg Simmel*. New York: Free Press.

3

"Our Eyes Behold Each Other"

Masculinity and Intimate Friendship in Antebellum New England[1]

KAREN V. HANSEN

A 23-year-old box factory worker, J. Foster Beal, wrote to his friend, Brigham Nims, a teacher, in 1834, expressing a teasing camaraderie between the two and the importance of caregiving in their friendship.

> Well Brig:
> I suppose you have got to be a school master, since you was in Boston, you need not be so stuck up (as jock Downing says) because you are tucked down in the least post of Nelson, I have been there myself, I guess you have forgot all about you being at Boston last Sept. when you was so sick, and I took care of you, doctored you up, even took you in the bed with myself; you will not do as much, as, to write me.—(Beal to Nims, December 17, 1834)[2] (See Appendix for a list of all historical documents.)

To share a bed in nineteenth-century Boston was not uncommon; with the lack of space in most homes, visitors frequently shared beds with their hosts. What is striking in the above passage, however, is the tender image of Beal nursing Nims. We can imagine Beal sitting beside the bed mopping his brow, feeding him, perhaps reading aloud to pass the time. The concept of nursing, historically a female vocation, practiced by Beal challenges our conception of men's relations with one another and of the acceptable boundaries of male behavior in the nineteenth century.

Beal's relationship with Nims was complex, as the letter reveals. He chides Nims for his success (becoming a schoolteacher) and reminds him of his more humble past (recently being a box factory worker). Although in jest, these comments have a hostile edge. They reveal the importance of their shared class background and the threat of social and economic mobility to their relationship. At the same time, Beal reminds Nims of the affectionate time they spent together and his own role in nursing Nims through an illness. While not necessarily a representative document of all working-class men in antebellum New England, the letter represents one of the many ways men's friendship was expressed in the nineteenth century, and it falls within the acceptable parameters of men's behavior.

In late twentieth-century America, there exists a widespread belief that men and women have different capacities to be intimate (Chodorow, 1978). Even when people disagree about why and how those capacities exist, there is agreement that men's intimacy is expressed differently than women's (Rubin, 1985). While not necessarily taking issue with this body of research, this chapter delimits some of the historical boundaries to this understanding of working men's intimate lives. By looking at several cases of friendship in the antebellum period, this chapter challenges the notion that working men did not have intimate relationships with other men and women. Such an investigation reveals the historical variation in men's friendships and, in the process, uncovers human agency in the construction of the boundaries of acceptable masculine behavior. In documenting the historical variation in men's experiences, the social construction of masculinity (and femininity) becomes evident.

In her search for transcendent public life, Hannah Arendt (1968) believes that intimate friendships are not noble ventures, between either men or women.[3] In her mind, the friendship worth striving for is cool and sober, not sentimental. Ideal friendship should be embedded in politics and public activity. While her portrait of the honorable comradeship of public life is compelling, even inspirational, it implicitly devalues the importance of private intimacy and common everyday life activities. This chapter begins with a contrary assumption. It is rooted in the notion that private and social friendship and the expression of intimacy are fundamental to providing a full range of human experience in addition to building communities.

This chapter presents selected findings from a larger study on social life of antebellum working women and men. It poses questions about how to understand the elastic boundaries of manhood in the antebellum period. What was the nature of friendships for men who were artisans, day laborers, and farmers? How did it differ from men of the middle and upper classes? Were men's friendships with women different from those with men? Was there a *male* "world of love and ritual" in the early nineteenth century that paralleled that of women?

Manhood in Historical Context

Industrial development, urbanization, and Western expansion began to reorder American society in the pre-Civil War period. All three resulted in massive shifts in population as marginal farm workers sought jobs in newly established shoe or textile factories, moved to the city to learn a trade, or migrated West to the ever-expanding frontier to homestead cheap land or pan for gold. While the majority of American citizens lived in rural areas until 1920, industrialization in particular had a tremendous impact on the organization of social and economic life. It resulted in the movement of production out of the household, theoretically creating a separation between "home life" and "work life." But as long as a majority of Americans lived in rural areas through the nineteenth century (Bureau of the Census, 1975), it was not uncommon for men and women to go back and forth between factory and farm employment, and city and country living arrangements. On the farm the proto-industrial economy organized a division of labor and social life different from that in the city, even after industrialization and commercial agriculture were introduced into the countryside. But even with the industrial organization of textile production, workers fluctuated between farm and factory; and they manipulated, to the extent possible, their work experience within the factory to fit their needs and habits (Dublin, 1979).

To what extent either the city or the farm produced a strict separation of work and home is debatable. One school of thought claims that the division of labor into paid production and unpaid reproduction created physically, emotionally, and culturally separate spheres of influence and activity for men and women (Degler, 1980; Sacks, 1975). The assumption is that men had little to do with the domestic sphere and its activities. The prescriptive cultural manifestation of the separation of home and paid work was the "cult of true womanhood," propagated by middle-class reformers, such as Catharine Beecher (Sklar, 1973). The burgeoning domestic advice and religious literature of the 1830s and 1840s encouraged wives and mothers to be "true women." That is, they should guard their sphere and rightful place—the home—with all the virtues imbued in a proper wife-mother: "piety, purity, submissiveness and domesticity" (Welter, 1966, p. 152). While the ideology had a solid audience within the urban middle class, the extent to which it resonated with working-class, poor, and rural women is unclear. The domestic ideology failed to influence some people for economic, cultural, and geographic reasons. It was particularly problematic for young farm girls because it was they who populated the first textile factories in New England. They were the ones to leave the domestic sphere for factory work, not their fathers. At the same time, the message capitalized on the widespread fear and insecurity that resulted from geographic mobility and the shifting modes of production that marginalized large numbers of women workers (Ryan, 1981, p. 118).

The dominant school of feminist thought accepts the assumption of the nineteenth-century emergence of separate spheres for men and women (Cott, 1977; Halttunen, 1982; Smith-Rosenberg, 1986). Smith-Rosenberg, for example, claims that this staunch geographic separation of home and workplace, coupled with a deep cultural division between men and women, led middle-class women to develop emotional relationships with those whom they shared their everyday lives and cares: other women. She argues that women shared a common experience based on gender roles and biological rites of passage, and their relationships functioned as mutual support systems, providing security, companionship, and self-esteem in a self-contained world that was whole and integral without men. "Such female relationships were frequently supported and paralleled by severe social restrictions on intimacy between young men and women. Within such a world of emotional richness and complexity, devotion to and love of other women became a plausible and socially accepted form of human interaction" (Smith-Rosenberg, 1986, p. 60).[4] Other studies have also found evidence of this same intense romantic emotionality in friendships between middle- and upper-class women (Faderman, 1981; Strouse, 1980).

What did this separate life mean for men? Men were to be "the movers, the doers, the actors," those who provided for and protected the family (Welter, 1966, p. 159). In his study of self-made men, Byars (1979, p. 197) describes the emergent middle-class man as someone who exhibited ambition, courage, strength, and "who was almost ascetically devoted to the work-related virtues." That said, however, the virtue required concerted effort because the new man was vulnerable to the lure of vice and evil, particularly under the influence of women. Rotundo (1989, p. 18) points to the critical transition from youthfulness to middle-class manhood that involves a strong commitment to a career, marriage, and a house of one's own. "The identity of a middle-class man was founded on independent action, cool detachment, and sober responsibility." And at least in the advice manuals that Byars (1979, pp. 36, 143-144) studies, "There was a persistent sense that home was an appendage to a man's life. It did not contribute much to his sense of personal identity." Some went so far as to reject those aspects of life that held feminine associations—religion, culture, the home, and women themselves.

Portraits of American working men in the nineteenth century are more rare and, when they do exist, attend less frequently to issues of masculinity and identity. Stearns (1979) characterizes working-class men as physical, enamored of authority, and somewhat rigid. Frontier men are portrayed by Faragher (1979) as strong, self-indulgent, adventurous, and competitive. Although historical time and geographic location shape these portraits, their development is rooted in laboring activities (e.g., Baron, 1989). More positive images have been attributed to the artisan, the "model citizen of the republic" (Clawson, 1989, p. 153), whose power was based on his skilled work and economic self-sufficiency. For men involved in trade associations, masculinity was deeply tied to their work. It was in part a reflection of craft pride, which symbolized independence and adulthood (Wilentz, 1984). Clawson notes that, ironically, even when women entered the paid labor force, masculine identity was largely defined by artisanal identity. This was because "apprenticeship was not only an institution for the inculcation and acquisition of craft knowledge; it was a vehicle of masculine socialization" (1989, pp. 153-154). These formative investigations of antebellum working-class culture leave the personal dimensions of a composite working-class/artisanal/agrarian masculinity to be explored in further research.

Friendship and Homoeroticism

Did separate spheres create separate emotional worlds for men and for women? Smith-Rosenberg asserts that middle-class women had homosocial work lives and emotional circles. Dublin's (1979) study of New England mill workers demonstrates that women who left the farm to work in factories also existed largely in female worlds due to the gender-segregation of textile factories and boardinghouses.

Smith-Rosenberg (1986) argues that the close bonds between women often became passionate and sometimes erotic. In their homogeneous world, even at great distances and in the context of heterosexual marriage, women professed their great love to each other in letters. For example, Molly Hallock wrote to Helena, her friend from school:

> Imagine yourself kissed a dozen times my darling. Perhaps it is well for you that we are far apart. You might find my thanks so expressed rather overpowering. I have that delightful feeling that it doesn't matter much what I say or how I say it, since we shall meet so soon and forget in that moment that we are ever separated . . . I shall see you soon and be content. (Smith-Rosenberg, 1986, p. 57)

Smith-Rosenberg convincingly argues that explicitly loving relationships between women as expressed in a literary form were seen as normal, natural, and acceptable by their families, neighbors, and society. In one illustrative court case in early nineteenth-century Scotland, two women were accused of having sexual relations with each other. They were acquitted, however, because the court found that "to be willing to involve oneself in totally committed female friendship was an indication of the seriousness of one's moral character" rather than the opposite (Faderman, 1981, p. 150-151). However, Smith-Rosenberg's research has sparked a debate about the degree to which women's affection for one another expressed the cultural romanticism dominant in the early nineteenth century, reflected a unique women's culture, or revealed a lesbian sexual practice. Smith-Rosenberg recommends that rather than try to label the behavior normal or deviant, we should consider it a part of a sexual continuum ranging from homosexual to heterosexual.

Clawson (1989), D'Emilio and Freedman (1988), and Pleck and Pleck (1980) argue that, like their female counterparts, men encountered and created opportunities to socialize independent of women, which enabled them to develop relationships with each other, some of them intimate. They point to the all-male worlds of battlefields, the work place, the wild Western frontier, and fraternal societies as environments where men congregated together and discovered friendship and the secrets of same-gender intimacy.

D'Emilio and Freedman and Pleck and Pleck argue that, parallel to the experience of women, men's distinct social world allowed them to develop their own culture and "encouraged manly intimacy and affection, a love between equals, which was often lacking in sentiments toward the other sex" (Pleck & Pleck, 1980, p. 13). They point to the men-only spaces that nurtured male culture in the Colonial and antebellum periods—lodges, clubs, militia, fire departments, taverns, and voluntary associations. All of these institutions, however, would have encouraged verbal rather than written affection, hence leaving little documentation of the interpersonal dimension of their relationships behind.

Clawson (1989) sees these all-male spaces in a somewhat different light. In her investigation of fraternal organizations, such as the Masons and Odd Fellows, in the nineteenth century, she argues that the rise of male organizations, fraternal orders in particular, met a specific need in a turbulent and uncertain nineteenth-century society. In contrast to Carnes (1989) who argues that "fraternal ritual provided solace and psychological guidance during *young men's troubled passage to manhood* in Victorian America," (p. 14, emphasis added) Clawson asserts that the fraternal orders functioned as a defense against threatened manhood. She convincingly demonstrates that artisanal manhood was under assault because of industrial capitalism, the rise of female values, and the cultural critique of masculinity. The effect of these sacred bastions of masculinity "was to promote solidarity among men to reinforce men's separation from women, and thus to validate and facilitate the exercise of masculine power" (Clawson, 1986, p. 41). I would argue, therefore, that the form of male-bonding within the orders and lodges, with its valorization of that-which-was-not-female, would be a place for activity, networking, camaraderie, but not for the type of intimacy so commonly displayed in friendships between women.[5] Together these studies indicate that indeed there was a world of male ritual. But, the question remains, was there also a world of love and intimacy?

The subject of men's friendships with men have only recently been investigated from a feminist perspective.[6] The research on contemporary society shows that male relationships are less personal and less intimate than female ones (Pleck, 1975; Rubin, 1985; Sherrod, 1987). While men and women have about the same number of friends, women are more self-disclosing and seek friends who feel the same way, while men are more interested in doing things and want companionship and commitment. Sherrod finds that men reveal more to their female friends than male friends. Pleck and Rubin claim that men's expectations for emotional intimacy focus on women in contemporary society; men need women for emotional expression. Do contemporary forms of male friendship extend back in time? Is this *male* behavior? Or is it a phenomenon unique to late twentieth-century men?

Crowley (1987) makes a convincing argument that nineteenth-century culture was homosocial and had erotic undercurrents. The culture associated male homosociality with childishness and powerlessness, but it was not a cause for shame or scorn, and certainly did not provoke the virulent homophobia evident in the twentieth century. In the mid-nineteenth century, Thoreau wrote that friendship between those of the same sex was easier. In a middle-class world of separate spheres where men had little knowledge of women, this seems plausible. Because of the paucity of information, the nature of relationships between working men needs to be the focus of further research.

Conclusive evidence reveals that elite men had romantic correspondence with other men in the nineteenth century.[7] In foraging archives for evidence of gay relationships throughout history, Katz (1976) unearthed a variety of romantic letters written by male political and literary figures to other men. Using one example from the eighteenth century, he cites a letter from Alexander Hamilton to John Laurens, a friend and fellow soldier, in South Carolina during the American Revolution, written in April 1779:

Cold in my professions, warm in [my] friendships, I wish, my Dear Laurens, it m[ight] be in my power, by action rather than words, [to] convince you that I love you. I shall only tell you that 'till you bade us Adieu, I hardly knew the value you had taught my heart to set upon you. (Katz, 1976, p. 453)

In another letter, dated September 11, 1779, Hamilton wrote:

I acknowledge but one letter from you, since you left us, of the 14th of July which just arrived in time to appease a violent conflict between my friendship and my pride. I have written you five or six letters since you left Philadelphia and I should have written you more had you made proper return. But like a jealous lover, when I thought you slighted my caresses, my affection was alarmed and my vanity piqued. I had almost resolved to lavish no more of them upon you and to reject you as an inconstant and an ungrateful——. But you have now disarmed my resentment and by a single mark of attention made up the quarrel. You must at least allow me a large stock of good nature. (Katz, 1976, p. 455)

When Hamilton becomes engaged to be married he acknowledges himself as a "benedict" and speaks grudgingly of relinquishing his liberty. He later marries, while Laurens dies at the hands of the British.

Although the title and content of his book frame the letters as homoerotic, like Smith-Rosenberg, Katz rejects the impulse to label the relationships homosexual. The term *homosexual*, with its emphasis on same-sex genital contact directed toward orgasm, is particularly inadequate as a means of encompassing and understanding the historical variety of same-sex relations. Katz says, for example, that the loving letters of Alexander Hamilton to John Laurens present the dilemma of interpreting to what extent it is an honest expression of emotion, referring to some deeply felt, perhaps physical, relation. Katz (p. 451) argues that the mere existence of these letters, so casually kept, "suggests more lenient social attitudes toward male-male intimacy" than we would expect of late eighteenth- or nineteenth-century society, and than we find today. Other historians range in their assessment of the material from a conviction that the language reflects only a spiritual love (Richards, 1987) to a skeptical ambivalence about the innocence of the erotic messages (D'Emilio & Freedman, 1988). There is great difficulty in studying same-sex relationships in a heterosexist and homophobic society because of the tendency to distort innocent relations, to read consummated sexual activity into passionate innuendos, or because of an inability to put aside twentieth-century biases in order to be sensitive to a pre-Freudian epoch. For these reasons the notion of a sexual continuum is most useful in capturing historical nuance.

Rotundo's (1989) research on middle-class male friendships shows that men in the nineteenth century formed friendships throughout their lives, but established *intimate* relationships with men virtually only in the period between boyhood and manhood (supporting Crowley's findings). He defines intimacy as "a sharing of innermost thoughts and secret emotions" (p. 1). During their youth, he asserts that men psychologically break from their families and seek to establish themselves in the world, "a time when a young male had reached physical maturity but had not yet established the two identifying marks of middle-class manhood —a career and marriage" (p. 13). This was a time, according to Rotundo, that a young man passed "from the security and moral rectitude of women's sphere to the freedom and competitive rigor of men's sphere" (p. 13). So, we must ask, was it only while affiliated with the female world that men had female-type friendships and intimacy?

The male-male relationships studied by Rotundo ranged from casual to intimate to romantic (sometimes incorporating all three dimensions), and men's letters spoke of a physical component, which may or may not have been explicitly sexual but at least included hugs, kisses, and sleeping together. Men recognized the range of acceptable physicality between men, each drawing their own boundaries based on personality and cultural heritage. For example, W. D. Howells, a prominent literary figure in the late nineteenth century and editor for many years of the *Atlantic Monthly*, recalled: "when [H. H.] Boyesen told me that among the Norwegians men never kissed each other, as the Germans, and the Frenchmen, and the Italians do, I perceived that we stood upon common ground" (Crowley, 1987, p. 304).

The casual relationship provided companionship for socializing, working, drinking, playing sports, and going to events. The intimate one included a sharing of secrets and a serious attachment that may or may not have included physical intimacy. For example, Rotundo likens the relationship between Daniel Webster and Hervey Bingham to a comfortable but happy marriage. Webster wrote, "Seven years' intimacy has made him dear to me; he is like a good old pen knife, the longer you have it the better it proves, and wears brighter till it wears out" (p. 4). Like the Hamilton-Laurens correspondence, James Blake's friendship with Wyck Vanderhoef ventures into romance, speaking of love: "After an acquaintance of nearly three years I have chosen [Wyck] as my friend, and he has reciprocated; May he live long and happy, and may the tie of pure friendship which has been formed between us, never be severed, but by the hand of death . . . ever keep us as we now are in oneness, one life, one interest, one heart, one love" (Rotundo, 1989, p. 5).

Rotundo finds that physical expression of affection—embracing, sharing a bed—carried no real stigma for the men in the nineteenth century and in fact was culturally supported. Rotundo (p. 5) gives an example from the diary of James Blake about Wyck Vanderhoef: "We retired early, but long was the time before our eyes were closed in slumber, for this was the last night we shall be together for the present, and our hearts were full of that true friendship which we could not find utterance by words, we laid our heads upon each other's bosom and wept, it may be unmanly to weep, but I care not, the spirit was touched." As Rotundo notes, it was not the physical closeness that Blake felt embarrassed about, but the fact that he wept. My own research also shows that emotional self-control indicated manhood for working men. When Francis Bennett, Jr., son of a fisherman, left his Gloucester home to work as a clerk in Boston, he wrote: "I found it pretty hard to keep from crying on leaving the home of my childhood. But I had resolved to be as manly as possible about it. Mother would not say goodbye" (Bennett Diary, August 28, 1854). Rotundo argues that manhood was not threatened by physical intimacy because the word *homosexual* was not in the nineteenth-century vocabulary. Individuals did not self-consciously worry about their behavior. They did not fear same-sex relationships. In addition, the culture as a whole did not stigmatize the behavior. "The modern terms *homosexuality* and *heterosexuality* do not apply to an era that had not yet articulated these distinctions" (D'Emilio & Freedman, 1988, p. 121; see also Katz, 1990). Again, the concept of a sexual continuum ranging from verbal endearment to genital play or intercourse better explains same-gender friendships than discrete categories.

When comparing them to Smith-Rosenberg's female relationships, Rotundo finds middle-class men's friendships similar in their social acceptability, daily content, and physical manifestations. The primary difference he observes is that the male relationships were bound by the life cycle; they did not continue into married life, as did their female equivalents. Can we assume that what was true of the elite was also true for working men?

Working Men's Friendships

Visiting and Sociability

Working men were firmly ensconced in the prevalent social ritual of visiting acquaintances, friends, neighbors, and relatives. As Pleck (1975) reviews the literature in the twentieth century, he finds that while men may avoid intimacy, they socialize extensively. So too in the nineteenth century, men observed visiting conventions (who is supposed to call on whom, how often, and when) and other labor-intensive obligations that they sometimes incurred. Visits were often occasions for the exchange of labor and services—such as making quilts, preparing cider, building barns, or caring for those who were sick—central to rural economic life. One tenant farmer in central Massachusetts, Leonard Stockwell, a failure in most of his ventures, felt pride at being a good host, "he was decidedly a home man and liked to have everything comfortable and make those welcome who came to visit him" (Stockwell Memorial, c. 1880, p. 38). And he found it difficult to forego visits when he was ill. In sum, men were active as visitors and hosts, laborers and nurses—all central roles in making social ties and building communities. Friendship was a linchpin of this culture of exchange, reciprocity, and mutual aid.

Friendship

A case study illuminates the possibilities and range of emotional expression open to men who worked at different kinds of manual labor. Brigham Nims, the recipient of the letter previously cited, broke many stereotypes of nineteenth-century manhood. He was born in 1811 to farmers Matthew and Lucy Nims; he lived and died on the family homestead. He worked seasonally as a teacher over a period of 19 years. As with most teachers in the 1830s and 1840s, he had other jobs as well because he taught only 16 weeks of the year and was paid low wages.[8] To supplement his income, he was intermittently employed as a clerk in his brother Reuel's store, as an itinerant tailor (living at people's homes while he sewed for them), as a blacksmith and carpenter, as a stone splitter in the farm's rock quarry, as a farm day laborer, and, most important, as a farmer.[9]

When Nims was 20, he made the acquaintance of Jacob Foster Beal, who became a close confidant. Their friendship may have begun while they both worked in a box factory in Boston or while enmeshed in their overlapping social worlds in Cheshire County, New Hampshire. The few clues to their relationship exist only in a small collection of letters from Beal to Nims from 1832 to 1834. It is not clear how long the friendship continued. Beal married in 1838 and it appears he died before 1849.[10] Regardless, the letters reveal a vital, loving friendship sustained in spite of the geographic distance (Nims was teaching in Nelson and Roxbury, New Hampshire, and Beal was based in Boston) but probably also because of their shared New Hampshire heritage.[11]

The earliest letter reveals a rowdy joyfulness in their relationship, with a decidedly masculine physical component:

Dear friend Sir B—Boston March 21st 1832
I received your letter by G Tuffs which I read with the greatest pleasure I rejoice to hear that you are in good health, and the rest of your friends I want to see you very much indeed to have a good box with you which you said you should like to have with me I think if you are as fat as I be we should puff and blow. (Beal to Nims, March 21, 1832)

In contrast to other men's romantic letters, such as those of Hamilton-Laurens or Blake-Vanderhoef, it does not speak of love. If we compare the above exchange to those between middle-class women, we find it more jovial, less romantic and flowery. Beal's letter reflects a casual friendliness and conveys a sense of delight in the friendship. Beal's teasing seems to ignore Nims' self-portrait as a man with whom others have difficulty getting along: "I know that my owne temper and disposition is not so easily governed as I would wish" (Nims to Gould, August 1, 1853). The physicality embodied in the letter—organized play, rambunctiousness, and competitiveness—reflects male expressions of affection (and sometimes attraction).

Their letters were not a literary exercise as they were for elite men who cleverly hinted at romance. They were written by a teacher/farmer and box factory hand, frequently punctuated with misspellings and grammatical errors.[12] And their purpose was not about work but about all matters related to their friendship and community of shared acquaintances.

The letters contained a broad range of information and moods. Most letters included some gossip—news of people, events, greetings from others who knew Nims. For example, Beal records a notable piece of news: "Wm Buckminster said there had been a weding to Old Father [Wonderell] Harriet was married, he and [Lucy] stood right up by the side of them, all the time—by the flash of [Gimblets] if it didn't make his eyes weep, when he come to tie the nott————" (Beal to Nims, December 17, 1834). Again, it is interesting to observe that the tears of a man were worthy of gossip.

On a more serious note, some letters revealed an uncertainty in Beal's life, a soul-searching, an attempt to find a promising future: "I still remain at Mr. Huntings and how long I shall stay, I cannot tell—I come very near of going to the Ohio this spring so near that I did not go, but I do not know but I shall go next fall or spring" (Beal to Nims, April 1, 1834). Later in the letter, Beal pondered the death of his mother, the difficulty, even at age 23, of relinquishing his attachment to her, and his wretchedness at not being more emotionally tied to God:

It is almost three years since we first formed an acquaintance, time has rappidly passed on by and wrought changs that time nor eternity can replace when I look around me, I see many of my fellow [mortels] deprived of health many going down to an early grace and still I am bless with perfet health, why is this distinction yet I hardly think of [him] God that made me; my ungrateful [heart] clings to its mother [dead] and there alone it seeks for happiness. (Beal to Nims, April 1, 1834)

Beal clearly trusted Nims to be his sympathetic philosophical sounding board. He continued to talk about his struggle to separate from his parents, but did so in the third person.

Some passages in the Beal letters read more in the romantic tradition of the 1830s and are similar to the letters exchanged between women who were intimates:

can not forget those happy hours [th]at we spent at G. Newcombs and the evening walks; but we are deprived of that privilege now we are separated for a time we cannot tel how long perhaps before our eyes behold each other in this world. (Beal to Nims, March 21, 1832)

In fact, this passage, like Nims' diary entry, if not clearly attributed, could easily be read as written by a female hand. At the end of the letter, after signing his name, Beal wrote a poem:

O be on the tenne[sse] to night
Look as far as your blue eyes can see
Remember each star in your sight
Will be gilding my cottage and me
Take one from the many and think
That Foster has singled it to
Still bound by one lingering link
To Boston, great City and you. (Beal to Nims, March 21, 1832)

Its romantic simplicity connects the two men who were separated due to the demands of their work. Beal's poem situates their relationship within a greater context—the universe—as a means to maintain their link to one another.

It is important to note that despite what might appear as deviant behavior, historical records indicate that Nims was not treated as an outcast. There is nothing in any of the correspondence to indicate that Beal or Nims felt secretive or uncomfortable about their relationship or behavior. Nims was a respected member of the community. Very active in civic affairs, over the course of his life he was a town selectman, a representative to the general court, the town treasurer, a member of the school committee, and school superintendent. However, to keep perspective, his prominence was limited to a remote geographic area with a population of less than 300. Respected citizenship in Roxbury, New Hampshire, meant something quite different than it did in proper Boston. His obituary referred to him as "a man of prominence." "He was interested in every good work, was a man of integrity and industry, possessed a vigorous mind and body, and was strong in his convictions. In politics he was a staunch Republican" (Nims Obituary, June 5, 1893).

That said however, the Beal-Nims correspondence was the only collection I found in my search for letters between farmers, artisans, and working-class men that were not relatives. The dearth of documents can be interpreted several ways. One is that scarcity of such letters reflects the rarity of the friendship. Another is that working-class men had friendships, and although literacy was high for native-born Yankee men, they had little occasion for writing to one another. Yet another is that the biases inherent in preserving documents of non-elites would render "pedestrian" letters that might have existed not worth preserving, therefore leaving few today, except those between family members.

Men's Friendships with Women

Unquestionably, it was difficult and unusual for male-female relationships to be exclusive, intimate, and yet non-romantic unless they were between relatives. That is not to say that some men did not have close women friends, because they did. Evidence of this type of relationship in my study comes more from women's diaries than from letters. For example, Sarah Trask, a young shoebinder living in Beverly, Massachusetts, spoke repeatedly of a male friend of her boyfriend Luther (who was away at sea), and her exchanges with him about the status of her romantic involvement. He was a touchstone that brought her closer to her beloved Luther, a barometer registering Luther's feelings and helping her interpret them. But, at least in her diary, their relationship was safely defined by their mutual friendship with Luther.

Another case that demonstrates the obstacles to male-female friendship involves correspondence between John Burleigh and Ann Dixon. A former teacher of Dixon's, Burleigh corresponded with her after her placement at her own teaching job. After a while he stopped writing to her because of gossip that had been circulated about them by "an *(afraid she should be)* old maid," despite his assertion that their correspondence had been "from the purest motives" (Burleigh to Dixon, April 30, 1841, emphasis in the original).[13]

However, the vast majority of letters examined in the study that were between men and women were between either family members or lovers. At least in their childhood years, men almost unavoidably shared households with women—their mothers and sisters. Atkins (1988) persuasively argues that conceptions of separate spheres ignore the fact that men often had homes and families where women also lived. By looking at men's relationships with their sisters, we are forced to rethink the gendered character of the home, and men's capacity for intimate friendship.

Men experienced a range of relationships with their sisters. If we look to a privileged literary family as an example, we see that Alice James—sister in the remarkable, intellectual family of Henry and William James —was somewhat estranged from two of her brothers, faced verbally seductive flirtation from a third, and shared an intimate camaraderie with the fourth (Strouse, 1980). If we look to artisanal and farm men, we see that their relations with their sisters could be romantic, formal, fraternal, obligatory (where siblings have nothing in common except parents), or they could embody an intimate friendship between peers.

This latter type of friendship—supportive, purposely self-revealing—between brother and sister was not unusual. In 1820 Chloe Adams wrote to her brother James in Portland, Maine, responding to his suggestion about the level of honesty in their friendship:

> My dear brother
> Have retired alone to my chamber & taken my pen to answer your truly affectionate letter which was duly received. Altho it has caused some unpleasant anxious feelings. yet that does not lessen its value, but renders it more acceptable, for I shall ever esteem it a favor to be made acquainted with the feelings & anxieties of Brother James tho they may be different from what I could wish. You wish me to write with as much 'freedom & plainness' as you did. I will if it is in my power. (C. Adams to J. Adams, August 2, 1820)

To return to a now-familiar example, Brigham Nims, we find a few letters between him and his sister, Laura Nims, in the 1830s, and numerous entries about her in Nims' diaries. This correspondence suggests that, like other siblings in the nineteenth century, Nims did have an intimate relationship with a woman—his sister. The letters reveal a shared understanding, a knowledge of each other. In one letter in May 1834 from school, Laura wrote: "Dear Brother, I steal away a few moments to addss a friend" (L. Nims to B. Nims, May 1834). Other letters expressed joy in seeing him and hearing from him. Not surprisingly, the intimacy with Laura differed from that between Nims and Beal. While she displayed similar levels of comfort with Brigham and with familiar and direct forms of address, her letters to Brigham reported on her working conditions and her school activities, rather than focusing on their relationship. She *demonstrated* her intimacy with him—through a show of trust and her expressed desire to be in his company—but she did not *speak* of it directly. Nims and Laura were constant companions and shared secrets. One letter in particular reveals Brigham's trust in her; he closes with: "Foster stands laughing over my shoulder who can write. I am the same do not expose this B. Nims" (B. Nims to L. Nims, September 18, 1839). Especially before she married in 1845 at age 30, she and Nims were constant companions and at one point journeyed together to upstate New York to visit relatives.

Separate spheres did not dissociate these two siblings, even in their adulthood. Laura may have had a host of women friends as well, with whom she confided her deepest desires. However, she sustained a companionship with her brother, she worried about his religious salvation, and he confided secrets to her. They shared the profession of teaching and both made their base at the Nims homestead in Roxbury. When Laura married, Nims toured the countryside, inviting guests to come to the wedding, as was a custom at the time (Rothman, 1984). More important, he helped bake her wedding cake and afterward carefully recorded the recipe in his diary (Nims Diary, August 22, 1845).[14]

While not all brothers and sisters were intimates, the capacity for friendship existed, was socially accepted, and was acted upon by working men and women.

Class and Gender Implications

The character of contemporary male friendships does not simply extend backwards in time. This chapter demonstrates the importance of historically situating men and the range of emotional expression available to them, while investigating the role of overarching economic and cultural forces in shaping social possibilities. The political economy of antebellum New England wrought dislocation in rural communities while creating new working conditions in the cities. Great geographic mobility acted as an incentive for people to become literate and write letters (Zboray, 1987).[15] And the culture of the 1830s, the "sentimental years," promoted the unprecedented expression of feelings, while not sanctioning individuals who professed their passion to those of the same gender.

The small body of evidence on which this paper is based does not tell us what was typical in antebellum New England, but rather what was possible. Brigham Nims was not so different from his contemporaries in his work history, his family life, and his place within his community. While we cannot generalize the experience of Brigham Nims, we can assess reactions to his behavior. He was not regarded as deviant, but was a respected member of his village and region. Neither Nims nor Beal display any discomfort with their relationship, nor do they express any need for secrecy regarding their claims of affection. The absence of negative reaction suggests it was acceptable for men to reveal their feelings to one another and to write about it. It also indicates that, unlike the twentieth century, the suppression of emotion was not required in order to demonstrate manliness. This chapter raises many more questions than it answers; and in doing so, it suggests strategic areas for future research.

Extant research on fraternal societies convincingly demonstrates that working-class men did construct a world of ritual. But did their world of love overlap with the world of ritual, as it did for women? Nims' friendship with Beal suggests that a world of love between working men did exist. How many people participated in such a world remains to be explored in future research. Nims' experience opens a window onto the full range of friendship between working men—the intimacy, the camaraderie, the physicality, the romance, and the sparring. The Nims-Beal friendship existed apart from the framework of fraternal or trade organizations, indicating that it did not necessitate an exclusive, male-identified group context in which to thrive.

How different was their friendship from relationships documented between middle-class and elite men? Rooted in shared employment and a common culture, Beal and Nims developed a friendship that transcended the workplace. Beal and Nims spoke a less eloquent language than their middle-class contemporaries; nevertheless, it was a language of caring and friendship. The friendship germinated and flourished while the two were single and in their early twenties, rendering it similar to those transitional relationships of youth described by Rotundo. On the basis of one case study it is impossible to assess to what degree their friendship represents other working men and how they might differ categorically from middle-class men's friendships. I strongly suspect that many other such relationships existed because such intimacy was not unacceptable. And although on the surface the case seems consistent with those of the middle-class, class definitions of acceptable masculinity diverge by the turn of the twentieth century. These differences may be rooted in the ante- bellum period and tied to the evolving class structure in ways that only further research can uncover.

In some ways the Nims-Beal relationship was also similar to the intense romantic friendships of middle-class white women. If men's and women's friendships were more similar in the 1830s than they are today, what made them change? Oliker (1989) makes the distinction between romantic friendship and intimate friendship. She claims that for women romantic friendship declined after the nineteenth century, but intimate friendship continued. Romantic friendship declined because of greater mixed-gender socializing, increased dating, the spread of psychoanalytic assumptions about pandemic eroticism, the rise of consumer culture and advertising, the increased value on companionate marriage, and the change in the structure of work and occupations (pp. 29-30). In part, romantic friendship was replaced by romantic marriage, but the practice of intimacy in friendships continued for women.

The evolution of friendship was different for men and had more restrictive consequences. For men, there was not only a shift from romantic friendship to romantic marriage, but also a decline in the value placed on intimacy, and a constriction of the arenas in which intimacy was appropriately expressed. In the late twentieth century, while marriage or partnership might be a place where men can be intimate and vulnerable (although this varies by class), men's ideal friendship no longer includes intimacy. Physically and emotionally intimate relationships are no longer a part of the acceptable range of behavior for "masculine" men. This dramatic change, a result of the many factors Oliker outlines above, but especially the now omnipresent fear of identification as homosexual, is a profound loss for men, gay and straight. It is only with the second wave of feminism that some of this lost ground has come to be reclaimed.

How should we evaluate antebellum relationships that today would unhesitatingly be labeled homosexual? The twentieth-century context alters how we interpret sexual innuendo between friends of the same gender. In antebellum New England it is impossible to separate romantic friendship from other kinds of friendship. A continuum of affection between friends always existed, with sexuality inevitably an undercurrent but not threatening the relationship. Since neither the heterosexual nor the homosexual label had been coined, and consequent stigmas were not part of the cultural consciousness, intimate friendship did not reflect negatively on masculinity. The friendship between Nims and Beal threatened neither their manhood nor their respectability in the community. Only after Freud, and changing economic and social relations, do prescriptions of masculinity so rigidly constrict friendship patterns.

Men could and did have friendships with women; how frequently and in what context remains to be explored in future research. Within this study, cross-gender friendships were more rare than those between men, unless the women were related to the men. If the female friends were not relatives, their interactions were monitored and circumscribed by gossip and community sanction. The one safe arena for friendship with women was the family. A man's relationship with his sister was not necessarily an intimate friendship, but it had the capacity—socially and personally—to be so.

The friendships investigated in this chapter were private, but not exclusionary or antisocial. The nineteenth-century culture did not force a mutually exclusive choice between intimate friendship and sociability. And contrary to Arendt's conception, men's visiting and intimate friendship forged important ties within the community that transcended mundane and personal interests. The bonds were reciprocal, entailing mutual economic and social obligations crucial to the well-being of the community. There are more arenas for the social overlapping of genders in the twentieth century. Ironically, the present is similar in some ways to the Colonial period, where there was less separation of work and family life than in the nineteenth century, creating greater potential for friendship between men and women who are not related, as well as those who are.

The study of historical variation in intimate behavior reveals dramatic fluctuations over the past two centuries. A most important message emerges: Gender arrangements change historically through the influence of culture, human practices and attitudes, and economic relations. Evidence from this study reveals that the capacity for intimacy was not determined by gender or by class. In a culture that broadly defines masculinity and femininity, and that accepts fluidity between the categories rather than imposing rigid boundaries between them, people engage in an expansive range of feeling, expression, and behavior. Early nineteenth-century society allowed for more varied interpretations of manhood than the late twentieth century. The recognition of human agency in the construction of definitions and behavioral boundaries spurs hope that the twenty-first century can restore a similar flexibility in gender arrangements.

Notes

1. Many thanks to Carol Brown, Andrew Bundy, Michael Kimmel, Peter Nardi, Jo Anne Preston, Andrea Walsh, and an anonymous reviewer for comments on an earlier version of this paper. For the purposes of this study, "working" people refers to those who worked for a living, did not attend college, and did not own more than $2,500 of property in 1850. The study therefore includes shoebinders, textile workers, carpenters, teachers, farmers, and seamstresses.

2. All primary documents quoted are presented with the spelling, punctuation, and capitalization as they appear in the original. Brackets are used to indicate words that were not decipherable.

3. For a fuller discussion of Arendt's work, see my "Feminist Critiques of Public and Private: A Critical Analysis," *Berkeley Journal of Sociology, 32,* (1986), 105-128.

4. Smith-Rosenberg (1986), Cott (1977), and others (e.g., Berg, 1978) have argued that the distinct women's culture that developed in this homogeneous environment provided the shared experience and consciousness that gave birth to nineteenth-century feminism. Recent scholarship, particularly that which investigates the working class, challenges the notion that divisions were absolute. Ryan (1981) argues that even for middle-class women, the boundaries were more fluid than domestic ideology purported, at least until after the Civil War. For example, in contrast to the demands of the cult of true womanhood, women's labors in the home were often a part of the local economy, and significant numbers of women were gainfully employed outside of the home. In addition, women were actively involved in the church and in voluntary associations and charitable organizations.

5. I assume Clawson would concur. However, the different kinds of evidence available—organizational records versus personal correspondence—make conclusions impossible. Also, friendship, even fraternity, was not necessarily the primary reason for joining an organization.

6. There has been a popular and scholarly assumption, particularly prior to the women's movement, that men bonded together in solidarity. The women's movement and the research of those such as Smith-Rosenberg (1986) and Cott (1977) have debunked the stereotype of women as competitive, petty, and incapable of friendship. However, the reinterpretation of men's relationships with one another is also a result of second-wave feminism.

7. The question of whether this behavior is age-specific remains unanswered.

8. Nims' wages were $15 a month in 1850—more than twice as much as women teachers were paid. For a discussion of the teaching profession, see Mattingly (1975) and Preston (1989).

9. Given his employment as both artisan and laborer, and the fluctuating social and economic status of each, Nims' class location is difficult to define. However, in the 1830s and 1840s, the period under investigation, he was decidedly not middle class and was not a property owner (partly a function of his age).

10. As with that of other ordinary working men, Beal's life has been extremely difficult to trace. He married Sarah Jane Day in 1838, and she remarried in 1849. There is no official record of his death in Massachusetts, but in 1851 Sarah Jane Travers sought alternative guardianship for her only son, Foster Ellenborough Lassells Beal. The petition she filed with the Worcester County probate court states that the boy's father had died.

11. It is important to note that we have a record of it only because of the distance between them. People in the same town, organization, or workplace rarely had occasion to correspond.

12. Grammatical errors in middle-class letters were sometimes intentional, used as a form of endearment, a kind of baby talk that took a less literate form.

13. That said, and despite his protestations of innocence, other parts of his letters were sexually suggestive. If he acted the way he wrote, the "old maid" would not have needed jealousy to prompt her speculation about romance. This supports the observation that sexual tension was assumed to exist between men and women, except within the safety of a defined situation such as a family.

14. The recipe begins: "6 lbs Butter, 6 lbs Flour, 6 lbs Sugar, $4\frac{1}{2}$ lbs Currants, 3 lbs Raisins, 6 lbs or $4\frac{1}{2}$ dozen eggs with the Spices . . ."

15. The postal service load increased from 1.61 letters per capita in 1840 to 5.15 in 1860.

Appendix

Beal, J. Foster, Roxbury, New Hampshire; Correspondence, 1881-1838; Roxbury Town Records, New Hampshire State Archives.

Bennett, Francis Jr., Gloucester, Massachusetts; Diary, 1852-1854; American Antiquarian Society, Worcester, Massachusetts.

Carpenter, Edward J., Greenfield, Massachusetts; Diary, 1844-1845; American Antiquarian Society, Worcester, Massachusetts.

Chandler, Horatio Nelson, Chesterfield, New Hampshire; Diary, 1839-1842; New Hampshire Historical Society, Concord, New Hampshire.

Dame Sister Letters, Lowell, Massachusetts, 1830-1850; New Hampshire Historical Society, Concord, New Hampshire.

Dixon, Ann Lilley, Worcester, Massachusetts; Correspondence, 1841-1863; American Antiquarian Society, Worcester, Massachusetts.

Foster, John Plummer, North Andover, Massachusetts; Diary, 1848-1888; Essex Institute, Salem, Massachusetts.

Metcalf-Adams Letters, Maine and Massachusetts, 1796-1866; Museum of American Textile History, North Andover, Massachusetts.

Nims, Brigham, Roxbury, New Hampshire; Diary, 1840-1888; New Hampshire Historical Society, Concord, New Hampshire. Correspondence, Roxbury Town Records, New Hampshire State Archives.

Nims Obituary; June 5, 1983; Nims Family Association.

Parker Smith, Rhoda, West Newburyport, Massachusetts; Correspondence, 1824-1854; Essex Institute, Salem, Massachusetts.

Stockwell, Leonard M., Massachusetts; Memorial, c. 1880; American Antiquarian Society, Worcester, Massachusetts.

Trask, Sarah, Beverly, Massachusetts; Diary, 1849-1851; Beverly Historical Society, Beverly, Massachusetts.

References

Arendt, H. (1968). *Men in dark times.* New York: Harcourt, Brace & World.

Atkins, A. (1988). *Brothers, sisters, and shared spheres: An introduction to a work in progress.* Paper presented at the Pacific Coast Branch Meetings of the American Historical Association.

Baron, A. (1989). Questions of gender: Deskilling and demasculinization in the U.S. printing industry, 1830-1915. *Gender & History, 1,* 178-199.

Berg, B. J. (1978). *The remembered gate: Origins of American feminism,* New York: Oxford University Press.

Bureau of the Census. (1975). *Historical statistics of the United States, Colonial times to 1970.* Washington, DC: Author.

Byars, R. P. (1979). *The making of the self-made man: The development of masculine roles and images in ante-bellum America.* Unpublished doctoral dissertation, Michigan State University.

Carnes, M. (1989). *Secret ritual and manhood in Victorian America.* New Haven: Yale University Press.

Chodorow, N. (1978). *The reproduction of mothering.* Berkeley: University of California Press.

Clawson, M. A. (1986). Nineteenth-century women's auxiliaries and fraternal orders. *Signs, 12*(1), 40-61.

Clawson, M. A. (1989). *Constructing brotherhood: Class, gender, and fraternalism.* Princeton, NJ: Princeton University Press.

Cott, N. (1977). *Bonds of womanhood.* New Haven: Yale University Press.

Crowley, J. W. (1987). Howells, Stoddard, and male homosocial attachment in Victorian America. In H. Brod (Ed.), *The making of masculinities* (pp. 301-324). Boston: Allen & Unwin.

Degler, C. (1980). *At odds: Women and the family in America from the Revolution to the present.* New York: Oxford University Press.

D'Emilio, J., & Freedman, E. (1988). *Intimate matters: A history of sexuality in America.* New York: Harper & Row.

Dublin, T. (1979). *Women at work: The transformation of work and community in Lowell, Massachusetts, 1826-1860.* New York: Columbia University Press.

Faderman, L. (1981). *Surpassing the love of men: Romantic friendship and love between women from the Renaissance to the present.* New York: William Morrow.

Faragher, J. M. (1979). *Men and women on the Overland Trail.* New Haven: Yale University Press.

Halttunen, K. (1982). *Confidence men and painted women: A study of middle-class culture in America, 1830-1870.* New Haven: Yale University Press.

Katz, J. (1976). *Gay American history.* New York: Harper Colophon.

Katz, J. (1990). The invention of heterosexuality. *Socialist Review, 20,* 7-34.

Mattingly, P. (1975). *The classless profession.* New York: New York University Press.

Oliker, S. J. (1989). *Best friends in marriage: Exchange among women.* Berkeley: University of California Press.

Pleck, E., & Pleck, J. (1980). *The American man.* Englewood Cliffs, NJ: Prentice-Hall.

Pleck, J. (1975). Man to man: Is brotherhood possible? In N. Glazer-Malbin (Ed.), *Old family/new family* (pp. 229-244). New York: Van Nostrand.

Preston, J. A. (1989). Female aspiration and male ideology: School teaching in nineteenth century New England. In A. Angerman, G. Binnema, A. Keunen, V. Toels, & J. Zirkzee (Eds.), *Current issues in women's history* (pp. 171-182). New York: Routledge.

Richards, J. (1987). "Passing the love of women": Manly love and Victorian society. In J. A. Mangan & J. Walvin (Eds.), *Manliness and morality* (pp. 92-122). New York: St. Martin's Press.

Rothman, E. K. (1984). *Hands and hearts: A history of courtship in America.* Cambridge, MA: Harvard University Press.

Rotundo, E. A. (1989). Romantic friendships: Male intimacy and middle-class youth in the northern United States, 1800-1900. *Journal of Social History, 23,* 1-25.

Rubin, L. (1985). *Just friends.* New York: Harper & Row.

Ryan, M. P. (1981). *Cradle of the middle class.* New York: Cambridge University Press.

Sacks, K. (1975). Engels revisited. In R. Reiter (ed.), *Towards an anthropology of women* (pp. 211-234). New York: Monthly Review Press.

Sherrod, D. (1987). The bonds of men: Problems and possibilities in close male relationships. In H. Brod (Ed.), *The making of masculinities: The new men's studies* (pp. 213-239). Boston: Allen & Unwin.

Sklar, K. K. (1973). *Catharine Beecher: A study in American domesticity.* New York: Norton.

Smith-Rosenberg, C. (1986). *Disorderly conduct.* New York: Oxford University Press.

Stearns, P. N. (1979). *Be a man! Males in modern society.* New York: Holmes & Meier.

Strouse, J. (1980). *Alice James: A biography.* Boston: Houghton Mifflin.

Welter, B. (1966). The cult of true womanhood: 1830-1860. *American Quarterly, 18*(2-1), 151-174.

Wilentz, S. (1984). *Chants democratic: New York City and the rise of the American working class, 1788-1850.* New York: Oxford University Press.

Zboray, R. J. (1987). The letter and the fiction reading public in antebellum America. *Journal of American Culture, 10,* 27-34.

PART TWO

FRIENDSHIP AND SOCIAL STRUCTURAL VARIATIONS

4

The Spatial Foundations of Men's Friendships and Men's Power

DAPHNE SPAIN

Friendships seem to represent the most spontaneous of social relationships. They are established by mutual consent between two or more people and represent an attraction based on personal choice. Yet such choices are a consequence of each individual's location in the social structure. Like marriages, friendships tend to occur between people with similar social characteristics. Thus friendships are more likely to develop within (rather than across) categories of age, race, gender, education, or income (Allan, 1989).

The rigidity of the social structure within which friendship bonds are formed varies by society. Caste is an immutable facet of stratification in India, for example, while race restricts interaction more pervasively than class in the United States. Indian cross-caste or American interracial friendships are thus rare events. When social distinctions are reinforced by spatial separation, friendship boundaries become more pronounced. Interracial friendships are atypical in American society partly because of the high degree of racial segregation characteristic of residential neighborhoods. The spatially separate places in which blacks and whites carry out daily activities hinder the formation of friendship ties.

Men and women are also spatially segregated in ways that affect the formation of friendships. Like race, gender is often the basis of group

AUTHOR'S NOTE: Thanks to Peter Nardi, Michael Kimmel, and an anonymous reviewer for comments on an earlier draft. Recognition should go also to Bettie Hall for manuscript preparation, to Martin Whyte of the University of Michigan for providing the data, to Steve Ainsworth for coding, and to John Jarvis for creation of the computer file.

59

identities, so that concepts of masculinity and femininity develop in relation to one another (Kimmel & Messner, 1989). The purpose of this chapter is to examine the ways in which spatial separation between women and men is associated with the development of male friendships and with gender differences in power. The first hypothesis is that male friendships are strongest in societies with a high degree of gender segregation. Second, the spatial separation that enhances male friendships is hypothesized to reinforce men's power advantage relative to women. That is, structural supports provided by separate places that nurture men's friendships are proposed to solidify those friendships to men's social advantage. These hypotheses are tested using nonindustrial societies for which gender segregation is measured by the presence or absence of a men's ceremonial hut. My perspective places more emphasis on correlation than causation. In other words, it is irrelevant whether men's initial power advantage creates gender segregation or whether such segregation leads to more power for men. Each reinforces the other in a reciprocal relationship that perpetuates power differences by gender.

Spatial Segregation in Nonindustrial Societies

A primary form of gender segregation in many nonindustrial societies is the ceremonial men's hut. Anthropologists have described the separate living arrangements of men (especially characteristic of Melanesian societies) by a variety of names. Whether called a ceremonial house, bachelors' hut, or club house, all serve a similar function: They are places where men congregate with other men to the exclusion of women. In some societies men sleep in the houses apart from their wives and children, while in others they use the houses only for informal meetings or formal initiation rites. The physical structure of the men's house varies from being more elaborate than typical dwellings to being in worse repair. Whatever their built form, however, men's houses are places in which men gather for religious ceremonies, initiation rites, and to make major decisions affecting the village (Bateson, 1958; Herdt, 1981; Hogbin, 1970; Maybury-Lewis, 1967: Mead, 1949; Newman, 1965; Read, 1965).

The men's hut is a place of ritual where men go to gossip, debate, and organize the activities of hunting, fishing, and warfare. In societies with little stratification, status in the community often is achieved by public displays of conspicuous behavior in the men's house. Bateson depicted the traditional Iatmul men of New Guinea as engaging in continuous rivalry for status within the ceremonial hut. All men worked together, however, to impress women outside the hut with periodic rituals. Men would don masks and costumes in the privacy of the hut and then emerge to perform a dance before the women. Bateson (1958, p. 128) observes that "the ceremonial house serves as a Green Room for the preparation of the show," in other words, as a staging area for appropriate displays of masculinity to a feminine audience.

The ceremonial hut is thus a separate place in which men develop personal ties apart from women and also display solidarity toward women as a group. Such solidarity is often revealed in friendship rituals in nonindustrial societies. Among the Azande of the upper Nile, men cement friendships with an elaborate blood-brother ceremony before the entire community, while Nzema men of southern Ghana "marry" their best friends in a public celebration (Sherrod, 1987). These displays of "male bonding" highlight the centrality of masculine relationships to preservation of the social order, a social order that typically allocates greater power to men than to women (Rosaldo & Lamphere, 1974; Schlegal, 1977; Whyte, 1978).

The Spatial Foundations of Men's Power

Sociologists Max Weber and Georg Simmel identified men's houses in nonindustrial societies as repositories of power from which women were excluded (Simmel, 1950, p. 364; Weber, 1978, p. 907). The religious ceremonies, initiation rites, and discussions taking place within the walls of the men's huts are protected by secrecy. Controlling access to secret rituals thus becomes one way of distinguishing insiders from outsiders. Insiders—all men—have access to highly valued social resources, while outsiders—primarily women—are excluded from such access.

Although the essential purpose of secret male clubs in nonindustrial societies is to emphasize differences between men and women (Simmel, 1950, p. 364), not all males are admitted to ceremonial huts. Some might be too young, for example, or from a different kinship group. Men who are not strong warriors are relegated to the outside as symbolic "women." In war-prone societies, definitions of masculinity are intertwined so closely with battle skills that lacking such skills means one is less than a "real" man. Not surprisingly, warriors are accorded the highest status and greatest power in such societies. And rituals of the men's hut reinforce insiders' definition of the social order (Weber, 1978, p. 1144).

Women are barred from participation in ceremonial huts and there-fore excluded from the training in practical and symbolic skills neces-sary for positions of status and power. Men's huts thus create spatial segregation by gender that reinforces men's potential for friendship and greater power, while reducing women's access to the knowledge neces-sary for the acquisition of power. For example, initiation rites among boys of the same age cohort teach them to depend on one another for such endeavors as hunting and fighting. While boys are learning these highly valued skills within the men's hut, girls are learning the less prestigious skills of cooking and child care outside its walls. Initiation rites recreate the same hierarchy of authority found in the patriarchal family by placing young boys under the supervision of older men. Wo-men's lack of authority within the family is translated into a total absence from the secret society. That is, their symbolic lack of presence within the family authority structure becomes a corporeal lack of presence in the men's hut. Thus secret fraternal associations contribute to male dominance outside, as well as inside, the family (Clawson, 1980).

Weber drew heavily on work by Schurtz in identifying men's houses as military barracks where warriors lived "as a communistic associa-tion, apart from wives and households" (Weber, 1978, p. 906). Although removed from the household, warriors periodically reasserted their authority over women, as the following passage demonstrates:

> In order to secure their economic position, which is based on the continuous plundering of outsiders, *especially women*, the consociated warriors resort under certain circumstances to the use of religiously colored means of intim-idation. The spirit manifestations which they stage with masked processions very often are nothing but plundering campaigns which require for their un-disrupted execution that, on the first sound of the tom-tom, *the women and all outsiders* flee, on pain of instant death, from the villages into the woods and thus allow the "spirits" conveniently and without danger of being un-masked to take from the houses whatever may please them. . . . Obviously, the warriors do not believe at all in the legitimacy of their conduct. *The crude and simple swindle* is recognized by them as such and *is protected by the magical prohibition against entry into the men's house by outsiders and by the draconic obligations of silence which are imposed upon the members* (Weber, 1978, p. 907; emphasis added).

"Outsiders" here include both women and strangers who are excluded from knowledge of the ceremonial secrets. That knowledge is reinforced both by spatial segregation and by the "obligations of silence" prevent-ing men from betraying knowledge of the spirit masquerade. Men's prestige is weakened when their secrets are revealed by the indiscretion of a member or by a missionary's intervention (Simmel, 1950, p. 364; Weber, 1978, p. 907).

Men's Huts, Men's Friendships, and Power Differentials

Among the Akwe-Shavante of Brazil, induction into the bachelors' hut occurs among boys united in the same age-set (typically ages 7 through 12), a type of cohort identification that separates its members hierarchically from other members of the society and forms the central core of Shavante stratification. During their 5 years in the hut, boys are taught practical and symbolic skills in the making of weapons, ceremonial regalia, songs and dances. The seclusion serves both to develop a "corporate spirit" and to expose the boys to older men for leadership training through example and emulation. Boys are collectively socialized into masculine traits most admired by the Shavante, such as wrestling, singing at night to demonstrate they are "wakeful," and stamping their feet in dances (Maybury-Lewis, 1967, p. 113).

The boys' corporate solidarity is structurally supported by the institution of ceremonial partnerships. While in the bachelors' hut, each boy acquires one or two *i-amo* (literally "my other" or "my partner"). These formal relationships are characterized by friendship (e.g., in game playing) and mutual assistance (e.g., in plaiting sleeping mats). Ideally, each boy sleeps between his *i-amo* in the hut and dances between them during ceremonies. Shavante age-sets dance in a circle holding hands, making it theoretically possible for everyone to hold both partners' hands (Maybury-Lewis, p. 108).

Whether these patterns are actually carried out in practice is not as important as the concept that each boy enters into a special relationship with all the members of his age-set. "They are collectively his *i-amo* . . . and the important aspect of the institution is that a man is bound throughout his life by formal friendship ties to at least one member of his age-set . . ." (Maybury-Lewis, p. 108). The bond may be operative only during the years when the age-set is secluded in the bachelors' hut, but the ideal is that of lifetime connections.

Bonds formed during the years of communal seclusion are important for future positions of power in Shavante society. The age-set system plays a central role in the identification and recruitment of future leaders. While still living in the bachelors' hut, two boys are appointed by the chief to lead their age-set in all its activities. Expectations for these boys are high: They learn to organize hunting, fishing, and gathering trips; lead ceremonial rituals; and bear sacred flutes during initiation rites (Maybury-Lewis, p. 191).

Shavante girls are excluded from the age-set system and thus from the training necessary to become future chiefs. Women are also barred from participation in the nightly village meetings in which the affairs of the community are discussed, and in fact are not "supposed to approach the mature men's council *nor to hear its debates*" (Maybury-Lewis, p. 143; emphasis added). Even overhearing discussions of the men's council is considered disrespectful behavior for women and younger men. The taboos that prevent women from listening to the men also reinforce a knowledge differential between the sexes. The importance of these men's councils cannot be overestimated. Everything happening in the community (and in neighboring communities) is discussed there, disputes reconciled, and decisions affecting communal life made. The men's council is so important that it often overrules the chief on a variety of issues (Maybury-Lewis, pp. 144, 199, 200).

Shavante girls marry between the ages of 8 and 10 and typically have sexual intercourse before their first menses. Traditional Shavante society is a polygamous one in which wives are considered an economic asset. Divorce is rare since men do not need to divorce one wife in order to take another. Women who divorce are required to leave the community, a severe penalty since it means leaving an extended kinship network (Maybury-Lewis, pp. 76, 82, 94). Women who are married as children, are banished from their communities if divorced, and do not participate in public decision-making have relatively little power by standards of nonindustrial societies.

The Sambia of New Guinea provide another example of pronounced gender segregation and men's greater social power. Relations between men and women are highly polarized among the Sambia. Ritual taboos forbid men and women from performing each other's hunting and gardening tasks, and the hamlet is divided into male and female spaces to insure gender segregation. Boys enter the men's house when they are 7 to 10 years of age, and for the next 10 to 15 years undergo a series of initiation rites that eventually turns them into men. Avoidance of women is crucial throughout this period. Segregation taboos are enforced with shamings, beatings, and ultimately death if ritual secrets are revealed (Herdt & Stoller, 1990).

Sambian women have little power, either within or outside the family. Hamlet authority is held by male elders and warriors, and men are in charge of public affairs. Men's rhetoric disparages older and younger women alike; wives are thought to be inferior to husbands. In all aspects of life (except reproduction), "male is the socially preferred and valued sex" (Herdt & Stoller, 1990, p. 56).

Herdt's work among the Sambia revealed another facet of friendship among members of the men's house: the erotic homosexual component of the relationships among initiates and elders. The Sambia believe that females mature naturally because their bodies contain menstrual blood, which hastens physical and mental development. Males, however, do not mature as quickly as females because their bodies do not naturally contain semen. Therefore men require inseminations and magical rituals for many years to catch up with women and become strong, masculine men (Herdt, 1981).

Daily homosexual encounters are thus a crucial part of the maturation process for Sambian boys. Depending on the stage of initiation, males progress through an exclusively homosexual behavioral period, to a briefer bisexual period, and finally to exclusive heterosexual relationships with wives when they leave the men's hut. The failure to negotiate these transitions is considered a failure of masculinity (Herdt & Stoller, 1990). This relationship between homosexual behavior and the presence of a men's house is also characteristic of other Melanesian cultures (Herdt, 1984).

I propose that the same spatial arrangements fostering men's friendships also enhance men's power by reducing women's access to knowledge of highly valued social resources. The walls of the men's hut both enclose men in a space promoting male solidarity and exclude women from the songs, dances, and transmission of hunting and warfare skills that reinforce the status quo. Masculine traits associated with greater power are located within the walls of the men's hut; feminine traits associated with lesser power are located outside its walls.

Data from the Human Relations Area Files are used to test the hypotheses that men's friendships are strongest in societies with the greatest gender separation, and that men's power relative to women's is associated most strongly with men's friendships when those ties are structurally supported by gender spatial segregation.

Data and Methods

The data are a subset of Murdock and White's (1969) Standard Cross Cultural Sample and consist of 93 Human Relations Area File (HRAF)

cultures randomly drawn by Whyte (1978) for his study of gender stratification in nonindustrial societies. Frequencies and a detailed description of the sample are available in *The Status of Women in Preindustrial
Societies* (Whyte, 1978). Whyte's coding used the original sources and
required each variable to meet stringent inter-coder reliability standards.
A research assistant conducted additional coding (from the Human
Relations Area Files and from Whyte's original sources) for the presence of a men's house. Any reference to a men's house was coded as
one, while no reference was coded as zero. At least two sources were
consulted for each culture. This procedure may have underestimated the
presence of spatial segregation, since there may have been references
overlooked. However, ethnographies typically include a description of
the physical layout and living arrangements of the village, and oversight
of a ceremonial men's house would be rare.

The current research is based on ethnographies of cultures existent
primarily in the nineteenth and early twentieth centuries (41% of the
cultures in the sample refer to time periods before 1900, and 59% to
cultures studied since 1900). Thus the term "nonindustrial" is meant to
identify reliance on hunting and gathering, horticultural, or agricultural
economies rather than a specific period of history. The majority of the
sample reflects the "anthropological present" and should not be considered evolutionary precedents of industrial or advanced industrial societies.

Gender *spatial segregation* is defined as the presence or absence of
a ceremonial men's hut. Twenty-two of 81 societies (27%) for which
information was available had men's huts. *Men's friendship* is opera-
tionalized as a 4-item Guttman scale constructed by Whyte to measure
"male solidarity," ranging in value from 1 (least) to 5 (greatest) solidarity. It is based on the following variables: presence of male activities
that exclude females; ritualization of such male activities; ranking of
men hierarchically within these activities; and training for warfare as
part of the activities (Whyte, 1978). This definition of solidarity (or
"male bonding", as Tiger [1969] would call it) represents several aspects of friendship and thus qualifies as an adequate proxy measure.
The strength of the variable is its emphasis on activities, a commonly
recognized element of male friendships (Sherrod, 1987). The variable's
weakness is the absence of components dealing with emotional ties or
possible homosexual behavior.

Since *men's power* exists relative to women's lack of power, it is necessary to examine men's power in relation to that of women. Those societies
in which men's power is greatest will be those in which women's is lowest.

This study uses three measures of power typically used in stratification research: control of labor, control of property, and participation in the public sphere.

According to Blumberg (1978), control of the means of production and allocation of surplus influences a variety of life options. *Control of labor* is represented by a scale ranging in value from 1 (least male control) to 7 (greatest male control). The scale consists of the addition of two variables—control over male labor and control over joint male-female labor—calculated by Whyte (1978) and correlated at Gamma = .80.

A second type of formal power is represented by the ability to *control property*. In nonindustrial societies with few material goods, rules of inheritance often govern the allocation of property to men and women. The current research adapts Whyte's (1978) variable ranging from 1 (female preference) to 4 (male preference) in the inheritance of land, tools, animals, orchards, or produce. The third indicator is *participation in the public sphere*. There are relatively few nonindustrial societies in which women hold positions of political power, making it necessary to use a broad definition of community participation. Therefore, Whyte's dichotomized variable indicating degree of public activity is adapted to reflect participation in community gatherings (such as village meetings or activities not specifically religious or political in nature). The variable ranges in value from 0 (least male participation) to 1 (greatest male participation). These three dependent variables are only weakly related. Partial correlations range in value from −.01 to .40.

In addition to these three measures of formal power, four measures of informal power are analyzed. *Husband's dominance* is a dichotomous variable represented by the absence (0) or presence (1) of an explicit statement that men should and do dominate their wives. *Male aggression valued* is a 3-point scale of the value attached to men's aggression, strength, and sexual potency; it ranges from 1 (least emphasis) to 3 (greatest emphasis). Belief in *female inferiority* is Whyte's dichotomous variable of the absence (0) or presence (1) of a clearly stated belief that women are generally inferior to men. The last variable, *control of women's sexuality*, is a 2-point scale reflecting least male control (1) to greatest (2) of the following items: premarital double standard; extramarital double standard; ease of remarriage for women; and spouses' relative ages at first marriage.

With the exception of the relationship between the male solidarity scale and the presence of men's huts, relationships between variables are not statistically significant. The small sample sizes and qualitative nature of the data make statistical significance difficult to achieve. The data should be interpreted, therefore, as descriptive of this sample only. Gamma is the statistic used to quantify the strength of the relationships between ordinal-level variables.

Analysis

The first hypothesis is that male friendships will be strongest in societies in which men and women are most spatially separated. The existence of a separate place in which men gather without women reinforces bonds of male friendship and elaborates differences between appropriately masculine and feminine behaviors. Table 4.1 demonstrates the strong positive association (gamma = .61) between the presence of a men's hut and the 5-point scale of male solidarity. The mean score on male solidarity for the 59 societies without men's huts is 1.7 (SD = 1.3) compared with a mean score of 2.95 (SD = 1.5) for the 22 societies with men's huts (data not shown).

Men's power is divided into two categories: formal and informal. Table 4.1 reports gamma coefficients for the cross-tabulations of male solidarity by each measure of men's power. The hypothesis that men's power is greater in societies with stronger men's friendships would predict positive coefficients for all variables. Among examples of formal power, men's control of property and control of labor are greater in societies with greater male solidarity, as predicted. Men's control of public affairs is not related to male solidarity in the hypothesized direction, however. Greater male solidarity is associated with greater female participation in public activities. Since Whyte's coding of women's activities includes those segregated from men, it may be that societies with men's huts are those in which women stage separate ceremonies among themselves. Another possibility is that greater male solidarity emerges *in reaction to* women's participation in public life. That is, men's friendships become more intense when women's activities threaten the definition of public events as masculine. Men's friendships then reproduce, often in the privacy of ceremonial huts, privileges perceived as lost to women in the public sphere.

Among examples of informal power, all four of the relationships are in the anticipated direction. Husband's dominance within the family, the value attached to male aggression, a general belief in women's inferiority, and control of women's sexuality are all positively associated with male

Table 4.1 Male Solidarity by Measures of Gender Segregation and Men's Power

Association Between Male Solidarity and:	*Male Solidarity Scale*	
	Gamma Value	*(N)*
Gender Segregation		
Presence of a men's hut	.61	(81)
Formal Power		
Men's control of property	.09	(71)
Men's control of labor	.11	(81)
Men's control of public affairs	−.10	(62)
Informal Power		
Husband's dominance	.30	(63)
Male aggression valued	.20	(81)
Belief in female inferiority	.12	(93)
Control of women's sexuality	.13	(92)

SOURCE: HRAF data from Whyte, 1978

solidarity. In sum, six of the seven measures of men's power are positively, although weakly, associated male solidarity.

The second hypothesis leads to an examination of the relationship between male solidarity and men's power within the context of spatial segregation. The hypothesis is that men's power will be greatest in societies where male solidarity is reinforced by spatial segregation. Table 4.2 reports gamma coefficients for the relationship between male solidarity and each measure of men's power, controlling for the presence of a ceremonial men's hut. Support for the hypothesis would be demonstrated by consistently higher positive coefficients among those societies with men's huts.

Partialling out the effects of a men's hut demonstrates the importance of a physical place in strengthening the relationship between men's friendships and men's power. In societies *without* men's huts, men's control of property, labor, and public affairs is actually negatively related to male solidarity, while in societies *with* men's huts, men's formal power and male solidarity are related in the hypothesized positive direction. In other words, men's formal power increases with their degree of solidarity only in societies with a men's hut. In societies without a men's hut, men's formal power *declines* as their degree of solidarity increases.

The pattern is similar for three of the four measures of informal power. Male solidarity is more strongly associated with husband's dominance,

Table 4.2   The Relationship Between Male Solidarity and Men's Power, Controlling for Gender Segregation

| | Ceremonial Men's Hut | | | |
| Association Between | Absent | | Present | |
Male Solidarity and:	Gamma	(N)	Gamma	(N)
Formal Power				
Men's control of property	−.18	(48)	.42	(16)
Men's control of labor	−.10	(51)	.30	(20)
Men's control of public affairs	−.41	(39)	.31	(17)
Informal Power				
Husband's dominance	.36	(38)	.41	(16)
Male aggression valued	−.02	(50)	.53	(21)
Belief in female inferiority	.10	(59)	.50	(22)
Control of women's sexuality	.57	(58)	.03	(22)

SOURCE: HRAF data from Whyte, 1978.

the valuation of male aggression, and a belief in female inferiority in societies with a men's hut than in societies without a men's hut. The opposite is true of the relationship between male solidarity and men's control of women's sexuality. Men's control of women's sexuality is more weakly associated with male solidarity in societies *with* men's huts. Apparently men must impose their physical presence on women to most effectively enforce standards of sexual conduct. Such a finding would be consistent with homosexual practices as exemplified by the Sambia. To the extent that men in societies with ceremonial huts are not engaged in sexual relations with women for a significant number of years, sustaining this particular form of control would be less relevant to men's informal power advantage than sustaining ideologies buttressing husband's dominance, male aggression, and female inferiority.

Among the seven relationships described in Table 4.2, six were in the hypothesized direction. In general, male solidarity and men's power are more strongly related in societies with men's huts than in those without men's huts.

Conclusions

Men's friendships and men's power appear to be enhanced by gender segregation in this sample of nonindustrial societies. The presence of a ceremonial men's hut is positively associated with male solidarity, and male solidarity and men's power are more strongly associated in societies with a men's hut than in those without men's huts.

The literature on nonindustrial societies with men's huts suggests that these are places in which men may compete internally for status, but from which they present a united front to women and other outsiders. The physical walls of such huts provide the enclosure necessary to protect ritual secrets. Further, the sense of belonging to a particular communal group is enhanced by sharing a space separate from those who do not belong. Outsiders are most typically women. However, men who are too young or who fail to display typically "masculine" characteristics may also be excluded from the men's hut.

Men's power is reinforced by such spatial separation to the extent that physical barriers help create the arena in which important decisions are made. Especially in regard to formal power, the rules determining inheritance of property, control of labor, and participation in public affairs will remain biased in favor of the more powerful group. As long as that decision-making process is not accessible to outsiders, the rules will change slowly (if at all).

In terms of informal power, social control is easier to exert if a place exists in which men's authority can be expressed without challenge from women. The ability to control women's sexuality appears to be an exception to this generalization. Male solidarity is most strongly associated with control of women's sexuality when there is *no* spatial segregation between the sexes. Perpetual vigilance is apparently an important component of monitoring acceptable sexual behavior.

Men's friendships seem most responsive to socially generated supports such as built structures. The construction of a ceremonial men's hut occurs for a variety of cultural, mystical, or religious reasons, all of which are socially created. If it is plausible that fraternal associations recreate a patriarchical hierarchy, as suggested by Clawson (1980), then it is possible that the existence of a shared structure further emphasizes the family analogy. Thus men's friendships would be strengthened by association with a dwelling modeled after a family dwelling, and the relationship between men's friendships and men's power would be strongest where such spatial supports exist.

Although it is inappropriate to make inferences about advanced industrial societies based on data for nonindustrial societies, several speculative observations about current spatial supports for men's friendships and men's power are possible. Men's friendships in industrialized societies tend to be oriented around activities rather than intimacies (Sherrod, 1987). Bonds of friendship are most likely to form when these activities are accompanied by opportunities for socializing in a separate place from women, for example, a clubhouse or tavern (Allan, 1989). Men's friendships often are enhanced by such gendered spatial arrangements: The houses occupied by college fraternities and the lodges housing Elks' and Freemasons' meetings are examples. These separate places in which large groups of men gather help reinforce the tendency for men's friendships to be more impersonal and to include more people than women's friendships. Having fewer public spaces in which to develop friendships in large groups, women's friendships tend to be more intimate and to include fewer people in more private spaces (Allan, 1989).

This difference in the public versus private nature of men's and women's friendships has implications for power differentials between women and men. Talking in private about private issues (as women do) does not have the same potential for social power that acting in public on public issues (as men do) has for social power. When the public activities in which men engage occur within the confines of a place segregated from women, the information conveyed by men's actions is accessible only to other men.

Traditionally, elite men have used male-only social clubs as places in which to engage in the public activities related to business and politics (Starr, 1987). Until their recently court-enforced integration, clubs such as the Cosmos and Metropolitan in Washington, D.C., were the contemporary equivalents of ceremonial men's huts (Feinberg, 1988; Pressley, 1988). Like ceremonial huts, these clubs have been as exclusive of some men (who do not meet appropriate criteria of ethnicity, race, education, or income) as of all women. The Supreme Court ruled that, far from being private organizations that could limit membership, these were places in which important public business was conducted. These clubs represented separate spaces in which men's friendships were instrumental in promoting relations of power and influence outside their walls. By banning their all-male policies, the court acknowledged the unequal socioeconomic advantages accruing to men by virtue of club membership.

In sum, men's friendships and men's power appear most strongly related when they are supported by spatial arrangements that separate men and women. Spatial barriers thus help differentiate appropriate masculine and feminine characteristics, contributing to a gendered society in which men's power is greater than women's.

References

Allan, G. (1989). *Friendship: Developing a sociological perspective*. Boulder, CO: Westview.

Bateson, G. (1958). *Naven* (2nd ed.). London: Wildwood House.

Blumberg, R. L. (1978). *Stratification: Socioeconomic and sexual inequality*. Dubuque, IA: William C. Brown.

Clawson, M. A. (1980, Summer). Early modern fraternalism and the patriarchal family. *Feminist Studies, 6*, 368-391.

Feinberg, L. (1988, October 12). 18 women end Cosmos Club's 110-year male era. *Washington Post*, p. B3.

Herdt, G. H. (1981). *Guardians of the flutes*. New York: McGraw-Hill.

Herdt, G. H. (1984). *Ritualized homosexuality in Melanesia*. Berkeley: University of California Press.

Herdt, G. H., & Stoller, R. J. (1990). *Intimate communications*. New York: Columbia University Press.

Hogbin, I. (1970). *The island of menstruating men*. London: Chandler.

Kimmel, M., & Messner, M. (Eds.). (1989). *Men's lives*. New York: Macmillan.

Mead, M. (1949). *Male and female*. New York: William Morrow.

Maybury-Lewis, D. (1967). *Akwe-Shavante society*. Oxford: Clarendon Press.

Murdock, G. P., & White, D. (1969). Standard cross-cultural sample. *Ethnology, 8*, 329-369.

Newman, P. L. (1965). *Knowing the Gururumba*. New York: Holt, Rinehart & Winston.

Pressley, S. A. (1988, June 26). Metropolitan Club ends ban on women members. *Washington Post*, p. B1.

Read, K. (1965). *The high valley*. New York: Scribner.

Rosaldo, M., & Lamphere, L. (Eds.). (1974). *Woman, culture, and society*. Palo Alto, CA: Stanford University Press.

Schlegal, A. (Ed.). (1977). *Sexual stratification*. New York: Columbia University Press.

Sherrod, D. (1987). The bonds of men: Problems and possibilities in close male relationships. In H. Brod (Ed.), *The making of masculinities* (pp. 213-240). Boston: Allen & Unwin.

Simmel, G. (1950). *The sociology of Georg Simmel* (K. Wolff, Ed.). New York: Free Press.

Starr, R. (1987, Fall). Men's clubs, women's rights. *The Public Interest, 89*, 57-70.

Tiger, L. (1969). *Men in groups*. New York: Random House.

Weber, M. (1978). *Economy and society* (2 vol.) (G. Roth & C. Wittich, Eds.). Berkeley: University of California Press.

Whyte, M. (1978). *The status of women in preindustrial societies*. Princeton, NJ: Princeton University Press.

5

Men in Networks

Private Communities, Domestic Friendships[1]

BARRY WELLMAN

Friends in Community Networks

Has the movement of North American friendships from public spaces to private homes affected the nature of friendship? My approach to this question is to see how friendships among men fit within a man's *personal community network* of active relationships, including his ties with kinfolk, neighbors, workmates, and women friends. Instead of assuming that men belong to communities that are traditional solidary groups —such as neighborhoods, kinship groups, or cliques of buddies—I treat each man as the center of his own Ptolemaic universe (see Figure 5.1). To set in perspective the analysis of friendships between men, I compare them with other community ties, such as women's friendships, friendships between men and women, and ties with kin, neighbors, and workmates.[2]

I suspect that the current situation of men's friendship is linked to transformations in the nature of community. Work and community have separated, and cars, phones, and planes have liberated community ties from being bound up in neighborhood, kinship, and work groups. One result has been that men's friendships now operate out of households rather than in public places. Husbands and wives now have more integrated friendships, men do not routinely rely on their friends to accomplish

AUTHOR'S NOTE: This chapter was written with the collaboration of Milena Gulia, David Tindall, and Karen Ramsay, Vince Salazar, Cristina Tahoces.

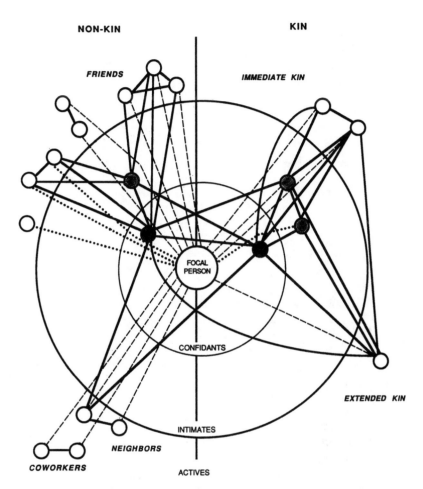

Figure 5.1. Typical Personal Network

important tasks outside of the household, and the intellectual climate now treats friendship as a relationship in which women excel.

My findings come from analyzing the accounts Toronto men and women give about their active relations with kith and kin. We interviewed 29 Torontonians (14 men and 15 women) for 10 to 15 hours in 1977-1978. Although the sample is small, we gained much more detail about many more ties than large-scale survey research usually elicits. Moreover, the congruence of our findings with those from large surveys gives us confidence in the general usefulness of studying this small sample (Wellman, 1982, 1988, 1990, 1992).

The respondents are predominantly British-Canadian, married (with children), working-class and lower middle-class. The men are variously employed as electricians, laboratory technicians, truck drivers, and in other skilled and semiskilled positions. The women hold white-collar and service jobs such as secretaries, insurance claims examiners, and waitresses. Hence these data cannot tell much about the friendships of the rich, the poor, the unmarried, segregated minorities.

These Torontonians told us about the 343 *active* members of their personal community networks: socially close *intimates* and the somewhat less intimate but still *significant* network members with whom they are in active contact (for details, see Wellman, 1982; Wellman & Wortley, 1989a, 1990).[3] Although these relationships comprise only a small fraction of the 1,500 or so informal ties that most North Americans probably maintain (Killworth, Johnsen, Bernard, Shelley, & McCarthy, 1990), they comprise most of a person's actively supportive ties (Erickson, Radkewycz, & Nosanchuk, 1988). Hence we have information about the strong ties that supply most resources and we ignore the many weaker ties important for obtaining information and integrating social systems.[4]

Public and Private Communities

The Privatization of Community

Men's Public Communities: My arguments about changes in men's friendships since earlier eras are speculative. They are my initial attempt to make some sense out of what I have found when studying contemporary male friendships. My findings made me wonder why intellectual discourse in North America now thinks that men's friendships are inferior to women's friendships, and whether changes in the nature of community since preindustrial times have fostered changes in men's friendships. To address these matters adequately would take many books. In this chapter, I can only begin the debate by sketching a preliminary account, which skips lightly over continents and centuries.

Urban men customarily have gathered in communal, quasi-public networks.[5] Although a popular metaphor has been the "old-boy networks," which allegedly run Britain, such male bonds have not just been elite shows (Cohen, 1974). Work groups spilled over into pubs after hours

(Kornblum, 1974; Wadel, 1969). Sports teams, even at the highest professional levels, often fostered supportive male friendships (Kramer, 1968; Messner, 1987; Pronger, 1990). Even casual street corners had their regular crowds of male buddies (Gans, 1962; Liebow, 1967; Useem, Useem, & Gibson, 1960; Whyte, 1943).

Such gathering places are what Oldenburg (1989) calls "the third place" in men's lives, along with home and work. They are "parochial" settings, neither private nor public (Hunter, 1985; Lofland, 1989). More accessible than private homes, they drew their clienteles from fluid networks of regular habitués with similar social backgrounds (Clawson, 1989; Kingsdale, 1973; Lofland, 1973; Oldenburg, 1989; Pleck & Pleck, 1980; Sennett, 1977; Wireman, 1984). Men could drop into the pub, cafe, fraternal club, or street corner "to eat well, drink wine, play cards and escape from the boredom of home life" (Tristan, 1991, p. 93). The high density of the city meant that they were likely to find many other men to talk with. In eighteenth-century Paris, a *vie de quartier* animated public places, with men gathering at wine shops, taverns, cafes, and barbershops (Garrioch, 1986).

> [T]he whole neighborhood overflowed [into the street] from nearby houses, workshops, shops and taverns. Around every inhabitant a *quartier* took on its shape, make up of daily contacts and changing reputations. Individuals worked round the corner from where they lived . . . (Roche, 1981, p. 246)

Communities focused around these places have been instrumental as well as communal. Although men went there to enjoy themselves, the communities controlled resources and accomplished work. In Colonial New England, "neighbors . . . assumed not only the right but the duty to supervise one another's lives" (Wall, 1990, p. 134). Men used their communities to organize politically, to accomplish collective tasks, and to deal with larger organizations.

Women's Private Communities: Such public community was a man's game.[6] "A woman going to a wine shop alone risked being taken for a prostitute, and to say that she was *'courait les cafes'* (ran around the cafes) was tantamount to calling her a whore" (Garrioch, 1986; see also Roche, 1981). Women stayed at home to tend the hearths and do paid work (Duby, 1985; Roncière, 1985). When women did go out to do paid work, they either did domestic work in someone else's home, or they returned directly to their own home after work (Elshtain, 1981; Mackenzie 1988; Shorter 1975; Tilly & Scott, 1978).

Consequently, women's communities were more private than men's. Women visited each other's homes in small numbers to provide companionship and domestic support (Duby, 1985; Garrioch, 1986; Gullestad, 1984; Mackenzie, 1988; Roche, 1981; Roncière, 1985; Sharma, 1986; Vicinus, 1985). In the nineteenth century, this separation of the men's public world and the woman's private world became even more pronounced in North America and Europe. The "cult of domesticity . . . [preached that while] men took on the care of business and politics, women devoted themselves to the life of the home" (Wall, 1990, pp. 144-145; see also Cott, 1977). Many women stopped working for wages inside and outside of the home and concentrated on making their homes their castles.

The continuing evidence of supportive women's friendships is enough to refute any Tigerish (1969) belief that men have uniquely innate propensities to form friendship groups.[7] Long-standing divisions of labor between men and women, together with the availability of public gathering places only to men, has encouraged men to form more permeable, more public, and less domestically oriented bonds. Where the recurrent public gatherings of men often led to somewhat corporate groups, women's friendships were more informally organized networks.

The Liberation of Community

The Separation of Work and Community: The reorganization of work in the Industrial Revolution has helped move friendships from shops (and nearby pubs) to homes. Zoning segregates big plants and offices from residential neighborhoods. Co-workers commute from many different neighborhoods and no longer come home together after work.

The nature of work also discourages many workers from forming friendly ties. Some workers are isolated from others, as the truck driver who told us:

> I generally keep problems to myself unless it is a problem that I can share with the wife. I don't try to give advice to anybody; they have their own lives to live.

Supervisors do not become friends with subordinates. For example, while a production manager formed a close patron-client relationship with an older manager who taught him the ropes, his position cut him off from friendships with other workers:

> My work is a manager's work. You have to get your work done through other people. You never hear anything good from them. You never see them if there's

not problems. There's obviously problems. Therefore you see them, and you don't like to see them!

Although co-workers continue to use informal ties to accomplish their work and get through the day (Halle, 1984), few relationships with co-workers continue after hours. Thus Toronto businessmen, making virtue out of reality, pride themselves on keeping their work and domestic lives separate (Erickson, 1991). "I try to keep my own circle of friends apart from work," says an accountant. Work is one world, community is another.

Moving Beyond Local Communities: Since World War II, telephones and cars have enabled people to maintain active community ties over long distances. Communities have been liberated from the constraints of space and the claims of neighborhood, work, and kinship groups. Each person (and each household) is at the center of a unique personal community, usually consisting of kin, friends, neighbors, and workmates; local, regional, and long-distance ties. It is fairly easy for people to maneuver through their networks, interacting more with compatible people and avoiding disagreeable neighbors, kinfolk, co-workers, and acquaintances (Wellman, 1988; Wellman & Leighton, 1979). A Toronto accountant asserts:

> I would rather have nobody than somebody who doesn't have much in common with me.

And an upholsterer warns:

> Family ties are great as long as they are just ties and not stranglables [*sic*]. Don't drive it into me that because we're related you've got to come see me.

Rather than gathering in public places where they may have to deal with all comers, Toronto men now have selective encounters with dispersed network members who live an average of 9 miles away. Compared to those of Toronto women, more of the men's ties are to people living outside of their neighborhoods (73% versus 50%). Most of the men's ties are with friends and relatives living outside of the neighborhood but still in the metropolitan area. Friendships depend more on accessibility than do kinship ties. Friends comprise only one-quarter of the men's active ties with network members living more than 150 miles away. The other three-quarters of these long-distance ties are with kin whose normative obligations and network density help them to stay together.

The preponderance of non-local relationships has changed the ways in which men contact network members. Rather than casual public encounters, they now meet in purposeful engagements. Toronto men telephone active network members almost as often as they see them and have some sort of contact with most network members at least once a week (Fischer, 1982; Wellman 1990; Wellman, Carrington, & Hall, 1988; Wellman & Tindall, 1992).[8] Nor are long-distance connections sustained only by telephone. For example, there was a daily average in 1985 of 447 charter (i.e., non-business) airline passengers between Toronto and Vancouver, 4,500 kilometers away (McKie & Thompson, 1990, p. 247).

The Composition of Personal Community Networks

The personal communities of Toronto men tend to have almost equal percentages of active ties with non-kin (45%)—friends, neighbors, and workmates—as with kin. Their active networks contain an average of 4.8 strong, intimate ties and 5.0 significant, but not intimate, ties. These networks usually contain four or five male non-kin, one female non-kin, two male kin, and two or three female kin (see Table 5.1).

Looked at more closely, the men's networks contain an average of two intimate male friends (including neighbors and workmates) and one intimate kinship tie (a brother, father, or adult son; Table 5.1). One out of every two men also has a woman as an intimate friend or neighbor, and an intimate tie to a sister, mother, or adult daughter. In addition to their intimate ties, Toronto men usually have significant, but not intimate, ties with two or three friends, workmates, or (more rarely) neighbors. Half also have a significant, non-intimate tie with a woman friend (or more rarely, a neighbor or workmate), and most have one or two significant, non-intimate ties with a grandmother, aunt, or woman cousin.

The networks of Toronto men are smaller than those of Toronto women, even though the men have more ties with women than the Toronto women have with men. The main reason for the smaller size of the men's networks is that the men have fewer significant, non-intimate ties with neighbors and extended kin (Table 5.1). The difference comes from the more extensive neighboring done by the many Toronto women who stay home all day to do domestic work. Indeed, the networks of those men and women who do paid work are almost the same size (Wellman, 1985).[9]

Toronto men engage in little of the public neighboring observed a generation ago on North American street corners. Most of the men's

Table 5.1 Mean Number and Percentage of Role Relationships in a Network, by Gender of Respondent and Network Member, and by Tie Strength

Respondents		Men N = 14				Women N = 15			
Network Members		Men N = 87		Women N = 50		Men N = 49		Women N = 157	
		mean #	%	mean #	%	mean #	%	mean #	%
Friend	Int	1.4	14	0.4	4	0.4	3	1.4	10
	Non	1.1	11	0.4	4	0.3	2	1.3	10
Neighbor	Int	0.3	3	0.1	0.7	0	0	0.7	5
	Non	0.5	5	0.1	1	0.3	2	2.7	19
Workmate	Int	0.2	2	0	0	0.1	0.5	0.1	1
	Non	0.9	9	0.1	0.7	0	0	0.5	3
All Non-Kin		4.4	45	1.1	10	1.1	8	6.7	48
Immediate Kin	Int	1.2	12	0.9	9	0.5	3	1.4	10
	Non	0.5	5	1.0	10	1.0	7	0.9	7
Extended Kin	Int	0.1	1	0.2	2	0	0	0.1	1
	Non	0	0	0.4	4	0.7	5	1.3	10
All Kin		1.9	19	2.4	25	2.1	15	3.8	28
All	Int	3.2	33	1.6	16	0.9	7	3.7	27
	Non	3.0	31	2.0	20	2.3	17	6.7	49
All Ties		6.2	62	3.6	36	3.2	24	10.4	76
Total Mean #		9.8				13.6			
Total %		98				100			

NOTE: Discrepancies due to rounding

contacts with neighbors are in couples and are quite casual. As an electrician asserts:

> I don't become involved. I know the guy's name next door is Bob. That's as far as it goes.

It is the wives of the Torontonians who actively maintain ties with neighbors in order to obtain important services that keep households running smoothly (Wellman, 1985; see also Moore, 1990). Thus an electronics technician reports:

> My wife has friends up and down the block, but I don't go looking for them. My neighbors end at the front doorstep and back doorstep. Any relation I have with my neighbors is directly due to the conduct of my wife.

The active friends of Toronto men are more apt to be socially close intimates than are their neighbors or workmates (Table 5.1). Indeed, half of the men regard a friend as their single most intimate relationship; the other half so regard a sibling or a parent. The low percentage of friends who have active, but not intimate, relationships is a consequence of the privatization of community. As a more voluntary relationship than kinship, friendship must be actively maintained. Yet the withering of public communities has lessened group support for friendships. Two friends must work by themselves to maintain their relationship. "A man, Sir, should keep his friendship *in constant repair*," warned Samuel Johnson (Boswell, 1991, p. 36).

Intimate friends gladly maintain their ties by themselves; weak acquaintances settle for unplanned, casual encounters. The most problematic relationships are those significant friendships that are not intimate enough for the participants to work actively to maintain them. Because there is a lack of group contexts to bring such friends together, the bonds are vulnerable to inadvertent neglect. A Toronto accountant complains:

I would like to see him [a friend] more often, but it's just inconvenient.

Hence, if friends are not intimate, people tend to regard them as "acquaintances," not as less-intimate friends.

By contrast to friendships, most immediate kin are active network members even when they are not intimates. Most of the active ties Toronto men have with women are with kin: Mothers, sisters, adult daughters, and in-laws are almost always active network members. These women kin are more important in the men's networks than male kin are in the women's networks (Fischer, 1982; Moore, 1990; Wellman, 1990; Wellman & Wortley, 1989a). The women work hard to hold kinship networks together and provide the men with emotional support.

The Domestication of Community

Home as Base for Community

The separation of work and leisure has increased the time men spend at home, while the development of birth-control techniques and household appliances has reduced the time women spend in domestic work. Men and women are more available to each other at home—to do domestic work and to play together (Langlois, 1990; Young & Willmott, 1973).

Just as urbanization once fostered public community among men, suburbanization now draws them away from public community. The neoconservative privatization of Western societies—the withering of collective, public services for general well-being—is being reflected in the movement indoors of community life. North American homes stand detached from their neighbors and have become guarded fortresses in the United States (Sennett, 1991). A chain of American stores in suburban shopping malls sells surveillance cameras for scanning one's lawns, electrical batons to shock intruders, and tear gas for personal defense ("Mace—just in case"). Even in Toronto, the safest North American metropolis, 36% of the residents feel somewhat unsafe walking alone in their neighborhoods at night (Duffy, 1991). This fear—coupled with the empty streets and long distances of suburbia—has made walking to public spaces difficult and unrewarding. Yet using cars affords fewer opportunities for casual contact en route than does walking through lively neighborhoods (Jacobs, 1961).

Public spaces have become residual places to pass through, to shop in, or to loiter in isolation (Hitt, Fleming, Plater-Zyberk, Sennett, Wines, & Zimmerman, 1990; Sennett, 1977; Whyte, 1980). Although churches still attract about one-third of North American adults weekly, they tend to be frequented by women (Gulia, 1991), and attendance has been declining (Mori, 1990). Annual movie attendance has decreased in Canada from 18.2 times per year in 1952 to 3.2 in 1987 (*Film Canada Yearbook*, 1990; Strike, 1990). Moreover, when Torontonians do go out to the movies, most (55%) go alone or in twos (Oh, 1991). The public community of the pub in the television show, *Cheers*, is appealing because it is so rare. Only 15% of all adult Canadian men (and 6% of Canadian women) go to a bar once a week or more.[10] Such a situation would have disappointed the carousing American author, Frank O'Hara, "The laughing in bars till we cried and the crying in movies till we laughed. . . . And in 1984 I trust we'll still be high together. I'll say 'Let's go to a bar' and you'll say 'Let's go to a movie' and we'll go to both" (1991, p. 57).

With the decline of public community, suburban shopping malls have become residual agoras, but for consumption purposes only—not for discussion. Unlike the public spaces of previous centuries, these privately owned, profit-oriented spaces sell goods primarily for private, domestic use. Their cafes are that only in name, deliberately using uncomfortable chairs, tiny tables, and inhospitable service to discourage lingering sociability and information exchange (Jacobs, 1984; Oldenburg, 1989). Indeed, former Canadian Prime Minister Pierre Trudeau warned the nation that it was on its way to being "a loose confederation of shopping malls" (Turner, 1990). Yet only in North America do fast-food chains order their employees to say "have a nice day" and expect their customers to stay less than a half-hour.

The separation of homes from public community has helped bring husbands and wives together. They are in no mood to go out after they wearily commute long distances from work. In any event, zoning regulations requiring the separation of residential and commercial areas ensure that there are no nearby public places to go to. Domestic pursuits dominate, and joint marriages flourish (Young & Willmott, 1973). Husbands and wives spend nights and weekends with each other instead of the men going off to pubs. Men spend more time in housework and minding children, even if they still spend much less time than their wives (Michelson, 1985). Large homes with special rooms for videocassette recorders and microcomputers have become encompassing environments, swallowing up their inhabitants from 6 p.m. to 7 a.m. Workaholic professionals bring disks home to their microcomputer instead of staying late at the office. Canadian men watch an average of 3.2 hours of television per day (in 1987) while women watched 3.8 hours (Young, 1990). To avoid conflict and increase privacy, 48% of Canadian homes had two television sets in 1987. To increase choice in viewing, 45% of Canadian homes had videocassette recorders in 1987, although almost none had them 5 years earlier (Devereaux, 1990).

Community has become domestic, moving from accessible public spaces to private homes. Men's friendships are now tucked away in homes just as women's friendships always have been. Rather than being accessible to others in public places, Torontonians overcome their isolation by getting together with friends and relatives in private homes and by telephone. Yet cars leave garages as sealed units, opened only on reaching the other's home, and telephones stay indoors, sustaining only closed duets between two persons.[11] The ties so easily reached remain out of view. As Torontonian Marshall McLuhan observed, North Americans go out to be private—in streets where no one greets one other —but stay in to be public—to meet their friends and relatives (1973, p. 16). Where Canadians in the 1950s often spent Saturday night going out for a movie and pizza, they now invite a few friends over to watch taped moves on their videocassette recorders and order a pizza for home delivery. The telephone number for Toronto's largest pizza delivery service, 967-11-11, has become so well known that Canadian immigration officers use it as a test to see if border crossers are real Canadian residents (Zimbel, 1991).[12]

Toronto men's friendships tend to be even more private than their other active relationships, rooted in the private worlds of homes (91%), phones (91%), letters (67%), and vacation cottages (26%) (see Table 5.2). Only a minority of these friendships operate in the public contexts of the neighborhood (21%), formal organizations (18%), or work (9%). Only intimate male friends usually get together in public for recreation or other informal activities (84%). The few women friends a man has are seen principally at home—in couples—and not invited up to the cottage or out for bowling, hockey, or other informal recreational activities.

Private Friendships

The domestication of community means that friendship does not often come in communal groups. Toronto men are not like Japanese men who carouse with workmates after hours and avoid wives ruling the domestic roost (Cole, 1971). Only 25% of the Toronto men are active in formal recreational groups, only 19% go to church regularly, and only 14% are active in their unions (Table 5.3). These men go home to have what they believe is a joint relationship with their wives, in which domestic work and companionship are shared (Young & Willmott, 1973).[13] Couples stay home together most evenings and weekends. They go out together to see friends and relatives, except for occasional male-only meetings with buddies (Table 5.3). Indeed, another Toronto study (Michelson, 1985) shows that if one spouse socializes a lot, so does the other—probably together. A firefighter talks about how he and his wife see their good friends:

> We would just get into the car and go over to their house and ring the bell, have a cup of tea, and shoot the breeze for a while. Then, we'd get back in the car and come home.

Similarly, a maintenance man reports:

> We usually have an evening. They will come out here or we will go in there for an evening. As far as going someplace, last year was the first time we have gone out as a foursome for anything like dinner and a show.

As friendships have moved into the home, homes have become less private. Where previous generations had confined friends to ground-floor parlors and dining rooms, friends now roam all floors and rooms

Table 5.2 Percentage of Friends and All Active Network Members Interacting in Various Contexts, By Gender of Respondent and Network Member, and by Tie Strength

Respondents Network Members Tie Strength		Men											Women											
		Men			Women								Men			Women								
		intim	non	all ties	intim	non	all ties						intim	non	all ties	intim	non	all ties						
Home	Friend	90	92	91	100	100	100						67	33	56	86	78	82						
	All	96	75	86	100	96	98						79	68	72	95	84	88						
Cottage	Friend	37	13	26	0	0	0						17	0	9	10	5	8						
	All	27	19	23	14	14	14						14	19	18	15	3	8						
Neighborhood	Friend	32	7	21	33	17	25						17	20	18	10	10	10						
	All	27	21	24	23	18	20						7	14	12	25	39	34						
Informal Activities	Friend	84	20	56	50	0	25						50	0	27	43	5	25						
	All	64	29	48	32	4	16						46	26	32	44	16	26						
Phone	Friend	95	86	91	67	67	67						100	100	100	100	82	92						
	All	87	63	76	82	78	80						100	95	97	100	76	87						
Letters	Friend	68	64	67	67	33	50						67	75	70	70	53	62						
	All	56	45	51	55	38	46						77	79	78	71	68	69						
Formal Organiz.	Friend	10	27	18	17	0	8						33	40	36	19	45	32						
	All	13	14	14	9	7	8						21	23	23	18	24	22						
At Work	Friend	0	20	9	17	0	8						0	0	0	10	5	8						
	All	13	38	25	5	7	6						14	4	7	12	11	12						

Table 5.3 Percentage of Toronto Respondents Active in Group
Activities, by Gender

Activities	Men	Women
Unions	0	0
Churches	19	25
Neighborhood Groups	6	0
Recreational Groups	25	17
Ethnic-Based Groups	0	0
Kinship Groups	7	0
Child-Centered Groups	7	18
Interest Groups	6	17
Occupation-Based Groups	14	6
Informal Sociability Groups	29	12
Formal Sociability Groups	7	6
Voluntary Groups	0	13
Other Groups	0	0

(Lawrence, 1987; Roncière, 1985).[14] The norm is *thirtysomething* domestic sociability, a few friends gathering in private homes. A Toronto maintenance man reports on the regular weekend get-together he and his wife have with the couple who are their best friends:

> We go to their place for dinner, or else they come over to our place and have a barbecue and perhaps a swim. (Sometimes they sleep over.)

Most of the Toronto men's friendships operate on their own or in small groups of three or four couples (85%) (see Table 5.4). Intimate friendships are even more likely to be private than significant, non-intimate friendships. Friends do not form large, densely knit friendship groups. For example, only 18% of the possible active ties among the friends of married Torontonians actually exist, and there are even fewer active ties between friends and kin (Wellman, Frank, Espinoza, Lundquist, & Wilson, 1991).[15] Although marriage enlarges networks, the friends of husbands and wives do not become fully connected with each other. A Toronto fireman, already married for 8 years, reports:

> We have so many different friends, but gradually we are starting to introduce each other to our friends now.

Table 5.4 Percentage of Friends and All Active Network Members, by Tie Strength, Interacting with Persons of the Same Gender, One-to-One, in Couples, or in Groups

		Man-Man			Woman-Woman		
	Tie Strength	Intimate	Non-Intimate	All Ties	Intimate	Non-Intimate	All Ties
One-to-One	Friend	47	40	44	67	28	49
	All	42	37	40	55	37	44
Couple	Friend	16	13	15	24	44	33
	All	22	12	17	29	17	22
Group	Friend	37	47	41	10	28	18
	All	36	51	43	16	46	35

This low density means that friends rarely have the structural capacity to get together and communicate, coordinate or control the flow of resources to each other.

Women as Keepers of Domestic Community

Feminist urban scholars have pointed out that suburbanization has hurt women by segregating them from the corridors of power and production (e.g., Hayden, 1984). But the move to larger, more physically isolated homes has also enlarged women's domestic domain to such an extent that one pundit has warned of "Mom-ism" (Sebald, 1976). Women, regardless of whether they also do paid work, retain the key responsibility in most North American homes for keeping households going (Hochschild, 1989; Luxton, 1990; Michelson, 1985; Smith-Rosenberg, 1975). With the movement of men's activities into the household, women's work no longer remains "hidden in the household" (Fox, 1980), but becomes a centerpiece of everyday life.

Women have historically been the "kinkeepers" of Western society, with mothers and sisters keeping relatives connected (di Leonardo, 1987; Rosenthal, 1985). This has been a domestic activity, operated from the household rather than the street corner or the pub (Adams, 1968; Luxton, 1980; Stack, 1974). Toronto men stay in touch with parents, siblings, and children because kinship systems usually are actively maintained by a mother or sister (Moore, 1990; Piché, 1988; Rosenthal, 1985). A Toronto maintenance man refers to his mother as "the central switchboard." Similarly, a fireman says:

Laurel's mom does all of that. She keeps us in touch with what is happening, or we phone my sister to find out what somebody is doing at the other end.

One result of the privatization and domestication of community is that community-keeping has become an extension of kinkeeping, with both linked to domestic management. Women now define the nature of friendship and keep much of it going for their husbands as well as for themselves. With the greater participation of men in household activities, informal ties among women friends, neighbors, and relatives form the basis for many of the men's friendship relations between couples. Wives recruit most new friends and neighbors and arrange most get-togethers between couples and family members (including in-laws). A Toronto mechanic calls his wife "the communications officer." A firefighter's wife tried to build up new ties by "having a reunion for our band, trying to get everyone together."

Where Toronto men's friendships have largely become sociable ends in themselves, Toronto women rely on their ties for important domestic work. Network members help with daily hassles and crises; neighbors mind each other's children; sisters and friends provide emotional support and advice on caring for children, husbands, and elderly parents.[16] Consequently, Toronto men are less likely than Toronto women to value having frequent contacts with network members (47% of the men value this, compared with 78% of the women), to value having network members live nearby (31% versus 50%), or to value having densely knit networks (31% versus 56%).

Because Toronto men worry less about their personal communities, they tend to be more relaxed than women about the state of their social relationships (Michelson, 1988). As one Toronto truck driver confessed:

My wife is the birthday rememberer, also phone numbers and dates. I wouldn't even go out and buy a birthday card. She signs both our names. She can remember everything but where our socks are.

While women are taking on the burden of maintaining friendships for their husbands as well as themselves, most women also do paid labor. To cope with overwhelming demands (Cochran, Larner, Riley, & Henderson, 1990; Luxton, 1987, 1990), working women cut back on friendship relations, one of the few discretionary uses of their time (Cochran, et al., 1990; Hochschild, 1989; Michelson, 1985; Sharpe, 1984; Wellman, 1985). As one secretary laments:

I don't go out much during the week because I always promise myself that I am going to get home early, and I never get home early.

Because women are the community-keepers and are pressed for time, men become even more cut off from male friendship groups. Private contact with familiar friends replaces public gregariousness. Rather than getting together in permeable public spaces, where friends-of-friends can meet and bystanders can join in conversations, current visits are by invitation only. Possibly their wives prefer such private contact: 83% of the women students at a University of Toronto cafeteria avoid eye contact with strangers, as compared with only 30% of the men (Wong, 1991).

The result of this domestication of community is that Toronto men have companionship and social support but they—and especially their wives—must work at it. They must invite people over or deliberately call them on the telephone. There is little possibility for casual contact or the expansion of networks. There is little group support. Each friendship tie must be maintained separately and reinforced directly. I suspect that one consequence is that men feel that they lack friends even when they have many supportive network members.

Social Support Through Friendship

Support Is Widespread, but Specialized

Network members give Toronto men many kinds of social support, from communicating acceptance, to giving advice on marital problems, to renovating homes. The respondents told us about whether they received 18 different kinds of social support from each network member. Factor analysis of all of the respondents' active ties (Wellman, 1992; Wellman & Hiscott, 1985; Wellman & Wortley 1989a, 1989b, 1990) showed that different network members tend to provide different "dimensions" of social support: *Emotional Aid,* provided in some form by 62% of the network members (the kinds included are minor emotional aid, family problems advice, major emotional aid); *Small Services,* provided by 61% of the network members (minor services, major emotional aid); *Small Services,* provided by 61% of the network members (minor services, lending or giving household items, minor household aid, aid in dealing with organizations); *Large Services,* provided by 16% of the network members (major repairs, regular help with housework, major services);

Table 5.5   Mean Number of Support Dimensions Provided by Network Members, by Gender of Respondent and Network Member, and by Role Relationship

	All Respondents: 2.2			
Respondents	*Men: 2.2*		*Women: 2.1*	
Network Members	*Men: 2.4*	*Women: 2.0*	*Men: 1.8*	*Women: 2.2*
Friend	2.4	1.9	1.6	2.3
Neighbor	2.5	2.0	2.4	2.4
Co-Worker	2.1	5.0	2.0	1.7
Immediate Kin	2.6	2.1	2.1	2.7
Extended Kin	2.0	1.4	0.8	0.9

Companionship, provided by 59% of the network members (discussing ideas, doing things together, fellow participants in an organization); *Financial Aid,* provided by 16% of the network members (small loans/gifts, large loans/gifts, large loans/gifts for housing); *Job/Housing Information,* provided by 10% of the network members (job information, job contacts, housing search).[17]

Male friendships, like other activities, tend to be specialized. They usually provide two or three out of the six dimensions of support (mean = 2.4; see Table 5.5). Thus a typical friend might provide companionship and small services, but not large services, emotional aid, financial aid, or help in looking for a job. Female friendships are even more specialized, providing a mean of 1.6 dimensions of support.[18]

Friends provide more specialized support than do immediate kin (brothers, sisters, adult children, mothers and fathers) but broader support than do extended kin (cousins, grandparents, aunts and uncles; see Table 5.5). Intimate friendships are more broadly supportive than non-intimate friends. Unlike with friendship, the likelihood of immediate kin providing support is not contingent on the two kinfolk being intimate (Wellman & Wortley, 1989a; see also Rossi & Rossi, 1990).

Companionship

Companionship is a key defining characteristic of most men's friendships. The Torontonians report that 79% of their male friends are companions. As this is the highest percentage in Table 5.6, it means that male friends are the most likely of all active members to be regarded as companions. Male friends also comprise the largest proportion of active companions in the Toronto men's networks: 22% of their companions are intimate male friends, while another 11% are non-intimate, but still significant male friends (see Table 5.7). Indeed, male non-kin—friends, neighbors, and workmates—comprise more than half (56%) of the Toronto men's active companions. By contrast, brothers and sisters are the only kin who are likely to be companions. Like friends, they tend to be people of the same generation and lifestyle as the Torontonians, and they have the additional bond of sharing extensive life histories. Women network members, kin and non-kin, comprise about one-quarter of the Toronto men's companionship ties (Table 5.7). About half of the small number of women friends in the Torontonians' networks (the average number of women friends in a network is one) are likely to be companions (Table 5.6).

Despite the domestication of men's networks, Toronto men still rely less than Toronto women on their neighbors for companionship (11% versus 33%) and more on their friends (41% versus 35%), workmates (15% versus 6%), and kinfolk (29% versus 23%). Where friends comprise the largest number of Toronto men's companions, neighbors comprise the largest number of Toronto women's companions (see Table 5.7). Those women who work at home stop socializing with their female neighbors when their husbands come home. The couples stay home together, socializing at night or on weekends with immediate kin or intimate friends. As the wife of an electronics technician reports:

> He is not a person that likes partying or even entertaining. There is no way you're going to get him to go out to a dance because he doesn't dance. We are stay-at-homers. He is quite content just to come home, work around his own place and stay home until it's time to go to sleep.

Couples: The Toronto men's friends are either the husbands of married couples seen jointly or male buddies seen alone. Get-togethers between couples are almost always arranged by the wives. A fireman reports: "My wife and his wife are on the phone quite often"; while a sales manager remembers how his household's closest friendship started:

> We were basically co-workers. Then he was going with his future wife, and I was going with my future wife. They hit it off, and they were good friends. Harry and I became good friends anyway.

Table 5.6 Percentage of Friends and All Active Network Members Providing Each Dimension of Support By Gender of Respondent and Network Member

Respondents Network Members	Men					Women				
	Men		Women		All Ties	Men		Women		All Ties
	friends	*all ties*	*friends*	*all ties*		*friends*	*all ties*	*friends*	*all ties*	
Companionship	79	70	58	45	61	73	50	73	59	57
Small Services	66	64	64	58	62	45	55	67	63	61
Large Services	12	19	0	8	15	18	20	10	16	17
Emotional Aid	56	54	73	73	61	27	41	82	67	61

Table 5.7 Percentage of Supportive Ties Provided by Different Role Relations

Respondents Support Dimensions Network Members		Men								Women							
		Companionship		Small Services		Large Services		Emotional Aid		Companionship		Small Services		Large Services		Emotional Aid	
		men	women	men	women	men	women	men	women	men	women	men	women	men	women	men	women
Friend	Int	22	6	18	6	20	0	13	6	4	17	2	14	6	9	1	16
	Non	11	2	7	2	0	0	8	4	4	10	2	7	0	3	2	10
Neighbor	Int	4	1	5	1	15	0	2	1	0	9	0	8	0	6	0	8
	Non	5	1	5	1	10	0	2	0	4	20	4	22	6	23	0	18
Workmate	Int	4	0	1	0	0	0	4	0	0	2	1	2	0	0	1	1
	Non	10	1	6	1	0	0	5	1	0	4	0	1	0	0	0	2
All Non-Kin		56	11	42	11	45	0	34	12	12	62	9	54	12	41	4	55
Immediate Kin	Int	16	6	16	10	25	10	13	12	4	10	3	14	6	20	4	15
	Non	2	5	5	9	10	10	4	12	4	5	6	6	11	9	6	8
Extended Kin	Int	0	1	1	2	0	0	2	4	0	2	0	0	0	0	0	0
	Non	0	2	0	1	0	0	0	2	1	3	3	4	0	3	2	5
All Kin		18	14	22	22	35	20	19	30	9	20	12	24	17	32	12	28
Subtotal		74	25	64	33	80	20	53	42	21	82	21	78	29	73	16	83
Total		99		97		100		95		103		99		102		99	

NOTE: Discrepancies due to rounding

A typical pattern is for two or three couples to visit, either in each other's house or, less frequently, in a restaurant or other public place (see Tables 5.2, 5.3, and 5.4 above). A fireman describes his social life:

A typical get together is really nothing planned. I'll phone or my wife will phone (or they'll phone) and say, "Are you doing anything?" If they aren't doing anything, we'll take steaks or chicken there, or they'll come here and we'll have a barbecue during the summer. Or we'll just go out for a walk or something and knock on their door. Once you get there, you have a couple of drinks and the kids have fun.

Often, the men like each other and their wives, but that is not necessary. As long as the wives like each other, mere toleration on the part of the men is all that is necessary. These are ties built around social compatibility between two women (or two couples) rather than relationships relying on each other for crucial goods, services, information, and status (Albert & Moss, 1990; Miller, 1983; Silver, 1990; Wellman, 1985). A municipal official complains, "I seem to cater to Elaine's desire to associate with her friends; I sacrifice my friends"; while an electronics technician complains, "She has her own friends, and I don't have any." With their wives arranging so much of their social life, it is not surprising that a higher percentage of men (83%) than women (67%) sometimes feel torn between the demands of different social circles.

Buddies: The other typical pattern is for two or more male buddies to get together by themselves. Buddies enjoy the sheer pleasure of being with each other, not talking much, and not having to deal with the burdens of home or work. They are friends to pass the time with, to accomplish minor tasks with, and, perhaps, to reaffirm (masculine) self-worth (Bly, 1990). These friendships are kept out of the home and center around sports and occasional nights out. As Laurence Olivier puts it, "I have often fallen gratefully into the warming change of male companionship" (1982, p. 234). More prosaically, a Toronto maintenance man feels that if his best friend "has been uptight or if I have been uptight, we get together and have a couple of drinks. We enjoy each other's company and we can relax." An unemployed Torontonian values a friend as "just someone to do things with and not have to worry about him putting a lot of demands on you." A sales manager lends credence to the stereotype of men's interactions being "side by side":

We weren't close or anything like that, but he'd phone me up and say, "I haven't seen you for a while. Let's go out and golf." So we'd golf. Or I'd say the same to him. Just a relationship that was not particularly close in a personal way, but was very friendly.

A printer and his buddies use CB radio to maintain their friendships and arrange get togethers. The printer sees friendship as "having a good time, but if you need help it is there." Sometimes wives and girlfriends tag along for a drink or dinner, but most often the printer and his buddies drive 150 miles to their lakeside vacation cottages to be alone together, snowmobiling, ice fishing, water-skiing and, inevitably, drinking beer. To some extent, such get-togethers continue the practice of male friends meeting in public places. However, because Toronto men rarely know their neighbors and because their get-togethers often do not take place near their homes or workplaces, they meet in anonymous public places where there is little likelihood that they will encounter anyone else they know.

Small Services

It has become a cliché to say that men prefer to do things with each other rather than say intimate things to each other. Certainly, male friends stand out. They are the most likely network members to provide small goods and services: 66% provide small services, the highest percentage of any role relationship (see Table 5.6). Moreover, they are the most numerous providers of such help in the network, comprising 25% of those active network members who provide small services (see Table 5.7).

There is a division of labor in the kinds of services men and women provide. Where women help each other with domestic chores and routine health care, male friends repair and improve homes and fix cars and household machines. For example, an electronics technician phones his best friend to say:

"I need your help. I'm doing aluminum siding. What are you doing this weekend?" He said, "Fine. I'm on holiday this week and I'll earmark the weekend for you." He stayed till Monday.

To reciprocate a year later, the electronics technician "went over to his place and helped him to do a few things, and he helped me but that's as far as it went." No books are kept, but the men remember who helped them and for what. Thus a truck driver helped build one friend's game room while another mutual friend did electrical work at his house and provided financial advice for his business. The help saved money, reduced anxiety, provided satisfaction, and strengthened the network. It was an important contribution to the household's informal economy.

Large Services

The large services that network members provide—most commonly, extended health care—usually are long-term health care or other substantial investments of time, money, or energy. As such services are not often needed—health care is free in Canada—and are harder to provide, it is understandable that only 16% of the active network members have provided them to the Torontonians.

Large services are usually provided by kin and neighbors rather than by friends (Tables 5.6 and 5.7). The structurally and culturally enforced obligations of kinship and the proximity of neighbors foster major supportiveness. Male friends comprise only 20% of the active ties providing large services, while kin comprise 55%, and neighbors 25% (Table 5.7). Immediate kin form the bulk of the supportive "reserve army," to be mobilized in terms of serious need. A Toronto firefighter says of his brother, "If I needed anything, money or help or assistance, he would be right there, as well as I would." Kinship is supportive across gender boundaries: Mothers and sisters help men, but women friends do not.[19] As a maintenance mechanic says:

> You have a duty to your family if they require assistance. It is a fact. Because if your family can't tell it to you, who can they tell it to?

Although none of the female friends of the Toronto men provide large services, some male friends of the Toronto women have provided large services for fixing homes and machinery (see Tables 5.6 and 5.7). One businessman visits a widow weekly to do chores. She appreciates his aid but chooses to interpret it in terms of male assertiveness:

> Phil's a very ambitious person. His idea of relaxing when he comes up here is doing things, so he'll be out digging in the garden. I'll say, "I wish I could get that done," and next thing he'll be doing it.

Emotional Aid

The data are ambiguous about the emotional supportiveness of men's friendships. Almost all Toronto men get emotional support from at least one male friend. Yet a smaller percentage of male friends (56%) provide Toronto men with emotional support than the 82% of female friends who provide Toronto women with emotional support (see Table 5.6). However, male friends still comprise the second largest component (23%) of emotionally supportive relationships in the men's networks (see Table 5.7). The largest component is female immediate kin (24%)—mothers, sisters, and daughters—followed by male immediate kin (17%) and female friends (10%).

Clearly, women are more likely than men to be emotionally supportive. The minority of women in Toronto men's networks comprise nearly half (42%) of the Toronto men's emotionally supportive relationships (Table 5.7). Even the female friends of the Toronto men are more likely than their male friends to be emotionally supportive, 82% versus 56% (see Table 5.6).

Yet to say that men are less likely than women to provide emotional support is not to say that most men are not emotionally supportive. A majority of all role relationships, except male neighbors and workmates, provide men with emotional support. It is a Zen question of how analysts perceive the glass: Is it half-empty or half-full? When analysts focus on statistically significant differences between men and women, they can easily confirm the prevailing belief that men are less emotionally supportive than women. But "less" does not mean "none" or even "little." Most Toronto men have a number of emotionally supportive relationships with male friends and other male network members. The difference is that men get emotional support from both men and women, while women get it predominantly from women—and from a higher proportion of women in their networks (Table 5.7).[20]

Male friends tend to give Toronto men different specific types of emotional support than do their kinfolk and women friends. Male friends specialize in providing support for minor upsets about work or family. Companions are handily available when men want to unburden themselves. "Thus [Schiller gave] sympathy and impulse. . . . He excited Goethe to work. . . . He urged him to finish what was already commenced, and not to leave his works all fragments" (Lewes, 1991, p. 71). Every writer needs a friend such as this!

Toronto men function like Goethe and Schiller, even if to less grand effect. A sales manager had a friend who "needed somebody to talk to. A lot of stuff came out, and it was because he was able to use me as the wall to bounce his problems off." Although Canadian medical and psychiatric care is free and of high quality, the men prefer to rely on network members, not professionals, for emotional support in major crises as well as in routinely stressful situation (see also Wellman, 1991). As one respondent told us:

> I might talk it over with someone, I wouldn't go to a doctor. All he'd do is stick you on tranquilizers.

However, intimate friends rarely provide large-scale emotional aid to Toronto men, and non-intimate friends hardly ever do. Because friendships function as isolated ties between individuals or couples (and not as solidary groups), there is little means or obligation for friends to organize major, sustained help. By contrast to male friends, immediate kin preeminently provide Toronto men with major emotional aid, and non-intimate immediate kin are as likely as intimates to be emotionally supportive (Wellman & Wortley, 1989a, 1990). Toronto men often confide in their mothers or sisters when they have marital problems because they believe that women have more empathetic understanding of what makes relationships work. An East York municipal official reports:

> [She] is my idea of a mother, a person I can confide in. Anything personal I say, I know she won't say it to anyone else. I have told her things I haven't told my own brother or my own wife.

By contrast to Toronto men, Toronto women rely on their female friends for emotional support as much as they rely on their kin. Unlike Toronto men, Toronto women rarely get emotional support from the opposite sex —not even from their fathers or brothers, much less their male friends (see also Wellman & Wortley, 1989a). The movie, *When Harry Met Sally*, is a mythical portrayal of a supportive male-female friendship that does not fit the Toronto reality, and recall that Harry and Sally inevitably wind up as lovers and spouses.

Hugging and Beyond

Friends in Personal Community Networks

The Toronto data show that male friends are important members of men's networks. They comprise a large portion of active relationships, and they are the preeminent suppliers of companionship and frequent small services. They are the second most numerous purveyors of emotional support, allegedly a woman's domain.

The liberation of community has allowed men to maintain friends over long distances, and it has freed them from having to rely heavily on less voluntary ties of kinship and neighboring. Toronto men do not live at the economic or social edge, relying on friends and relatives for survival at home and work. They need everyday sociability and assistance from their friends, plus the assurance that major help will be there from somewhere in their network when needed—usually immediate kin. If these men went out to purchase the social support that they receive from network members, they would not get the same combination of frequent, flexible, nuanced, and inexpensive assistance that network members supply. Hence, they are willing to invest the time and effort necessary to maintain their ties (and consequent social support) than they are to spend money to buy equivalent help.

While men's friendships flourish, they are different from what they used to be. Although the situation varies over time and between localities, friendships between North American men now operate out of homes rather than in public spheres. The separation of home from work, and the development of introverted homes set off in areas without usable public spaces, have affected the kinds of friendships men can have. At the same time that men have increased their domestic involvement, they have lost access to male hangouts. They have few ties to their neighbors. Friendships are now private affairs between residentially dispersed buddies or couples. This domestication of community is likely to continue as new means of telecommunications make it even easier for isolated people to maintain ties from the safety, comfort, and privacy of their own homes.

The move of men's friendships into households is not just a change in venue. It has affected how friendships are maintained, how they are interrelated, and how friendship itself is defined. Despite recent moves in the direction of symmetric marriages, homes remain women's domain. With their men at home, wives have added the burden of maintaining their husband's friendships to their traditional role of maintaining ties with their own friends and with their own and their husband's kin. The heavy involvement of women in paid work, combined with the separation of the workplace from the residence, has caused couples to focus their friendships on small domestic get-togethers. As husbands and wives work together in raising families, their friends become integrated and their kinship relations become similar to their friendship ties.

Defining Friendship: Masculine/Feminine

If men's friendships continue to flourish, why the contemporary intellectual shift to seeing friendship as something that women do better than men? I believe that such a shift has occurred, and that it is linked to the privatization of community and the domestication of friendship. It is also linked to the shift in the Western world's economy from an emphasis on manufacturing things to an emphasis on services and information-processing (Castells, 1989) and to the ways in which the feminist movement has altered perceptions of men and women.

As men's friendships have become domesticated, their emphases have changed. Private intimacy has replaced public sociability. No longer must men jockey for position in communal groups. Just as husbands and wives are more involved with each other at home, the focus of couples and male friends is on private, domestic relations. Men's friendships have come to be defined as women's always have been—relations of emotional support, companionship, and domestic services (Allan, 1989; Lyman, 1987; Pleck, 1975; Rubin, 1985). The nature and success of their friendships are being defined in domestic, women's, terms.

Concurrently, the growing dominance of the service sector in the economy means that the manipulation of people and ideas has acquired more economic and cultural importance than the industrial and resource-extraction sectors' manipulation of material goods. The basis of society, the workplace writ large, has become the very emphasis on social relationships that women have traditionally practiced at home. At the same time, the material comfort of most North Americans means they no longer need to rely on maintaining good relations with kin, friends, and neighbors to get the necessities for material survival. Although men and women do give each other important material help, these are matters of convenience, not necessity. Friendships have become ends in themselves, to be enjoyed in their own right and used for emotional adjustment in a society that puts a premium on feeling good about one-self and others.

Along with these shifts in the nature of friendships, intellectuals have changed the way in which they think about friendship. In the view of consciousnesses raised by women's liberation, the instrumental focus of old-boy networks reeks of male chauvinism. Much feminist writing now celebrates emotional supportiveness as the dominant theme of friendship, for men as well as women (Echols, 1989; Smith-Rosenberg, 1975). Rejecting efforts to become more like men, a significant portion of the feminist movement exalts women as uniquely more qualified than men to have the emotional openness necessary to form true friendships. Polemicists declare that men do not know how to be friends as well as women because men have been trained to exercise power and women to exercise intimacy (Griffin, 1981; MacInnis, 1991; Sherr Klein, 1981). A pundit proclaims on television that "men just don't have friends the way women have friends. Men just don't like to make themselves vulnerable to other men."[21]

Patriarchal arguments for male superiority in accomplishing great deeds are being replaced by arguments for female superiority in holding social groups together. Writing in a key periodical for intellectuals, *The New York Review of Books,* Murray Kempton (1991) extols Nicaragua's president:

> What has so often troubled our encounters with women of state in recent years is how like the men of state they seem, and how susceptible to the false masculinity that has been the baneful weakness of politicians everywhere. But Violeta Chamorro reminds us again of the blessings of what used to be thought of as sensibilities uniquely feminine. The world has been wearied and brought low by movers and shakers; what it cries out for now are healers to whom words like kind and gentle are not rhetoric but the feelings that rule every minute of the day. . . . If we listen to that spirit, we may begin to think of all around us as our own family; unless we do, we will break apart and die of loneliness and hatred.

Research from a number of areas identifies women as specialists in emotionally supportive relations. Socialization analysts report that North American sons form weaker childhood ties with their fathers, the primordial male bond, than daughters do with their mothers (Chodorow, 1978; Kemper, 1991). Sociobiologists note that high male levels of testosterone produce more instrumental behavior (Kemper, 1978, 1990; Treadwell, 1989). Young men persist in defining the male role in terms of status, toughness, and anti-femininity (Gaskell, 1983; Thompson & Pleck, 1987). Lexical analysts and social psychologists note that women use more cooperative, empathetic words such as "like," while men use more assertive, power words such as "push" (Ashmore, Del Boca, & Wohlers, 1986; Russell & Fournier, 1989; Sapadin, 1988). A media analyst notes that male heroes are aggressive, victorious, and emotionless (Garfinkel, 1985). Social psychologists report that women have more complex understanding of close relationships than do men (Ross & Holmberg, 1990). Medical sociologists note that women care more about the problems of others (Kessler & McLeod, 1984; Thoits, 1982; Turner & Avison, 1989). Gerontologists report that adult daughters are more likely than adult sons to take care of their elderly mothers *and* fathers (Connidis, 1989; Stone, 1988; Wolf, 1988). "Women express, men repress," is the way two social psychologists summarize the research literature (Perlman & Fehr, 1987, p. 21).[22]

As we have seen, male friendships continue to flourish. Yet, as friendships have become domesticated and redefined, North American men must now defend the legitimacy and importance of their relationships. Abandoning their celebration of friendship as semipublic male bonds that get things done, they now argue that they can be as emotionally supportive as women.[23] Traditional sexist discourse, seeing women as inadequate men, is being questioned and sometimes reversed. Vagina envy—the alleged longing for empathy and acceptance among men— may have become the new-age successor (MacInnis, 1991) to penis envy— the longing for power and assertiveness that Freudian myth contends is prevalent among women (Chodorow, 1974; Lyman, 1987; O'Neil, 1981).

The debate is becoming widespread. A columnist for *The New York Times* (Kimbrell, 1991) identifies "a crisis" requiring a "male manifesto." Men must reject the Industrial Revolution's credo of efficiency and power and rediscover "such traditional masculine traits as husbandry, honor, relation to community and land" so they can "re-establish ties with one another, their families, communities and the earth." Pulitzer Prize winning columnist Russell Baker warns (only semi-ironically): "Real men do not meet to drink beer, thus wallowing in the joys of male bonding" (1991). He asks if anything can be done about "people [who] invent phrases like 'male bonding' . . . like cutting off their research grants or making them read Keats." Nevertheless, scholars work to rethink masculinity (Kimmel, 1987). Humorist Dave Barry warns that testosterone has been declared a controlled substance. A best-selling book warns Americans that the fall of public community means that older generations no longer initiate men into manhood. The results, the author fears, are that either aggressive blustering or fearful acquiescence has replaced men's inner strength (Bly, 1990; see also Stearns, 1990). These concerns are spotlighted in mass magazine cover stories: the American *Newsweek* (1991) asking *"What Do Men Really Want?"*, and the French *Le Nouvel Observateur* (1991) wondering *"Ça Va, Les Hommes."*

Although the assertion that women have greater capacity for friendship has raised much consciousness, it is an idea that is time-bound, culture-bound, and empirically unsound. By isolating friendship analytically, scholars neglect the ways in which relatives, neighbors, and workmates join with friends in social networks. It ignores the millennia during which men's bonds defined friendship (see also Allan, 1989; Brain 1976; Paine 1969). By reducing friendship to emotional support, the assertion assumes that the world is as materially comfortable as North American intellectuals. Moreover, to say that a lower percentage of North American men are emotionally supportive is by no means the same thing as finding that most men are unsupportive. The Toronto data show that most male friends provide important emotional support in addition to their companionship and frequent services.

In less comfortable parts of the world, friends do even more things for each other in addition to hugging. Consider how Eastern Europeans use friends for economic, political, and social survival: Greek men still socialize and argue in cafes, Hungarian men cooperate extensively with male friends and relatives in building new homes (Sik, 1988), while Albanians naturally expect sons, not daughters, to nurture the elderly (Tarifa, 1990). Even in more affluent Britain, people value getting services and information from friends about as much as they value getting esteem and affection (Argyle, 1990, p. 165). It is probably true that people worldwide want to be wanted and to be cheered up. Yet even in North America, male friends do important things for each other. To define friendship solely as emotionally supportive companionship is to limit one's worldview to a California hot tub.

Notes

1. I thank Milena Gulia and Cristina Tahoces for their help with finding relevant quotations and illustrations, Milena Gulia and Karen Ramsay for preparing tables, and David Tindall and Vince Salazar for doing the computer runs that were the basis for the tables. They all gave much useful advice, along with Graham Allan, Bonnie Erickson,

Bonnie Fox, Muriel Hammer, Theodore D. Kemper, Martin Kimmel, Lyn Lofland, Suzanne Mackenzie, Peter Nardi, Stacey Oliker, Louise Tilly, Bev Wellman, and Scot Wortley. My thanks, also, to D. J. Enright and David Rawlinson for their timely editing of *The Oxford Book of Friendship* (1991).

Financial support for this research has been provided by the Social Sciences and Humanities Research Council of Canada, Health and Welfare Canada, and the University of Toronto. The Centre for Urban and Community Studies has been a supportive home. This paper is dedicated to Leslie Howard, an old and good friend.

2. For more on the network approach to the study of personal community networks see Wellman (1979, 1982, 1988); Wellman and Leighton (1979).

3. *Intimate* network members are defined (identically to Wellman, 1979) as persons whom respondents "feel closest to you outside your home." *Significant* network members are non-intimates identified by respondents as those who "are in touch with [you] in your daily life and who are significant in your life." Intimate and significant network members together make up the respondents' sets of *active* network members. If a respondent named a couple jointly as a relationship, we counted the first person named as the effective network member; that is, a tie to "Bob and Carol" is treated as a tie to Bob.

The respondents are a subsample of the 845 randomly sampled residents of the Toronto borough of East York that our research group had first surveyed in 1968 (Wellman, 1979). The greater statistical reliability of the first, large-sample study gratifyingly supports the more nuanced validity of the current study.

4. For descriptions of the quantitative and qualitative methods used in our analyses, see Wellman (1982), Wellman and Baker (1985), Wellman and Sim (1990), and Wellman and Wortley (1989b, 1990).

5. For my purposes here, I do not need to enter the debate about whether men's public communities were inherently linked to early urbanization. Analysts of hunter-gatherer and subsistence agriculture society point out that their tighter social and spatial integration of work and home fostered public women's communities (Boserup, 1970; Draper, 1975). Indeed, Kalahari !Kung women developed strong public communities because they stayed near home to rear children and gathered most of the band's food while the men went off to chase game (Draper, 1975; Howell, 1979).

6. See the reviews in Allan (1989); Bell (1981); Brain (1976); Duby (1985); Farrell (1986); Hammond and Jablow (1989); Hartmann (1976); Paine (1969); Pleck and Pleck (1980); and Sennett (1977).

7. See also Maryanski and Ishii-Kuntz, 1990, for a discussion of social support among female primates.

8. More precisely, the mean number of times per year that Toronto men have telephone contact with active network members is 43 (median = 24) while the mean number of face-to-face contacts is 75 (median = 24). In comparison, Toronto women have telephone contact with active network members a mean of 52 times per year (median = 12) and face-to-face contact a mean of 60 times per year (median = 14).

9. It is possible that men's active networks would be larger if we had also taken into account important work-only relationships (a possibility strongly suggested by Allan's [1989] review and Moore's [1990] research).

10. The percentages are only slightly higher for lower-income Canadians. These data come from Scot Wortley's special analysis for this article of the *1989 National Alcohol and Other Drug Survey*. The situation is quite different in Britain, where 65% of the men have gone out for a drink in the past month (Argyle, 1990, p. 156). It is unclear whether the domestication I am describing will continue to be only a North American phenomenon or whether North America is the forerunner of more broadly diffused world changes.

11. Conference calls are difficult to arrange, and multiple voices (without simultaneous visual contact) makes for confused and strained conversations. Although many households can have several people talking through extension phones or speaker phones, the confusion and strain of multiple voices occurs here also. Hence, almost all telephone conversations are between two persons.

12. Europe is also domesticating now. Suburbs and videocassette recorders are proliferating, and the average size of homes is growing. People are getting off buses and cycles and into private cars. Motorcycles deliver pizza to Parisian homes; no need to go out to sociable *brasseries* for a bite. Some Greek *tavernas* now welcome couples dropping by for a quick visit before going home to spend the evening.

13. The Toronto men do less domestic work than their wives, whatever the norms of equality (Wellman, 1985; Wellman & Wellman, 1992). This is consistent with time-budget data (e.g., Luxton, 1990; Michelson, 1985; Vanek, 1974).

14. Of course, earlier generations of the upper class often invited close friends and kin to sleep in extra bedrooms. Yet as *Les Liaisons Dangereuse* suggests, guests who penetrated the upper floors could rip apart households.

15. We defined an active tie between two network members in the same way as we defined an active tie between the respondents and their network members (see above). As these are relationships reported by the respondents about other persons (their network members), these data are less reliable than normal interview data.

To obtain the percentage of the potential ties that actually exist (the density of each respondent's network), we use the standard network analytic procedure of dividing the number of actual ties by the number of potential ties, the latter defined as all possible active ties among network members in each direction (Person A to Person B and Person B to Person A). In a network of 15 persons (excluding the respondent who is at the center, by definition), there would be $15 \times 14 = 210$ potential ties (see Knoke & Kuklinski, 1982, for more details).

16. See Cochran, Larner, Riley, and Henderson, 1990; Fischer and Oliker, 1983; Gullestad, 1984; Hochschild, 1989; Mackenzie, 1988; Moore, 1990; Oliker, 1989; Wellman, 1985; Wellman and Wortley, 1989a, 1990; Wellman and Wellman, 1992.

17. We do not discuss financial aid or job information in our analyses. Each is largely provided by a small, specialized group: immediate kin in the former case and workmates in the latter. Although the dimensions obtained depend in part on the questions asked and the analytic procedures used, other studies have obtained similar results (e.g., Barrera, 1986).

18. Note, though, that Campbell's (1991) much larger American survey found greater breadth among women's ties.

19. This finding is echoed by the recent literature on caregiving for the elderly, which finds immediate kin (especially daughters) to be the principal supporters for widows, but that the elderly also prefer to obtain companionship through similar-aged friends (see the reviews in Connidis, 1989; Wolf, 1984).

20. It is especially important here to distinguish between the proportion of different types of relationships that provide emotional aid (Table 5.6) and the proportion of a person's emotionally supportive ties provided by each type of relationship (Table 5.7). A high proportion of women friends, neighbors, and workmates provide emotional aid to men. Although symbolically (and sometimes locally) important, the small number of such relationships means that they do not comprise a substantial proportion of a man's emotionally supportive ties (see also Booth & Hess, 1974; Burda & Vaux, 1987; Campbell, 1991; Sapadin, 1988).

21. Maggie Scarf, author of *Intimate Partners*, on the *Oprah Winfrey* show, May 30, 1991.

22. See the research, reviews and arguments in Burda and Vaux (1987); Cancian (1987); Chodorow (1974, 1978); Echols (1989); Farrell (1986); Ferree and Hess (1985); Kessler and McLeod (1985); Oliker (1989); Pogrebin (1987); Sherrod (1989); Smith-Rosenberg (1975); Vaux (1985); Wright (1982, 1989).

23. Expanding the bounds of male emotional demonstrations may be an unanticipated consequence of the Kuwait war. After the American marines rolled into Kuwait, CBS newsman Bob McKeown reported, "I've been kissed by more Kuwaiti men tonight than I can count" (Associated Press, 1991).

References

Adams, B. (1968). *Kinship in an urban setting*. Chicago: Markham.

Albert, S., & Moss, M. (1990, August). Consensus and the domain of personal relations among older adults. *Journal of Social and Personal Relationships, 7*, 353-369.

Allan, G. (1989). *Friendship*. London: Harvester Wheatsheaf.

Argyle, M. (1990, July). *An exploration of the effects of different relationships on health, mental health and happiness*. Paper presented to the International Conference on Personal Relationships, Oxford.

Ashmore, R., Del Boca, F., & Wohlers, A. (1986). Gender stereotypes. In R. Ashmore & F. Del Boca (Eds.), *The social psychology of female-male relations* (pp. 69-120). Orlando, FL: Academic Press.

Associated Press. (1991, February 27). Euphoria widespread in freed capital. *Toronto Globe and Mail*.

Baker, R. (1991, March 19). Gosh, Ma! Nothing at all? *The New York Times*.

Barrera, M., Jr. (1986). Distinctions between social support concepts, measures and models. *American Journal of Community Psychology, 14*, 413-45.

Barry, D. (1991, June 22). The Illegal Gender. *International Herald Tribune*.

Bell, R. (1981). *Worlds of friendship*. Beverly Hills, CA: Sage.

Bly, R. (1990). *Iron John: A book about men*. Reading, MA: Addison-Wesley.

Booth, A., & Hess, E. (1974). Cross-Sex friendship. *Journal of Marriage and the Family, 36*, 38-47.

Boserup, E. (1970). *Woman's role in economic development*. London: Allen & Unwin.

Boswell, J. (1991). Excerpt from *Life of Johnson*. In D. J. Enright & D. Rawlinson (Eds.), *The Oxford book of friendship* (p. 36). Oxford: Oxford University Press. (Originally published 1755).

Brain, J. (1976). *Friends and lovers*. New York: Basic Books.

Burda, P., & Vaux, A. (1987). The social support process in men: Overcoming sex role obstacles. *Human Relations, 40*, 31-44.

Campbell, K. (1991, February). *Gender differences in support networks*. Presented to the Sunbelt Social Network Conference, Tampa, Florida.

Cancian, F. (1987). *Love in America: Gender and self-development*. Cambridge: Cambridge University Press.

Castells, M. (1989). *The informational city: Information technology, economic restructuring and the urban-regional process*. Oxford: Basil Blackwell.

Chodorow, N. (1974). Family structure and feminine personality. In M. Z. Rosaldo & L. Lamphere (eds.), *Women, culture and society* (pp. 43-66). Palo Alto, CA: Stanford University Press.

Chodorow, N. (1978). *The reproduction of mothering.* Berkeley: University of California Press.

Clawson, M. A. (1989). *Constructing brotherhood: Class, gender, and fraternalism.* Princeton, NJ: Princeton University Press.

Cochran, M., Larner, M., Riley, D., & Henderson, C., Jr. (1990). *Extending families: The social networks of parents and their children.* Cambridge: Cambridge University Press.

Cohen, A. (1974). *Two-dimensional man.* London: Routledge & Kegan Paul.

Cole, R. (1971). *Japanese blue collar.* Berkeley: University of California Press.

Connidis, I. (1989). *Family ties and aging.* Toronto: Butterworths.

Cott, N. (1977). *The bonds of womanhood.* New Haven: Yale University Press.

Devereaux, M. S. (1990). New necessities: Popular household appliances. In C. McKie & K. Thompson (Eds.), *Canadian social trends* (pp. 258-261). Toronto: Thompson Educational Publishing.

di Leonardo, M. (1987). The female world of cards and holidays: Women, families and the work of kinship. *Signs, 12,* 440-458.

Draper, P. (1975). !Kung women: Contrasts in sexual egalitarianism in foraging and sedentary contexts. In R. R. Reinter (Ed.), *Toward an anthropology of women* (pp. 77-109). New York: Monthly Review Press.

Duby, G. (Ed.). (1985) [1988]. *A history of private life: Vol. II. Revelations of the medieval world* (A. Goldhammer, Trans.). Cambridge, MA: Harvard University Press.

Duffy, A. (1991, June 7). Fear on streets of metro is increasing, poll shows. *Toronto Star.*

Echols, A. (1989). *Daring to be bad: Radical feminism in America, 1969-1975.* Minneapolis: University of Minnesota Press.

Elshtain, J. B. (1981). *Public man, private woman.* Princeton, NJ: Princeton University Press.

Enright, D. J., & Rawlinson, D. (Eds.). (1991). *The Oxford book of friendship.* Oxford: Oxford University Press.

Erickson, B. (1991, June). *Social exclusion and social networks.* Presented to the Canadian Sociology and Anthropology Association, Kingston, Ontario.

Erickson, B., Radkewycz, A., & Nosanchuk, T. A. (1988). *Helping hands.* Toronto: Centre for Urban and Community Studies, University of Toronto.

Farrell, M. (1986). Friendship between men. In R. Lewis & M. Sussman (Eds.), *Men's changing roles in the family* (pp. 163-197). New York: Haworth.

Ferree, M. M., & Hess, B. (1985). *Controversy and coalition: New feminist movement.* Boston: Twayne.

Film Canada yearbook. (1990). Toronto: Telefilm Canada.

Fischer, C. (1982). *To dwell among friends.* Berkeley: University of California Press.

Fischer, C., & Oliker, S. (1983). A research note on friendship, gender, and the life cycle. *Social Forces, 62,* 124-133.

Fox, B. (1980). *Hidden in the household.* Toronto: Women's Press.

Gans, H. (1962). *The urban villagers.* New York: Free Press.

Garfinkel, P. (1985). *In a men's world.* New York: New American Library.

Garrioch, D. (1986). *Neighbourhood and community in Paris, 1740-1790.* Cambridge: Cambridge University Press.

Gaskell, J. (1983). The reproduction of family life: Perspectives of male and female adolescents. *British Journal of Sociology of Education, 4*(1), 19-38.

Griffin, S. (1981). *Pornography and silence*. New York: Harper & Row.

Gulia, M. (1991, April). *Friends through faith*. Urban Sociology term paper, Department of Sociology, University of Toronto.

Gullestad, M. (1984). *Kitchen-table society*. Oslo: Universitetsforlaget.

Halle, D. (1984). *America's working man*. Chicago: University of Chicago Press.

Hammond, D., & Jablow, A. (1989). Gilgamesh and the Sundance Kid: The myth of male friendship. In C. Hendrick (Ed.), *Close relationships* (pp. 241-258). Newbury Park, CA: Sage.

Hartmann, H. (1976). Capitalism, patriarchy, and job segregation by sex. *Signs, 1*(3, part 2), 137-169.

Hayden, D. (1984). *Redesigning the American dream: The future of housing, work, and family*. New York: Norton.

Hitt, J., Fleming, R., Plater-Zyberk, E., Sennett, R., Wines, J., & Zimmerman, E. (1990, July). Whatever became of the public square? *Harper's*, pp. 49-60.

Hochschild, A. R. (1989). *The second shift: Working parents and the revolution at home*. New York: Viking.

Howell, N. (1979). *Demography of the Dobe !Kung*. New York: Academic Press.

Hunter, A. (1985). Private, parochial and public social orders. In G. Suttles & M. Zald (Eds.), *The challenge of social control* (pp. 230-242). Norwood, NJ: Ablex.

Jacobs, J. (1961). *The death and life of great American cities*. New York: Random House.

Jacobs, J. (1984). *The mall: An attempted escape from everyday life*. Prospect Heights, IL: Waveland Press.

Kemper, T. D. (1978). *A social interactional theory of emotions*. New York: John Wiley.

Kemper, T. D. (1990). *Social structure and testosterone*. New Brunswick, NJ: Rutgers University Press.

Kemper, T. D. (1991). Personal communication.

Kempton, M. (1991, June 13). Good housekeeping. *New York Review of Books*, pp. 58-59.

Kessler, R., & McLeod, J. (1984). Sex differences in vulnerability to undesirable life events. *American Sociological Review, 49*, 620-631.

Kessler, R., & McLeod, J. (1985). Social support and mental health in community samples. In S. Cohen & S. L. Syme (Eds.), *Social Support and Health* (pp. 219-240). Orlando, FL: Academic Press.

Killworth, P., Johnsen, E., Bernard, H. R., Shelley, G. A., & McCarthy, C. (1990, December). Estimating the size of personal networks. *Social Networks, 12*, 289-312.

Kimbrell, A. (1991, June 4). The male manifesto. *The New York Times*.

Kimmel, M. (1987). Rethinking masculinity. In M. Kimmel (Ed.), *Changing men* (pp. 9-24). Newbury Park, CA: Sage.

Kingsdale, J. (1973, December). The "poor man's club": Social functions of the urban working-class saloon. *American Quarterly, 25*, 472-489.

Knoke, D., & Kuklinski, J. (1982). *Network analysis*. Beverly Hills, CA: Sage.

Kornblum, W. (1974). *Blue collar community*. Chicago: University of Chicago Press.

Kramer, J. (1968). *Instant replay* (D. Schaap, Ed.). New York: New American Library.

Langlois, S. (1990). L'avènement de la société de consommation: Un tournant dans l'histoire de la famille [The coming of the consumption society: A turn in the history of the family]. In D. Lemieux (Ed.), *Familles d'aujourd'hui* [Today's families] (pp. 89-113). Québec, Qué: Instiut Québécois de Recherche sur la Culture.

Lawrence, R. 1987. *Housing, dwellings and homes*. Chicester, England: John Wiley.

Lewes, G. H. (1991). Excerpt from *Life of Goethe*. In D. J. Enright & D. Rawlinson *The Oxford Book of Friendship*, (p. 71). Oxford: Oxford University Press. (Originally published 1855).

Liebow, E. (1967). *Tally's corner.* Boston: Little, Brown.

Lofland, L. (1973). *A world of strangers.* New York: Basic Books.

Lofland, L. (1989). Private lifestyles, changing neighborhoods, and public life. *Tijdschrift voor Economie en Social Geografie, 80*(2) [Journal of Economic and Social Geography], 89-96.

Luxton, M. (1980). *More than a labour of love.* Toronto: Women's Press.

Luxton, M. (1987). Time for myself: Women's work and the "fight for shorter hours." In H. J. Maroney & M. Luxton (Eds.), *Feminism and Political Economy* (pp. 167-178). Toronto: Methuen.

Luxton, M. (1990). Two hands for the clock: Changing patterns in the gendered division of labour in the home. In M. Luxton, H. Rosenberg, & S. Arat-Koç (Eds.), *Through the kitchen window: The politics of home and family* (pp. 39-55). Toronto: Garamond.

Lyman, P. (1987). The fraternal bond as a joking relationship: A case study of the role of sexist jokes in male group bonding. In M. Kimmel (Ed.), *Changing Men* (pp. 148-163). Newbury Park, CA: Sage.

MacInnis, C. (1991, March 30). Time to stop apologizing for being male. *Toronto Star.*

Mackenzie, S. (1988). Building women, building cities. In C. Andrew & B. M. Milroy (Eds.), *Life spaces: Gender, household, employment* (pp. 13-30). Vancouver: University of British Columbia Press.

Maryanski, A., & Ishii-Kuntz, M. (1990, February). *A cross-species application of Bott's hypothesis on role segregation and social networks.* Presented to the Sunbelt Social Network Conference, San Diego.

McKie, C., & Thompson, K. (1990). *Canadian social trends.* Toronto: Thompson Educational Publishing.

McLuhan, M. (1973, February). Liturgy and the media. *The Critic,* pp. 15-23.

Messner, M. (1987). The life of a man's seasons: Male identity in the lifecourse of the athlete. In M. Kimmel (Ed.), *Changing men* (pp. 53-67). Newbury Park, CA: Sage.

Michelson, W. (1985). *From sun to sun: Daily obligations and community structure in the lives of employed women and their families.* New York: Oxford University Press.

Michelson, W. (1988). Divergent convergence: The daily routines of employed spouses as a public affairs agenda. In C. Andrew & B. M. Milroy (Eds.), *Life Spaces: Gender, Household, Employment,* (pp. 81-101). Vancouver: University of British Columbia Press.

Miller, S. (1983). *Men and friendship.* Boston: Houghton Mifflin.

Moore, G. (1990, October). Structural determinants of men's and women's personal networks. *American Sociological Review, 55,* 726-735.

Mori, G. (1990). Religious affiliation in Canada. In C. McKie & K. Thompson (Eds.), *Canadian Social Trends,* (pp. 28-32). Toronto: Thompson Educational Publishing.

Newsweek. (1991, June 24). Drums, sweat and tears: What do men really want? Now they have a movement of their own. [international edition], pp. 42-48.

Nouvel Observateur, Le. (1991, June 13). Ça Va, Les Hommes? pp. 6-76.

Oh, S. (1991, May). *A study of urban and suburban movie audiences and their patterns.* Urban Sociology term paper, University of Toronto.

O'Hara, F. (1991). John Button birthday. In D. J. Enright & D. Rawlinson (Eds.), *The Oxford Book of Friendship,* (pp. 56-57). Oxford: Oxford University Press. (Originally published 1965).

Oldenburg, R. (1989). *The great good place: Cafes, coffee shops, community centers, beauty parlors, general stores, bars, hangouts, and how they get you through the day.* New York: Paragon House.

Oliker, S. J. (1989). *Best friends and marriage: Exchange among women.* Berkeley: University of California Press.

Olivier, L. 1982 [1983]. *Confessions of an actor.* London: Hodder & Stoughton Coronet.

O'Neil, J. M. (1981). Patterns of gender conflict and role strain: Sexism and fear of femininity in men's lives. *Personnel and Guidance Journal, 60,* 203-210.

Paine, R. (1969). In search of friendship: An exploratory analysis in "middle-class" culture. *Man, 4,* 505-524.

Perlman, D., & Fehr, B. (1987). The development of intimate relationships. In D. Perlman & S. Duck (Eds.), *Intimate Relationships* (pp. 13-42). Newbury Park, CA: Sage.

Piché, D. (1988). Interaction with the urban environment: Two case studies of women's and female adolescents' leisure activities. In C. Andrew & B. M. Milroy (Eds.), *Life Spaces: Gender, Household, Employment* (pp. 159-75). Vancouver: University of British Columbia Press.

Pleck, E., & Pleck, J. (Eds.). (1980). *The American man.* Englewood Cliffs, NJ: Prentice-Hall.

Pleck, J. (1975). Man to man: Is brotherhood possible? In N. Glazer-Malbin (Ed.), *Old family/new family* (pp. 229-244). New York: Van Nostrand.

Pogrebin, L. C. (1987). *Among friends.* New York: McGraw-Hill.

Pronger, B. (1990). *The arena of masculinity: Sports, homosexuality, and the meaning of sex.* Toronto: Summerhill Press.

Roche, D. (1981) [1987]. *The people of Paris: An essay in popular culture in the 18th century* (M. Evans, Trans.). Berkeley: University of California Press.

Roncière, C. de La. (1985) [1988]. Tuscan notables on the eve of the Renaissance. In G. Duby (Ed.), *A history of private life. Vol. II: Revelations of the medieval world* (pp. 157-310). Cambridge, MA: Harvard University Press.

Rosenthal, C. (1985, November). Kinkeeping in the familial division of labor. *Journal of Marriage and the Family, 47,* 965-974.

Ross, M., & Holmberg, D. (1990). Recounting the past: Gender differences in the recall of events in the history of a close relationship. In J. Olson & M. Zanna (Eds.), *Self-inference processes* (pp. 135-152). Hillsdale, NJ: Lawrence Erlbaum.

Rossi, A., & Rossi, P. (1990). *Of human bonding: Parent-child across the life course.* Chicago: Aldine.

Rubin, L. (1985). *Just friends.* New York: Harper & Row.

Russell, D., & Fournier, H. (1989). *A study of gender bias in the Oxford English dictionary, 2nd edition.* Paper presented to the International Conference on "The Dynamic Text," Toronto.

Sapadin, L. (1988, November). Friendship and gender. *Journal of Social and Personal Relationships, 5,* 387-405.

Sebald, H. (1976). *Momism: The silent disease of America.* Chicago: Nelson-Hall.

Sennett, R. (1977). *The fall of public man.* New York: Knopf.

Sennett, R. (1991). *The conscience of the eye.* New York: Knopf.

Sharma, U. (1986). *Women's work, class, and the urban household: A study of Shimla, North India.* London: Tavistock.

Sharpe, S. (1984). *Double identity.* Harmondsworth, England: Penguin.

Sherr Klein, B. (1981). *Not a love story: A film about pornography.* Montreal: National Film Board of Canada.

Sherrod, D. (1989). The influence of gender on same-sex friendships. In C. Hendrick (Ed.), *Close relationships* (pp. 164-186). Newbury Park, CA: Sage.

Shorter, E. (1975). *The making of the modern family.* New York: Basic Books.

Sik, E. (1988). Reciprocal exchange of labour in Hungary. In R. Pahl (Ed.), *On Work* (pp. 527-547). Oxford: Basil Blackwell.

Silver, A. (1990, May). Friendship in commercial society: Eighteenth-century social theory and modern sociology. *American Journal of Sociology, 95*, 1474-1504.

Smith-Rosenberg, C. (1975). The female world of love and ritual: Relations between women in nineteenth-century America. *Signs, 1*(1), 1-29.

Stack, C. (1974). *All our kin.* New York: Harper & Row.

Stearns, P. (1990). *Be a man! Males in modern society.* New York: Holmes & Meier.

Stone, L. (1988). *Family and friendship ties among Canada's seniors.* Ottawa: Statistics Canada.

Strike, C. (1990). The film industry in Canada. In C. McKie & K. Thompson (Eds.), *Canadian social trends* (pp. 255-257). Toronto: Thompson Educational Publishing.

Tarifa, F. (1990). *Urban-rural comparisons for Albania.* Paper presented to the Centre for Russian and East European Studies, University of Toronto.

Thompson, E., Jr., & Pleck, J. (1987). The structure of male role norms. In M. Kimmel (Ed.), *Changing men* (pp. 25-36). Newbury Park, CA: Sage.

Thoits, P. (1982, October). Life stress, social support, and psychological vulnerability. *Journal of Community Psychology, 10*, 341-362.

Tiger, L. (1969). *Men in groups.* London: Nelson.

Tilly, L., & Scott, J. (1978). *Women, work and family.* New York: Holt, Rinehart & Winston.

Treadwell, P. (1989). Biologic influences on masculinity. In C. Hendrick (Ed.), *Close Relationships,* (pp. 259-285). Newbury Park, CA: Sage.

Tristan, F. (1991). Excerpt from *Promenades dans Londres.* In D. J. Enright & D. Rawlinson (Eds.), *The Oxford Book of Friendship* (pp. 92-93). Oxford: Oxford University Press. (Originally published 1840).

Turner, R. (1990). Modernity and cultural identity: Is there an alternative to the "loose confederation of shopping malls"? *Canadian Issues, 12*, 97-108.

Turner, R. J., & Avison, W. (1989, August). Gender and depression: Assessing exposure and vulnerability to life events in a chronically strained population. *Journal of Nervous and Mental Disease, 177*, 443-455.

Useem, R. H., Useem, J., & Gibson, D. (1960). The function of neighboring for the middle-class male. *Human Organization, 19*, 68-76.

Vanek, J. (1974). Time spent in housework. *Scientific American, 231*, 116-120.

Vaux, A. (1985). Variations in social support associated with gender, ethnicity and age. *Social Issues, 41*(1), 89-110.

Vicinus, M. (1985). *Independent women: Work and community for single women, 1850-1920.* Chicago: University of Chicago Press.

Wadel, C. (1969). *Marginal adaptations and modernization in Newfoundland.* St. John's, Newfoundland: Institute of Social and Economic Research, Memorial University.

Wall, H. (1990). *Fierce communion: Family and community in North America.* Cambridge, MA: Harvard University Press.

Wellman, B. (1979, March). The community question. *American Journal of Sociology, 84*, 1201-1231.

Wellman, B. (1982). Studying personal communities. In P. Marsden & N. Lin (Eds.), *Social structure and network analysis* (pp. 61-80). Beverly Hills, CA: Sage.

Wellman, B. (1985). Domestic work, paid work and net work. In S. Duck & D. Perlman (Eds.), *Understanding personal relationships* (pp. 159-191). London: Sage.

Wellman, B. (1988). The community question re-evaluated. In M. P. Smith (Ed.), *Power, community and the city* (pp. 81-107). New Brunswick, NJ: Transaction Books.

Wellman, B. (1990). The place of kinfolk in community networks. *Marriage and Family Review, 15*(1/2), 195-228.

Wellman, B. (1992). Which types of ties and networks give what kinds of social support? In E. Lawler, B. Markovsky, C. Ridegeway, & H. Walker (Eds.), *Advances in group processes. Vol. 9.* Greenwich, CT: JAI Press.

Wellman, B., & Baker, S. G. (1985). Using SAS software to link network, tie and individual data. *Connections, 8*(2-3), 176-187.

Wellman, B., Carrington, P., & Hall, A. (1988). Networks as personal communities. In B. Wellman & S. D. Berkowitz (Eds.), *Social structures: A network approach* (pp. 130-184). Cambridge: Cambridge University Press.

Wellman, B., Frank, O., Espinoza, V., Lundquist, S., & Wilson, C. (1991). Integrating individual, relational and structural analysis. *Social Networks, 13,* 223-249.

Wellman, B., & Hiscott, R. (1985). From social support to social network. In I. Sarason & B. Sarason (Eds.), *Social support* (pp. 205-222). The Hague: Martinus Nijhoff.

Wellman, B., & Leighton, B. (1979, March). Networks, neighborhoods and communities. *Urban Affairs Quarterly, 14,* 363-390.

Wellman, B., & Sim, S. (1990, February & May). Integrating textual and statistical methods in the social sciences. *Cultural Anthropology Methods Newsletter, 2.* (Part 1), 1-3, 10-11; (Part 2), 1-5

Wellman, B., & Tindall, D. (1992). Reach out and touch some bodies: How social networks connect telephone networks. In G. Barnett & W. Richards, Jr. (Eds.), *Advances in communication networks.* Norwood, NJ: Ablex.

Wellman, B., & Wellman, B. (1992). Domestic affairs and network relations. *Journal of Social and Personal Relationships, 9.*

Wellman, B., & Wortley, S. (1989a, Fall). Brothers' keepers: Situating kinship relations in broader networks of social support. *Sociological Perspectives,* 273-306.

Wellman, B., & Wortley, S. (1989b). Different strokes from different folks: Which types of community ties provide what kinds of social support? (Research Paper no. 174). Toronto: Centre for Urban and Community Studies, University of Toronto.

Wellman, B., & Wortley, S. (1990, November). Different strokes from different folks: Community ties and social support. *American Journal of Sociology, 96,* 558-588.

Wellman, Bev. (1991). *Pathways to back care.* Unpublished master's thesis, University of Toronto.

Whyte, W. F. (1943). *Street corner society.* Chicago: University of Chicago Press.

Whyte, W. H., Jr. (1980). *The social life of small urban spaces.* Washington, DC: Conservation Foundation.

Wireman, P. (1984). *Urban neighborhoods, networks, and families.* Lexington, MA: Lexington Books.

Wolf, D. (1984). Kin availability and the living arrangements of older women. *Social Science Research, 13,* 72-89.

Wolf, D. (1988). Kinship and family support in aging societies. In *Social and economic consequences of population aging.* New York: United Nations Department of International Economic and Social Affairs.

Wong, A. (1991, April). *A comparative study of men and women in formal and informal settings.* Urban Sociology term paper, University of Toronto.

Wright, P. (1982). Men's friendships, women's friendships and the alleged inferiority of the latter. *Sex Roles, 8,* 1-20.

Wright, P. (1989). Gender differences in adults' same- and cross-gender friendships. In R. Adams & R. Blieszner (Eds.), *Older adult friendship* (pp. 197-221). Newbury Park, CA: Sage.

Young, A. (1990). Television viewing. In C. McKie & K. Thompson (Eds.), *Canadian social trends* (pp. 231-233). Toronto: Thompson Educational Publishing.

Young, M., & Willmott, P. (1973). *The symmetrical family.* London: Routledge & Kegan Paul.

Zimbel, M. (1991, May 18). Playing the numbers game at Immigration. *Toronto Star,* p. F1.

6

Men's Families, Men's Friends

A Structural Analysis of Constraints on Men's Social Ties

THEODORE F. COHEN

Introduction

There are some rather familiar sketches of men's experiences of friendship and intimacy. Men are often described as lacking both an appreciation of and capabilities for intimacy (Bell, 1981; Rubin, 1983, 1985;
Stein, 1986). Men are inexpressive, rational, and competitive. In such
sketches, men are consistently described as being uncomfortable with
or incapable of expressing and confiding intimate thoughts and feelings
(Balswick & Peek, 1971; McGill, 1985; Rubin, 1976, 1983, 1985). This
is especially characteristic of, though not restricted to, the portrait of men's
relationships with other men (Bell, 1981; Levinson, 1978; McGill, 1985;
Stein, 1986). In such social relationships, men are described as unwill-
ing or unable to engage in intimate friendships. They are described, instead, as withholding feelings of vulnerability or affection because of the
impropriety attached to such expressions towards other males (Brannon,
1976). Homophobic concerns, growing out of a lifetime of male socialization, further trap men within narrow, somewhat superficial positions

AUTHOR'S NOTE: An earlier version of this paper was presented at the 2nd Annual
Conference on the Family, co-sponsored by the Ohio Council on Family Relations and Ohio
chapters of the American Association of Sex Educators, Counselors, and Therapists, and
the American Association of Marital and Family Therapists, October 1988, in Columbus,
Ohio.

vis-à-vis other men (Lehne, 1976). So consistent is this often anecdotal characterization of male-male friendships that one could easily conclude that men are socially impoverished, lacking real friendship and intimacy with other men.

In relationships with women, male inexpressivity is supposedly somewhat lessened as there are not the same sort and level of taboos around self-revelation and expression. Even there, however, men reportedly fall short of women's abilities and expectations for emotional intimacy. Women's experiences and expressions of friendship become the model against which men are compared and found wanting. This depiction of men's intimate experiences dominates the literature on gender-based differences in intimate relationships.

Equally dominant is the more or less individualistic explanation for the nature of men's friendships. Stein (1986) for example, cites four "barriers" to male friendship: competitiveness and its inhibiting effect on self disclosure; a lack of male role models in intimacy; homophobia; and a need to be in control, which also restricts men's willingness to be vulnerable. Thus, because of what men do and don't learn they fail to develop those qualities that are necessary if one is to enter into and maintain meaningful intimate relationships with other men. Bell (1981) also emphasizes the internalization of traits or characteristics that inhibit men's emotional lives. Noting the stoicism that is part of American concepts of masculinity and its exaggeration in the "cult" of machismo, Bell indicates that male friendships are narrow in both quantity and quality because of what American men learn while growing up male. Others echo these emphases (Rubin, 1985) in arguing that because of the nature of gender socialization, especially the gender-specific relationship between mother and child, men's friendships are destined to be limited and fragile. It is this characterization and its underlying individualistic assumptions that this chapter seeks to question.

While individualistic explanations dominate attempts to explain gender-based experiences of intimacy (see Risman & Schwartz, 1989) they are not without alternatives. Some scholars have incorporated more structural variables into their analyses of why men or women behave as they do within friendships and intimate relationships (Allan, 1989; Fischer, 1982; Hess, 1972; Risman & Schwartz, 1989). Emphasizing constraints imposed by the social context of everyday life and the structure of work and family responsibilities, structural arguments look beyond socialization and personality formation to account for the kind and quality of men's and women's experiences of intimacy. This is particularly evident in microstructural theory (Risman & Schwartz, 1989) which, in its extreme, suggests that the differences in male and female behaviors result from gender differentiated *opportunities and expectations*, the absence of which would lead to as nearly identical behavior between women and men as biological differences would allow.

Without the same label and terminology, other theorists have constructed comparable models to account for people's behavior within intimate relationships. In describing friendship across the life cycle, Hess (1972) suggests that friendships may, on occasion, compete with other roles and relationships for a person's time and loyalty. This is especially so at points in adulthood where individuals must respond to demands from a wide range of other relationships. In such competition, friendships frequently lose. Allan's (1989) analysis of friendship emphasizes the importance of the demands and restrictions on individuals' "personal space" that create constraints and limit the opportunities that one has for friendship. Economic, occupational, familial, and gender-related constraints consume much of the "space" or freedom people have to build and/or maintain friendships. While Allan recognizes that men's friendships may be characterized by inexpressiveness, he is much more concerned with the external, structural factors that shape men's and women's opportunities for and experiences of friendship.

Building upon the more structural arguments, I use data drawn from an exploratory study of the family and work lives of 30 Boston-area men to detail the impact of marriage, fatherhood, and work on the maintenance of informants' non-marital social ties. I argue that the combination of the inflexible demands of the workplace and the cultural expectations associated with familial roles and relationships are at least as powerful as determinants of the nature of men's social ties, as are whatever socially acquired capacities and preferences men might possess. Rather than question the compelling and consistent evidence indicating gender-specific definitions and styles of friendship (Swain, 1989), love (Cancian, 1985), and intimacy (Rubin, 1983, 1985), I examine some other determinants of the quality and kind of men's friendships with other men. After describing the processes through which these friendships change or end as men enter marriage and fatherhood, I examine the structural and cultural constraints that marriage, fatherhood, and work impose on men's temporal resources. As recognized by Hess and implied within Allan's notion of "personal space," relationships require *time* to either form or be maintained. Attention must therefore be paid to those familial and occupational claims on social time that constrain men's friendships by curtailing their accessibility. These constraints explain men's lack of male-male intimacy as much as any "missing ingredients" within the relationships themselves.

Study Design

The data reported come from intensive, semistructured interviews with a non-probability sample of 30 new husbands and/or fathers in the Boston, Massachusetts, metropolitan area about their experiences in becoming and being husbands and fathers. Sixteen of the 30 men were married and fathers of young children (average length of fatherhood = 2.1 years; married an average of 4.6 years), the remaining 14 were recently married, childless men (average length of marriage = 1.9 years). Ninety percent of the sample were in their first marriages; 13 of the fathers were first-time fathers. These sampling characteristics were thought to be important if I was to be able to explore the processes of *becoming* husbands and fathers as well as the role performances that make up *being* husbands and fathers.

I located the sample through three different sources: 12 men were located through community-based institutions in a working-class Boston suburb; 8 men were obtained by "snowball sampling" the original informants; and 10 men were referred to me by my network of colleagues, friends, and neighbors. The sample reflects some socioeconomic diversity: half of the employed men (13 of 26) worked in either traditional blue-collar or low-level white-collar occupations. The entire sample ranged from a high school-educated janitor to a Ph.D. in physics and contained three full-time graduate students and one full-time house-husband. Sixty percent of the sample had college educations (9 men) or more (9 men). Informants were less diversified in racial and religious characteristics. There were one non-white and one Jewish informant; the rest were spread across a variety of ethnic affiliations (Italian, Irish, Portuguese, and French Canadian).

I interviewed each informant once, covering his experiences entering marriage (questions about premarital relationships, marital expectations, and reasons for marrying), being married (questions about changes wrought by marriage, activities as a husband, satisfaction with marriage) and, where relevant, experiences entering and enacting fatherhood. All men were asked a series of questions about their jobs, designed mostly to qualitatively assess their attachment to work and its connections to their family lives. Most of the more than 100 items in the interview schedule were original to this study though there was some use of items from prior research (e.g., Oakley, 1980; Rubin, 1976). As ideas or themes emerged they were pursued and incorporated into subsequent interviews and analysis. I deliberately kept interviews somewhat informal in tone. This turned out to be an especially necessary strategy for interviewing men on issues that they rarely have occasion to reveal to another man. The average interview lasted just under 2 hours, though they ranged from slightly more than 1 to more than 3.5 hours.

All interviews were tape-recorded and eventually transcribed. The transcripts were then analyzed thematically. Some themes were derived from the literature on families or gender (e.g., LaRossa & LaRossa, 1981), others emerged from the interview material through the *constant comparative method* of qualitative analysis (Glaser & Strauss, 1967). Dominant patterns in men's accounts were used to build analytical categories, which were then modified and joined by new categories as variations on themes surfaced. The following discussion reflects those patterns that emerged in men's reports about their friendship ties and the ways in which such ties were affected by and, in return, affected men's families. The material is offered as a source for further inquiry and analysis and not as a series of generalizations to be applied to the population of men and their friends.

Findings and Discussion

Entering Marriage, Exiting Friendships

The process of becoming a husband, which began before and continued after official entrance into legal marriage, like that of becoming a father, radically altered informants' social ties with other men. The principal mechanism accounting for these alterations was the shift in temporal demands that accompanied marriage and fatherhood. Whereas prior to marriage informants' lives seemed to center around their relationships with male peers, the emergence of the relationship that ultimately became their marriage drove them directly from the peer group to a *coupled identity*. As the initially casual male-female relationship became increasingly serious and exclusive, men found themselves redefining and reallocating what available time they had. Time formerly shared within a small network of friends became the property of the now central male-female relationship, and this allocation of temporal resources was seen as both legitimate and appropriate. For example, the following comment from a 25-year-old stockroom clerk describes his gradual redistribution of his time and availability.

> I slacked down [*sic*] seeing my friends; I stopped partying a lot. I used to play hockey two or three times a week, go out after hockey and not come home until 3 in the morning . . . She slowed me down . . . I just decided I'd rather spend (my) time with her . . . I went from seeing her two or three nights a week and seeing my friends the rest of the time, to seeing her more, till I was seeing her every night.

Becoming a father had similar consequences in driving men both as individuals and as members of networks of couples into a kind of social isolation. But like the differences in the two role transitions (Cohen, 1987), the processes differed in their pace and perceived impact. In their transitions to marriage, men made more gradual reductions in their friendship ties than occurred within the transitions to fatherhood. Men reported "cutting back" on their availability to their friends, some to an occasional evening each week, others to an abbreviated appearance ("stopping by") after spending time with their future wives, while still others "made time" for friends by designating days or evenings during the week reserved for friends. Even in instances where more time was still being spent with male friends, more valued time (weekends versus weeknights) was spent with their future spouses.

Most commonly, friendships were reported to gradually diminish, eventually being supplanted by the emergent relationship between future spouses. This is that familiar situation whereby friendships fade and people fall out of touch. Others have commented on this process of men's friendships not surviving marriage (Berger & Kellner, 1974; Fischer, 1982; Komarovsky, 1967; Willmott, 1969). The interviews suggest, however, that much of this change occurs prior to marriage during the process of "coupling" (Cohen, 1987). As a 28-year-old retail manager commented: "By the time we were married it was an old situation . . ." This made marriage itself appear to be less of an explicit culprit, in that official marriage followed after the more difficult social restructuring had commenced. It is nonetheless part of entering marriage that led to diminished male involvement in friendship.

Informants recalled some interesting and telling reactions of friends to their shifting allegiance away from the group. Initial displays of group resistance to the departure of one of their members stemmed from both real and symbolic losses, but ultimately gave way to recognition and assistance. In a real sense, the network lost or saw sharp reductions in involvement from a valued member as men became less available. They could no longer count on doing the same kinds of things in the same ways with the same people involved to the level they'd always been (see also Komarovsky, 1967; Willmott, 1969). Symbolically, as men became increasingly involved within a male-female relationship, eventually marrying, the group was reminded of the inevitability of their own personal changes. Thus, they both mourn the real loss of the member and do some anticipatory mourning for a soon-to-be-passed life stage. These may explain the teasing and cajoling that characterized the peer group's "resistance" to such changes as well as friends' ultimate acceptance of what appeared inevitable.

Eventually, peers signaled their acceptance and understanding of the reduced priority they now had in informants' lives. At that point they actually assisted in the process of men's withdrawal by ceasing to make demands for active involvement on their former member "going off on their own," "moving on," and excluding informants from their plans and activities. As informants moved further along into official marriage, redefining themselves as husbands, friends seemed to redefine them and any social or personal claims on them as inaccessible and illegitimate. Even in some instances where this was contrary to how informants themselves defined their availability, peers demonstrated the presumption that marriage commands social and, thus, temporal priority over friendship. For example, a 26-year-old banker related the following anecdote.

> When we first got back from our honeymoon everybody stopped over to say "Hi . . ." Then, for about 4 months . . . we wouldn't get a phone call . . . I'd have to make those phone calls . . . It was like friends thought, "Well, you're married now, we can't impose . . ." Finally, I came point-blank to my best friend and asked, "What the hell is the matter? You guys used to call me . . . did I do something wrong? Are you mad at me?" He just said, "We didn't want to impose." But just because you're married it doesn't mean you can't do anything. It took *them* 4 months to get used to the idea that we were married.

While the behaviors of informants and reactions of peers may seem to indicate a low value or priority on male friendship, both reflect equally well cultural expectations about marital intimacy and temporal constraints.

Friendship in Marriage

Apparently, marriage was expected to become the relationship in informants' lives wherein they would seek and find companionship, intimacy, and emotional support and be the "place" where men were expected to spend the bulk of their nonworking time. This, in part, reflects the more recently emergent cultural ideology of the companionate marriage, where marital relations are expected to be built upon a foundation of intimacy and friendship, and where communication and self-revelation are more or less required of spouses. It also illustrates cultural expectations about legitimate expenditure of time. With only so much "interaction time" (Lewis & Weigert, 1981) at one's disposal, marriage is to claim the lion's share. Although this time is more flexibly structured than the time claimed by one's occupation, cultural expectations nonetheless helped dictate where and with whom one would engage in intimate ties.

Men's participation in such a "funneling of intimacy" left them forced to rely more heavily and exclusively on wives for the kind of social and emotional support otherwise characteristic of friendship. It accounts in part for informants' ambivalent assessments of marriage. Men's definitions of the husband role and reactions to marriage suggested a widespread acceptance of the ideology of "spouse as best friend." This was expressed in the following way by a 25-year-old warehouseman:

> To me it's (marriage is) so simplistic [*sic*]. It's something that was always there: it's having the best friend you can have. She's my best friend. It's very important to me and I'll always be her best friend, her feelings will always come before me . . .

The following quote from a 28-year-old computer operator echoes the same theme.

> Being married means living a good part of your life for somebody so that she might be able to fill some goals in her life, helping her to achieve things that she really desires . . . being a good friend (and) saying what needs to be said, that sometimes don't sound right but really are.

At the same time, men's accounts of the "rules of marriage" indicate the proscription attached to too much emphasis on nonmarital ties. While most commonly expressed regarding the unacceptability of extramarital sexual relationships, nearly one-third of the sample referred more generally to norms restricting nonmarital social relationships. For example, consider the following comments, first from a 31-year-old retail manager, then from a 28-year-old computer technician.

> Staying out late with the boys every night is a no-no. An occasional night out is necessary and good, but if you're going to be a husband, you start in the home.

> If you're not really working at it in all aspects of your life (and) confining how you relate to people to that first and then the others . . . it becomes too confusing.

Praised and valued most for the intimacy, companionship, and friendship to be found there, marriage was assailed most for the social constraints that it imposed on informants' lives. What seems to be an important though overlooked factor is that it seemed not to be men's inabilities or lack of interest in male-male intimacy that drove them more deeply into the emotional dimension of their marital relationships. Instead, it seemed largely the result of culturally imposed temporal priorities and constraints. More will be said of this shortly.

Fatherhood and Friends

Men's transitions to fatherhood were both occasions for further reductions in their already diminished social lives and opportunities to witness some of the effects of this funneling of intimacy. Despite reporting a variety of anxieties, fears, and/or concerns regarding pregnancy, childbirth, and, ultimately, fatherhood, men recalled making surprisingly little use of friends for information, social support, and/or reassurance. It might also be noted that men made equally little use of the vast available literature on pregnancy, childbirth, and parenthood. They explained this away by citing its irrelevance to *their* particular needs or concerns. Since much of that literature is written as if it will be read by women, there may be some validity behind men's claims. Less understandable is their failure to utilize other men (friends *or* family).

By men's accounts this stemmed mostly from a lack of opportunity; there were few to no available men to whom one could go with the concerns they acknowledged having had.

> Did you have anyone you could talk to about (it); friends who were fathers?

No, I really didn't, none my age who were immediately fathers. (27-year-old warehouseman)

I haven't really talked to anyone because there aren't that many—the people I know are either unmarried or are married and say they don't want to have kids. (29-year-old physicist)

I don't know any other men with kids . . . All of my male friends did not have children out of choice. When I told them what the situation was, they assumed the only reason I would be for it was because I had no choice. (30-year-old truck driver)

Whether in formal settings (e.g., childbirth classes), with friends, or at work, men who had earlier admitted having had concerns and worries reported not sharing those feelings with other men. For example, the following comment, from a 36-year-old househusband who had previously confessed having been worried about his wife's health and safety, about changes in his life and about *being* a father indicated that he saw *no reason* to seek out other men for support.

I don't remember specifically asking questions; we didn't have any specific questions that we didn't know the answers to.

So infrequently did informants turn to other men for emotional support and advice that they were clearly unaccustomed to doing so, even in an interview. This was expressed by a 37-year-old architect:

I just realized why I'm having so much trouble answering, and wasting so much of your tape. This is the kind of thing, what you're asking, that men don't ask men.

What is most interesting to note is that some of the same men, who had earlier expressed difficulty finding and talking with other men, spoke about frequent, lengthy, and/or intensive conversations with their wives. For example, a 28-year-old tool and die maker described what he and his wife had talked about during the pregnancy:

We would sit there all day and just talk—about what it was gonna be like; "I hope he looks like both of us," "I hope he's good," "I hope he's healthy . . ."

Thus, men's lack of male intimacy led them to rely heavily on their wives to be the major emotional support and source of information during pregnancy. This accounts, in part, for why a number of men reported "feeling closer" to their wives during pregnancy. While pregnancy and impending fatherhood raised the level of things felt, lacking available male intimates to turn to forced men to lean even more heavily on their wives. Yet this dependence on wives had important implications both within the marriage and for men's relations to other men. While some couples may have been brought closer together as husbands depended on their wives for advice, information, and emotional support, it is possible that some wives may have found this role a bit burdensome and grew resentful that their spouses didn't make greater use of other resources (both written and human). This was articulated as follows by the 29-year-old physicist, late in his wife's pregnancy:

I feel a little guilty . . . I ask her a lot of questions about things at which point she gets mad and says—"Well, why don't you read the books?"

More important for the moment, relying on wives for information and support meant that men continued not to turn to other men, not to learn from them, and not to share experiences with others. This may have perpetuated some of the mystique and mystery associated with fatherhood. It is important, however, not to assume automatically that the source of this behavior pattern rests exclusively in male socialization. Since the men had earlier made the temporal reallocation in keeping with contemporary cultural expectations of marriage and family life, their opportunities for support from intimate male peers were in short supply. Furthermore, with the increasingly heavy temporal demands emanating from the combination of job, marriage, and impending fatherhood, such intimate relationships were not likely to emerge and develop.

Because of the drama, suddenness, and irrevocability of the onset of parenthood in men's lives, the impact of fatherhood on men's friendship ties was more dramatic than the aforementioned more gradual process that accompanied marriage. It is again important to understand the mechanism responsible for altered peer relations. This is to be found in the nature of parental responsibilities. Thus, when men described the kinds of withdrawal from active friendship ties that they faced with fatherhood, it was their role responsibilities and not their socially acquired incapacities that were operating.

Few fathers in the sample reported any successful efforts to maintain active friendship ties after the arrival of their children. Instead, the more typical pattern was one of "cutting back," "telling people 'no,' " or not going out much. Two examples follow. A 33-year-old municipal administrator described altering his accessibility to friends in the following way:

> All your free time, all your relationships with everybody starts to change; you start telling people, "No, I can't come." You just don't go. I remember friends of mine would have children and then disappear for a couple of years. (I'd wonder) "Hey, where'd you go? What happened?" . . . But I never saw time disappear so fast and had so little time to do anything.

A 42-year-old teacher commented about his experience of the same process.

> I used to be more socially active . . . I think that is the area that I cut back most in . . . I write many fewer letters to friends over the last few months . . . I have less time.

Parenthood extended men's social withdrawal because of the needs of infants and the time demands that come with meeting those needs. Infants require "continuous coverage" (LaRossa & LaRossa, 1981), and parents find themselves faced with less and less time to be spent in ways they spent it prior to parenthood. While this becomes a source of conflict and negotiation between spouses, from which men emerge with still more free time ("down time") than wives (Allan, 1989; LaRossa & LaRossa, 1981), informants' social lives were not unaffected. Much more than with marriage, parenthood "embedded" men into a temporal context within which all other relations had to be fitted (Lewis & Weigert, 1981). Frequently, such a fit was impossible to accomplish to meet all the social claims on one's available "interaction time" (Lewis & Weigert). Within that broad level of time, competing claims are hierarchically ranked, much as the levels themselves are stratified (Lewis and Weigert). Friendship ties seemed always to rank behind both marriage and parenthood in terms of the salience and legitimacy of their claims on one's time.

Work, Family, and Friends:
Conflicting Claims on Social Time

While men's friendships lack both the cultural legitimacy and the priority that marriage and parenthood possess, neither friendship nor family asserts the kinds of temporal claims that one's work commands. Work makes the least flexible, most "temporally rigid" demands on workers' time and energies (Lewis & Weigert, 1981; Zerubavel, 1979). Of the variety of claims that might be made on one's temporal resources (i.e., self, peer, spouse, children, work), jobs make the least controllable and least avoidable claims. For most individuals, the number of hours one works and the scheduling of those hours are beyond the worker's immediate control.

Still structured around the idea of the "husband-economic-provider" (Gronseth, 1972) who can devote himself fully to his job while the family is tended to by women, most jobs force workers to participate in an occupational system that acts "as though" the family did not exist (Kanter, 1977; Piotrkowski, 1979). Demands for the time (and loyalty) of workers are made at the expense of time that could be devoted to other roles and interpersonal relationships (Margolis, 1979). With the uneven competition between work demands and family demands, individuals may often experience their family lives being fitted around their jobs. True in different ways for different kinds of jobs across the class spectrum, the result is the same. The first comment comes from my interview with a 28-year-old salesman. It is followed by similar statements from a 27-year-old warehouseman and a 26-year-old banker.

I put in 70 to 80 hours of work a week, 60-70 probably of solid work . . . It pulls away from our (marital) relationship . . . I don't have time during the week to go out, even to just go out and see a movie . . . to do that is precious sales time for me. Times that I do not have an appointment we'll definitely get together and do something . . . I like to . . . do that . . . but my paycheck is on a quarter basis. If I don't maintain the same level of production or even better, it doesn't feel good to live a quarter with a cut in pay.

Around Christmas it really bothered me because (working overtime) I'd be working, come home and sleep 7 hours and then go back to work. I'd have to sleep. I'd have to wake up. I'd have to go. That wasn't cool, I didn't like that at all.

We don't see each other enough . . . All of a sudden, the week is gone and we've spent all of an hour and a half with each other . . . That's lousy. Sure, I make good money but is it worth not seeing my wife?

Given the distress expressed in the above accounts over the lack of opportunity to spend time within one's family, it is hardly surprising to

see men cut back elsewhere. Having already sacrificed family involvements to the temporal structure of the workplace makes extrafamilial,
nonwork involvements more costly and therefore more expendable.

While other analyses have included the culture of the workplace,
particularly its competitiveness, as a barrier to male friendship (Bell,
1981; Rubin, 1985; Sherrod, 1987; Stein, 1986), the temporal dominance
of work is at least as important. Without sufficient financial resources
to sustain oneself if fired, or lacking job skills that could be taken elsewhere (or at least threatened to be), most individuals work within the
hours and to the level expected of them. As a result, the allocation of
temporal resources between work and family may fall short of one's
personal preference.

We would be remiss, however, if we failed to attend to cultural definitions and values, which suggest where we *ought* to spend the time we
more directly control ourselves. Within this dimension of temporal stratification, the family occupies a rather prominent place, especially in
comparison to friendship. These expectations leave little room for maintaining old or cultivating new extrafamilial friendship relationships.
This may be particularly true at certain life-cycle stages, most notably
during the early years of childrearing (Allan, 1989; Bell, 1981; Fischer,
1982; Halle, 1984; Hess, 1972). It may, therefore, have been overstated
some in the present analysis, given the ages and stages of family life of
my informants. Still, it is important to recognize that the prominence of
the family over friendships is not derived from the same sorts of factors
as the dominance of the job. The former is rooted in beliefs and values
about what one *ought to do* and where one *ought to be*; the latter is derived
from the reality of what one *must* do in order to survive economically.
Both, however, make claims to which men are compelled to respond.
Given opportunities to allocate time *as one chooses*, most informants
might have displayed different life structures from what we observed.
Perhaps both friendship and family would be recipients of more active
male involvement, regardless of men's earlier socialization. Lacking
that opportunity meant, however, that neither arena of informants' intimate lives received the same share of them that went to their jobs.

Like the possible effects of life-cycle stage, the process of social
withdrawal may be more acute for working-class men. Given tendencies toward marrying at an earlier age, working-class men are more
likely to go from peer group to marriage. Middle-class men may find
educational and/or occupational choices removing them from their peer
networks before they've even met their future spouses. After marriage,

class variations probably continue but possibly in the other direction. Evidence exists that suggests that working-class men may tolerate their jobs largely because of the peer relations that develop on the job (Halle, 1984). These relationships, Halle asserts, may "spill over" into the home in the same way that the careers of professional men do. If spending time with "buddies" away from the job and the home is a mechanism that allows working-class men to find otherwise missing gratification, they will probably be more protective of those ties. That a major source of marital conflict among Halle's working-class informants revolves around the competing claims friends make on men's time and allegiance suggests that wives, at least, embrace the cultural priority accorded to family over friends. Middle-class men, especially professionals, may find the work-related demands much more intrusive into their families and may respond by cutting back on those relationships that are perceived as "optional" (Stein, 1986). Regardless of these class differences, work and family constraints possess a degree of cultural legitimacy and structural dominance that friendship ties lack.

Summary and Conclusion

The thrust of the preceding argument is that informants' social lives are products of competing claims for their social time. Without the time needed to nurture and maintain existing friendship ties, informants gradually saw their emotional lives consolidated more and more in their marriages. Fatherhood extended this process as it exerted additional demands on their time. Without much time beyond the family and workplace to invest in new relationships, informants restricted much of their social and emotional life to their marriages.

This emphasis on social time and its effect on opportunities for social relationships is relevant if we are to understand what happens to men's peer relations over the early stages of the family life cycle and, perhaps also, why deep friendship ties don't emerge later. It cannot account for why men act as they do within their friendships (e.g., amount of self-disclosure), nor is it intended to. Clearly, there are social and cultural elements that operate in shaping how men and women express intimacy within social relationships. However, it is not the nature of these expressions that fully accounts for men's friendship patterns.

Some have questioned whether any emphasis on the temporal constraints on men's friendships is useful. For example, Rubin (1985) offers a strong case for something beyond time as a key explanatory variable for the ways in which men lack ties that women manage to maintain. She notes, for example, that even when faced with comparably demanding role sets, women "make time" or "find time" for maintaining active friendship ties. Thus, she dismisses men's claims about their lack of time as incomplete and inadequate. However, unless we have a situation in which women and men face more similar role expectations regarding work and family commitments—where work is one's "master role," demanding more than even one might willingly give and where family is an area in which there are emergent expectations for high levels of involvement—it will be difficult to claim that the gender difference is internalized in the personality or gender role and not as much a consequence of the constraints and opportunities that each gender faces. For instance, women in high-stress professional positions who are also married with children might be the best candidates for comparison with men. Do they resemble stereotyped images of women's intimacy or do they begin to resemble what Hunt and Hunt (1986) refer to as "sociological men"? This question needs to be answered before the more structural argument can be fully assessed.

References

Allan, G. (1989). *Friendship: Developing a sociological perspective*. Boulder, CO: Westview.

Balswick, J., & Peek, C. (1971). The inexpressive male: A tragedy of American society. *The Family Coordinator, 20*, 363-368.

Bell, R. (1981). *Worlds of friendship*. Beverly Hills, CA: Sage.

Berger, P., & Kellner, H. (1974). Marriage and the construction of reality. In R. Coser (Ed.), *The family: Its structures and functions* (pp. 157-174). New York: St. Martin's Press.

Brannon, R. (1976). The male sex role: Our culture's blueprint of manhood and what it's done for us lately. In D. David & R. Brannon (Eds.), *The forty-nine percent majority: The male sex role* (pp. 1-48). Reading, MA: Addison-Wesley.

Cancian, F. (1985). Gender politics: Love and power in the private and public spheres. In A. Rossi (Ed.), *Gender and the life course* (pp. 253-262). Hawthorne, NY: Aldine.

Cohen, T. (1987). Remaking men: Men's experiences becoming and being husbands and fathers and their implications for reconceptualizing men's lives. *Journal of Family Issues, 8*, 57-77.

Fischer, C. (1982). *To dwell among friends*. Chicago: University of Chicago Press.

Glaser, B., & Strauss, A. (1967). *The discovery of grounded theory*. New York: Aldine.

Gronseth, E. (1972). The breadwinner trap. In L. K. Howe (Ed.), *The future of the family* (pp. 175-191). New York: Simon & Schuster.

Halle, D. (1984). *America's working man*. Chicago: University of Chicago Press.

Hess, B. (1972). Friendship. In M. W. Riley, M. Johnson, & A. Foner (Eds.), *Aging and society. Vol. 3: A sociology of age stratification* (pp. 357-396). New York: Russell Sage.

Hunt, J., & Hunt, L. (1986). The dualities of careers and families: New integrations or new polarizations? In A. Skolnick & J. Skolnick (Eds.), *Family in transition* (5th ed.) (pp. 275-289). Boston: Little, Brown.

Kanter, R. M. (1977). *Work and family in the United States: A critical review and agenda for research and policy.* New York: Russell Sage.

Komarovsky, M. (1967). *Blue collar marriage.* New York: Vintage.

LaRossa, R., & LaRossa, M. (1981). *Transition to parenthood: How infants change families.* Beverly Hills, CA: Sage.

Lehne, G. (1976). Homophobia among men. In D. David & R. Brannon (Eds.), *The forty-nine percent majority: The male sex role* (pp. 66-88). Reading, MA: Addison-Wesley.

Levinson, D. (1978). *The seasons of a man's life.* New York: Ballantine.

Lewis, J. D., & Weigert, A. (1981). The structures and meanings of social time. *Social Forces, 60,* 432-462.

Margolis, D. R. (1979). *The managers: Corporate life In America.* New York: William Morrow.

McGill, M. (1985). *The McGill report on male intimacy.* New York: Perennial.

Oakley, A. (1980). *Women confined: Towards a sociology of childbirth.* New York: Schocken.

Piotrkowski, C. (1979). *Work and the family system.* New York: Macmillan.

Risman, B., & Schwartz, P. (1989). Being gendered: A microstructural view of intimate relationships. In B. Risman & P. Schwartz (Eds.), *Gender in intimate relationships: A microstructural approach* (pp. 1-9). Belmont, CA: Wadsworth.

Rubin, L. (1976). *Worlds of pain: Life in the working class family.* New York: Basic Books.

Rubin, L. (1983). *Intimate strangers: Men and women together.* New York: Perennial.

Rubin, L. (1985). *Just friends: The role of friendship in our lives.* New York: Harper & Row.

Sherrod, D. (1987). The bonds of men: Problems and possibilities in close male relationships. In H. Brod (Ed.), *The making of masculinities: The new men's studies* (pp. 213-240). Boston: Allyn & Unwin.

Stein, P. (1986). Men and their friendships. In R. Lewis & R. Salt (Eds.), *Men in families* (pp. 261-270). Beverly Hills, CA: Sage.

Swain, S. (1989). Covert intimacy: Closeness in men's friendships. In B. Risman & P. Schwartz (Eds.), *Gender in intimate relationships: A microstructural approach* (pp. 71-86). Belmont, CA: Wadsworth.

Willmott, P. (1969). *Adolescent boys of east London.* Baltimore: Penguin.

Zerubavel, E. (1979). Private time and public time: The temporal structure of social accessibility and professional commitments. *Social Forces, 58,* 38-58.

7

Self-Disclosure in Men's Friendships

Variations Associated with Intimate Relations

HELEN M. REID
GARY ALAN FINE

What does a man want—to talk about? How much will he reveal of himself? Does it make a difference if he is talking to a woman or a man? To a spouse, an intimate other, or a platonic friend? Does it matter if he is married, single with an intimate other, or single and unattached?

We explore these issues by studying platonic cross-gender friendships. Surprisingly, perhaps, there is little research on this topic, and this project, small and provisional though it is, sheds light on an important area of male friendships. In order to understand the dynamics of platonic friendships, we interviewed 32 white middle-class adults between the ages of 25 and 50 years, living in a large metropolitan area in the Midwest. Subjects were recruited through a random telephone survey and were interviewed during the spring of 1983. The interviews elicited data on topics discussed between male and female associates; additional data on self-disclosure were collected using a modified version of Jourard's (1971b) Self-Disclosure Questionnaire (SDQ). The focus of this chapter is on the responses by 16 heterosexual men about their friends, lovers, and spouses.

Self-Disclosure and Friendship

Self-disclosure has been defined by Derlega and Grzelak (1979, p. 152) as including "any information exchange that refers to the self, including personal states, dispositions, events in the past, and plans for the future." Interest in self-disclosure has burgeoned in the past two decades with the publication of volumes on this topic. Notable among these are Sidney Jourard's *The Transparent Self* (1971a) and *Self-Disclosure* (1971b), which generated interest by social psychologists, sociologists, psychologists, and psychiatrists (e.g., Chelune, 1979; Derlega & Berg, 1987). Jourard's (1971a) classic interpretation of the "lethal aspects of the male role" in which men suffer physically, psychically, and socially for their reticence was a launching pad for much research on disclosure throughout the seventies and eighties. Friendship as a topic of study has also produced considerable research, and the behavior of men in friendships is increasingly under scrutiny as researchers examine the implications of social support and interpersonal behavior for health and well-being.

Aspects other than an individual's physical or psychic health have captured the interest of sociologists and social psychologists. Among the major findings of interest to scholars in these areas are gender differences with respect to friendship and self-disclosure in same-gender and cross-gender dyads. Gender-role norms have been cited as mediating factors in self-disclosure (Hill & Stull, 1987). Other factors affecting friendship maintenance or disclosure within friendships are related to location within social structures. These factors include social class, occupation, mobility, stages in the life cycle, and marital status (Allan, 1989; Booth & Hess, 1974; Fischer & Oliker, 1983; Hacker, 1981; Pogrebin, 1987). Opportunities and normative constraints vary with structural factors, affecting the availability and depth of friendships.

After reviewing some of the literature on gender effects in self-disclosure, we will focus on the structure of interpersonal relations surrounding friendship dyads, in particular the effect of intimate relationships on the level of self-disclosure in friendships. Finally, interview data will be discussed in an effort to elucidate the variations observed among men in their disclosure with friends.

Disclosures Within Same-Sex and Cross-Sex Friendships

Women are generally credited with more expressive and intimate disclosures than are men and spend time talking with same-gender friends rather than doing activities with them, the preferred mode of interaction for males (Aukett, Ritchie, & Mill, 1988; Crawford, 1977; Rubin, 1985;

Sherrod, 1987; Wright, 1982). The tendency of women to trust a same-gender friend with sensitive personal information is frequently compared with the tendency men exhibit toward discussion of issues external to themselves, such as sports or politics (Aries & Johnson, 1983; Davidson & Duberman, 1982; Haas & Sherman, 1982). Men's reliance upon each other for companionship (Sherrod, 1987) is consistent with the conceptual framework of Wright (1982), who claims that male friendship, alleged to be superior to female friendship (Tiger, 1970), is not so much "better" as it is qualitatively different. Wright (p. 8) contrasts the characteristic "side by side" nature of male friendships with the "face-to-face" relationships found between women, highlighting socialization and gender role themes: Men exhibit instrumentality, activity-centeredness, and task orientation, whereas women emphasize personalism and interpersonal sensitivity oriented to the socioemotional aspects of the friendship.

Men reportedly disclose more intimate and personal information to their female associates than they disclose to other males (Aukett et al., 1988; Komarovsky, 1974), and derive therapeutic benefits from cross-gender friendships; for women, these benefits were found within same-gender friendships (Aukett et al., 1988). Hacker (1981) finds no gender effect in same-gender disclosures, but men confide more in their female friends than women confide in their male friends. When marital status is introduced, conflicting results emerge. While married men and women reported more confiding behavior with same-gender friends, Booth and Hess (1974) found single people, regardless of gender, more likely to disclose to members of the opposite gender.

A comprehensive review of gender effects in self-disclosure can be found in Hill and Stull (1987). Contradictions across studies are noted that highlight the lack of definitive results for the association between gender and self-disclosure.

We suggest two ways to improve consistency of results.[1] First, the level of intimacy within a cross-gender relationship should be controlled. It is necessary to distinguish disclosure within a sexually intimate cross-gender relationship from disclosure within a cross-gender friendship in which there is no sexual contact. We expect the level of disclosure within a cross-gender relationship to increase with sexual intimacy within that relationship. Second, the presence or absence of an intimate relationship external to the friendship dyad must also be controlled. Accessibility to a spouse or lover may serve disclosure needs; at the same time, normative pressures to limit disclosure outside the intimate relationship are expected to surface.

Relational Considerations for Self-Disclosure

The balance of this chapter highlights the two relational dimensions that are of primary importance in self-disclosure and talk between friends: relation of subject and target, and relations of the subject with significant others outside the friendship. Early studies by Jourard and Lasakow (1958) and Komarovsky (1974) analyze cross-gender disclosure patterns, but fail to adequately distinguish these dimensions.

Jourard and Lasakow found no overall differences between married and single subjects in disclosure to opposite gender associates. We find it problematic that the spouse and opposite-gender friend were not distinguished from one another but were "treated as equivalent target-persons" (Jourard & Lasakow, p. 96). Identifying a spouse with whom a subject is expected to share intimate feelings would seem to be critical.

Komarovsky's study was conducted with a male-only subject pool. Unfortunately, Komarovsky did not distinguish between the platonic female friend and the lover/girlfriend; they were lumped together as opposite-gender targets. She found that the female target receives higher levels of disclosures than the male friend, mother, father, sister, or brother —especially in sensitive aspects of self such as the personality and body dimensions of Jourard's SDQ. But this finding is based on a pooled average, rather than separate scores for lovers and platonic female friends.

We must distinguish between an intimate other and a platonic target to address the claim that men disclose at lower levels to other men than they do to women. If it can be shown that levels of self-disclosure to different targets vary by the intimacy of relations, we may infer that earlier failures to adequately identify these dimensions produced results erroneously ascribed to gender.

Aside from the relationship between the subject and the target of self-disclosure, intimate others in the relational domain of the subject must also be taken into account when reporting self-disclosure results. Jourard and Lasakow found that married subjects, while not differing in their overall disclosure to the opposite gender, differ from single subjects in that their disclosure becomes more concentrated toward the (opposite gender) spouse, to the relative exclusion of parents, siblings, and same-gender friends. This relational dimension is as important to distinguish as is the relation to the target. Whether a subject is married or intimately involved affects his or her level of disclosure to friends. Komarovsky (p. 679) hints at a possible correlation between the relational status of her male subjects and their disclosures to male and female friends: "In the sensitive area of Personality . . . for only 17 men was the closest friend a male. Of the latter 17 men, 12 were virgins." Komarovsky's subjects confide in other men when they are not in intimate sexual relationships with women. Rubin (1985) came to a similar conclusion regarding the few men she interviewed who reported intimacy (as opposed to her distinction with "bonding") in male friendships: Most of them were neither married nor living with a woman. We pursue this line of inquiry with our sample.

Self-Disclosure Questionnaire Results

The Self-Disclosure Questionnaire (SDQ) has been used by social scientists to explore, analyze or depict aspects of social interaction. We modified the scale[2] and compared mean disclosure scores within each of the following aspects of self: personal opinions and views, tastes and interests, work, money, personality, and body and health. The discussion that follows is based upon trends observed in preliminary data analyses. The limited size and lack of diversity of the sample, however, preclude reliance on the tabulation of statistical tests.[3] We acknowledge the small size of the sample and present these data as a provocative basis for further research.

Relational dimensions that served as independent variables were target of disclosure (cross-sex platonic friend, best friend of the same sex, and spouse or lover) and intimate relations of the subject. We distinguished between married men ($n = 8$), single men in intimate relationships ($n = 4$), and unattached single men ($n = 4$). We refer to this variable as relational status.

Target of Disclosure

In comparisons across targets, a male friend and a platonic female friend receive equivalent levels of disclosure, but a platonic female friend is the recipient of far less disclosure than a spouse or intimate other, in all six aspects of self. In comparisons between disclosure to a male friend and to a spouse or lover, a divergent trend for married men and single men begins to emerge. A wife receives more disclosure than a male friend, but the presence of a lover does not eclipse male-to-male disclosure to the same extent. Single men in intimate relationships appear not to differ in disclosures to their lover and their male friend in the areas of work, money, views, and tastes. However, in the sensitive areas of personality and body, the lover is the recipient of greater disclosure.

The level at which men reveal themselves to their associates seems to depend upon whether they are engaged in an intimate relationship, and to what degree they are committed to that relationship. The most significant trend is the attenuating effect that marriage has on disclosure to persons outside the marital relation, including other men. An emerging pattern of variation among men in differing categories of intimate relationship appears in disclosures to a male friend. Married men seem to disclose the least, while unattached single men disclose the most to their male friends in the areas of views, money, and personality. This trend is repeated in disclosure to the platonic female friend in the areas of views, personality, and body. Single men, regardless of relational status, appear to maintain some same-sex friendships in which they share relatively more of themselves than do married men. Unattached men exhibit the highest levels of disclosure to friends of both sexes, and appear to utilize other men as targets of disclosure to a greater extent than do men in intimate relations.

Variability among men in their disclosure patterns indicates that gender by itself cannot explain differential levels of disclosure. Knowledge of a man's intimate relations provides insight to disclosure patterns. To some extent, our findings address the fact that men may be predisposed to reveal themselves differentially, depending on the definition of the situation. Preliminary analysis of mean disclosure scores on the SDQ suggests answers about what the differences might be; we turn to the interview results to examine why they are so.

In the course of interviews, we asked about the nature of talk within platonic friendship dyads. Subjects were asked about frequency, method, and initiation of communications. Other questions elicited data on conversations, such as: What do you talk about with your platonic friend? Are there things you will talk about with this friend that you will not talk to anyone else about? Are there some things you would never discuss with this friend? These and follow-up questions also generated data about same-gender friendships; men volunteered descriptions of their same-gender conversations or contrasted conversations with male friends to conversations with platonic female friends. We analyze the data on same-gender friends, disclosures to platonic female friends, and men's reasons for the differences they report.

Talking With Men

A puzzling aspect of men's reported disclosure to other men is the degree to which it depends on intimate relations: It cannot be attributed solely to "maleness." Issues of privacy and boundary control are viewed by Derlega and Chaikin (1977, p. 110) as explanatory factors, but they also suggest that men's "absence of disclosure outputs may reflect a condition of isolation rather than an exercise of boundary control." An alternative explanation is that the "inexpressive male" is a result of the socialization process that prepares males to step into power roles for which they are headed as adults (Sattel, 1976). We found no explicit evidence for this explanation in our interviews, but neither can we exclude it. If one assumes that the acquisition of a spouse or a mate affords higher status to a man, then the greater levels of disclosure by unattached single men may be an indicator of relatively low status.

More relevant to our study is conceptual work regarding specific barriers to male intimacy (Lewis, 1978), which describes four barriers to intimacy among males: competition, homophobia, aversion to vulnerability and openness, and lack of role models. Lewis describes the first three barriers as traditional male role characteristics that result in lack of role models. Our interviews did not elicit discussion of role models, but we found evidence for the other three barriers; some were more evident among men in intimate relationships than among single men.

Competition

Several subjects cited competition as a reason for differences in the quality of their male and female friendships; all of these men were in intimate relationships. One married man explained:

> [A] lot of that information I would not disclose to my best male friend because I feel to some extent in competition with him and therefore would not be willing to tell my weaknesses to him, to tell him financial situations, as a rule . . . we're both similar in a number of ways. We're both engineers, we both have wives that are in the same profession. We both have houses that are similarly constructed. We both have a child approximately 2 years old. It's been somewhat of a basic competition, at least I feel it is, he probably doesn't . . . I've seen some traits in him that I would like to have and therefore I, I guess I probably tend to try to beat him at certain things to prove, possibly to myself, either that I have those traits or don't really need them to get by or to be successful.

A single man (with an intimate other) explained that competition affected what he does with his friends, as well as what he says to them:

> I think now when we get together, it's to play softball or touch football, it's still competitive to a certain extent. Or, who's making so much money and what they're doing now, things like that. And you don't run into that in a friendship with a woman . . . you can talk about things outside ordinary business-like topics and be accepted for it a bit more.

Acceptance for disclosures of a personal nature was a common theme for several subjects. The following excerpt is from a married man who mentioned competition when probed to explain what he meant by getting "a completely different viewpoint" from a woman than from a man:

> A man is generally concerned about his status, his performance as far as making money, how other men perceive him. And they're not so concerned with their feelings . . . they don't deal with them at all, pass over them, at least the men I know. I don't know about older men; younger men that I know are more concerned with just making money. Making money, I guess, is a bad term. But I guess that means being accepted by other men. They're more conscious as far as competition, as far as material possessions. They talk about different subjects. You can talk to some women and if they open up to you, you can get a different perspective because you're talking to them about their feelings, about how they feel. What hurts them, what bothers them. Where you can sit down and talk to a man and most times he won't tell you anything about himself. Not really, other than, where I work or what I'm gonna do with my life or how I'm going to achieve this, that and the other thing. But they don't really say, "I feel this, I feel that."

Men in intimate relationships seem more aware of competitive aspects of their male friendships, but the observations they make that their friends will not discuss personal issues are also noted by unattached men.

Vulnerability and Openness

The competitive characteristics of male friendship appear to be entwined with whether they will share feelings or personal aspects of their lives. Many men complain that their friends will not talk about personal or emotional subjects. They voice concerns about the reception their disclosures might meet and the level of reciprocity they can expect in disclosures with their male friends, rather than an outright aversion to openness. One single man reported an emotional "give and take" with his female friend that he found lacking in his male friendships. In fact, reciprocity and concern with acceptance were more common themes in our interviews than was competition. An unattached single man describes his experience:

> [M]en are much more guarded, much less willing to really share . . . you can tell them about feelings but they're not going to tell you about theirs—at least not at that point. They maybe will file it away and come back to it sometime later when they need info or something . . . Where the female perspective seems to be more open to discuss whatever they're feeling right now.

Formal measurement of disclosure reciprocity may require the conceptual refinements suggested by Hill and Stull (1982), who define measures to discriminate between equivalent exchange, covariant exchange, and turn-taking over time. Such measurements may be better suited for experimental design research of the kind carried out by Won-Doornink (1985) in her study of cross-sex disclosure by American and Korean students. Reciprocity patterns varied by acquaintance, friend, and best friend targets and by intimate and non-intimate topics.

Although we did not attempt any formal measurement of reciprocal disclosures, the problem of finding a male audience for feelings or personal experiences was expressed by both single and married men. One of our subjects said that his male friends were more able to be externally supportive, that he could get help from them for nonemotional things: "cars versus feelings." Men in our sample claim that they are willing to discuss intimate topics but are prevented from doing so by the behavior of their friends, as this married man explains:

> [My male friend] is somebody who if I were to talk to him about a career decision or a job decision or money, he would sit and listen. If I tried to talk to him about things that happened to me in the past, and there are very many things about me that he doesn't know. He doesn't know, you know, my father died when I was quite young. He has no comprehension of what it was like for me when I grew up; the things that I went through. Nor, I don't think, would he want to know about it, if I were to sit down and say, "Well, it was like this in my family." As a matter of fact, there have been times when I have actually started to talk about it and he just doesn't want to hear about it.

One single man solves the dilemma by discussing people with his intimate other and emotions with his platonic female friend. About his male friend he says:

[My male friend] rationalizes even emotions . . . And there's just some emotions that I have that I can't rationalize and there's just some things that I do that I can't rationalize. . . . we've been friends for a long time so he is not impatient with my thoughts, he just realizes that I'm different and so it is more of we sit around and talk about it in a quizative way. I'll say, "I feel like this," and he'll say, "That's interesting, because I don't feel like that at all, I feel like this." And then we start giving each other hypothetical situations and we tend to be very philosophical in our relationship. [We] have a very intellectual and philosophical relationship, but at times I get tired of that and so that's why before I said that if I want practical advice or emotional advice I will go to someone else.

Homophobia

Probably few heterosexual men have set out upon a journey to pursue other men for the sake of friendship. Stuart Miller's *Men and Friendship* (1983) chronicles his story of just such a journey. He came face-to-face with his male friends, and in the process of deepening his friendships, found himself questioning his own heterosexuality as a result of the intimacy generated by sharing with them increasing self-revelations. He concluded that what he experienced was a "tender energy." He writes:

My true problem, rather, is what to do with my tenderness toward him. How to remain honest in the expression of my love without having any desire to resort to sexual behavior or even imagery. For, indeed, what I feel toward him and want to express cannot be expressed sexually. (p. 140)

Our male subjects did not explicitly associate their levels of verbal self-disclosure with heterosexual orientations or homophobia, but they were aware that their touching behavior is limited by fears or discomfiting feelings. This indicates they have internalized pressures to avoid intimate physical contact with their male friends that may well extend to verbal intimacy. The following comments were elicited from a married man after discussing touching in platonic cross-sex relationships:

If I grabbed [male friend] on the ass, geez, he'd think I was gay, but I do it with [female friend] and yet I say it is not a sexual thing, it is just to show affection . . . I like [her] as much as I like my male friends, but it's funny how I would touch [her] and hug her where I would just shake hands with my other friends, my male friends, and I feel as close to them as I do to [her] and I don't know why there is a difference there.

After describing his reluctance to touch his female friend because he thinks, "maybe she'll take this wrong," a single man in an intimate relationship observes:

Yeah, but I would say that's the same way with guys . . . it's just, you know, I don't find it hard to touch my friends and stuff, it's just that too much intimacy, you think to yourself, "this isn't quite right" you know, "I wasn't," you know, "I wasn't supposed to do this." It's something that's learned, I think, it's not really how I feel, you know. I feel like touching them, and I feel like giving them hugs and things, there's just something that tells me "don't get too close to this person" for some reason.

One unattached single man describes his male friend and himself as an "odd couple." They have been friends since junior high school. By his description, this friendship is as rich and as solid as the friendship he describes with his female friend. He appears susceptible to homophobic pressures during the interview when he tries to explain why he and his friend have touched each other everywhere but their genital areas: They put suntan lotion on each other during vacations and trips to the beach. He has attempted to consummate a sexual relationship with his platonic female friend on many occasions, and the only difference he can cite between his male friend and his female friend is that he never "chases" his male friend. He concludes:

It's hard to say, her or [male friend] would be my best friend, it'd be hard to distinguish, you know. If they were both lined up and you make the decision, and one of them is going to go, you know, whether they're going to go off the plank, which one, it'd be awful tough to say, which one, you know if you, which one's gonna live, which one's gonna die or something.

Perhaps the most extreme evidence of alienation toward other men was provided by a married man:

I'm better friends with women than men, myself, but, and other men are not that way. Some men enjoy the camaraderie of other men, I don't particularly enjoy that. I don't like chitchat all that much . . . I like to get as much done as possible and I'm not gay so, you know, and I'm a sexual person so if I can have a relationship with someone that's both satisfying and sexual, why should I limit myself to one that's only satisfying? So, a friendship with a man can only go so far, it's not going to satisfy my sexual appetite. Whereas a friendship with a woman would do both, so . . .

This man was convinced that his platonic female friend remained a platonic friend in large part due to the fact that she has lived in another country throughout their friendship of 15 years.

The Reticence of the Married Male

Married men were the least disclosing of any of our relational categories in their friendships with men and women. Competition, concerns about vulnerability due to a fear that disclosures might not be reciprocated, and homophobia shed light on the differences found. Besides these traditional male role characteristics, there were two other commonalities among married men that contribute to the explanation of lower disclosure trends: a tendency to concentrate disclosures with their spouse and a tendency to assume that others already know about them.

Accessibility to an intimate relationship for sharing personal concerns obviates, to some extent, the need to seek a listening ear outside the marital relationship. Several of our married men indicated a preference for sharing with their wives over and above anyone else. As one man puts it:

> My wife is my best friend. I don't know if that says it all, she's above all to me. If you can go cry on her shoulder first before you . . . if she's not around you go cry on your best friend's shoulder or your platonic friend's shoulder.

Another married informant believes his wife should know more about him than his female or male friends. He simply states "that's the way it should be." The normative requirement of marital exclusivity regarding intimacy extends to the degree of disclosure married and single men in intimate relationships exhibit in their friendships.

After respondents completed the SDQ, we elicited comments about the questionnaire. Married men were more likely to expect others around them to already know things about them without explicit verbal disclosures:

> People know how I feel about things, many people and I don't necessarily, I don't sit down and say, "Now I feel this is what attracts me in a woman and I want this, that, and that." But that doesn't necessarily mean that my platonic friend doesn't know what I like . . . when you're around a person for a long time, you pick up through osmosis or whatever what a person likes and their religious beliefs to a certain extent.

Another married subject describes how his friend becomes known to him and, presumably, he becomes known to her. He talks about the revealing character of sharing events in each other's lives:

> I guess I see life as being a succession of them and each event will disclose something about a person's personality or character and therefore every event, every time anything happens, you learn more about the person.

We did not find this type of reliance on situation or "osmosis" among single men to reveal themselves to their friends.[4] The friends of single men know things about them because they tell their friends about themselves. There is an expectation that self-disclosures are cumulative; that their friends will not forget what they may have been told 5 or 6 years earlier. And to some extent, men express a degree of comfort in having someone in their lives who knows them well. One single man in an intimate relationship preferred bringing new problems to his female friend because she had once served in the role of his counselor at church and it was therefore unnecessary for him to "brief" her on past events that may be relevant to his current problems:

> [S]he's been a friend and she's been my counselor at church . . . she basically knows where I'm coming from, has a little bit better reality on me than my male relationships.

Platonic Friendships

In an earlier analysis of these data (Myers, 1984), the first author found that the definition of a platonic friendship depends upon successful strategies of maintenance and boundary negotiation. Friends negotiate the boundary between a platonic relationship versus a sexual relationship through discussion, decision making, and shared meanings: strategies that are internal to the friendship dyad. Structural constraints external to the relationship provide another strategic resource for maintaining the friendship as platonic. For example, the constant presence of a spouse or lover during interaction limits the depth of intimacy shared within the friendship dyad. The location of interaction within a work setting or other public place offers similar constraints to physical expression between friends.

The strategy relied upon most frequently by married persons, both male and female, to constrain behavior in a platonic dyad is to invoke the norms of marital exclusivity. Married people are less likely than single people to discuss the platonic nature of the friendship with their friends or to make a conscious decision to keep it that way. Single people in intimate relationships have "rules" regulating behavior that parallel the marriage code, that is, a "hands off policy" applies to those already engaged in intimate relationships.

The four basic challenges of cross-sex friendship discussed by O'Meara (1989) are: determining the type of emotional bond, confronting issues of sexuality, relationship equality in the context of gender inequality, and presenting the friendship as authentic to significant others in the social context. The talk and topics that fill interaction help to discriminate friendships from relationships with spouses or lovers. What kinds of communication do men report with their female friends; what is withheld and why?

Cross-Gender Disclosure

Relational status is a significant factor in disclosure to female friends in the areas of views, personality, and body. Boundary maintenance and appropriateness (Derlega & Chaikin, 1977; Derlega & Grzelak, 1979) may be relevant concepts in explaining lower levels of disclosure to women outside an intimate relationship by men with a spouse or intimate other, because controlling the information exchanged sets boundaries on the relationship. Two major boundaries are involved in self-disclosure: the *dyadic boundary* and the *self boundary*. The first regulates information retained within the dyad and is a precondition for self-disclosure; the second boundary is personal and is modified by self-disclosure (Derlega & Chaikin, 1977, p. 104). The appropriateness of a particular disclosure or general areas of self-disclosure is related to the nature of the relationship (Derlega & Grzelak, 1979).

A few informants discuss friendships with women in which dyadic boundaries around the friendship are honored. They enjoy trusting relationships with their friends in which self-disclosures are offered and respected, as the following quotes attest. The first is from a married man, the second from a single man in an intimate friendship.

> Not that you want to keep everything a secret but you know, if I go talk to her about anything personal, I know that's as far as its going to go.

That you can just kind of release yourself with and not worry about something coming back, mentioned to you. . . . we know it's not going to go any further, back to the husband, back to the lover.

Concerns with disclosure reciprocity did not emerge in friendships with women to the same extent as in friendships with men, even though many men in our sample indicated there are few differences in what they talk about with their male and female friends. Some men admit to "playing the listening role" and not sharing equivalent information that might make them appear "weak" to their friend. Yet most request information from their female friends to provide insight into their love relations, information they believe only a woman can provide. Gaining perspective, advice, and feedback from a woman who is not a mate was described as desirable and helpful in the areas of personal and work relationships.

While relationships in a general sense may be discussed, it was most common that men in intimate relationships (either married or single) withheld information from their female friend or avoided certain topics in order to preserve the dyadic boundary of their intimate relationship. The two main areas in which men indicate they will not disclose are sexual behavior and intimate issues between their mates and themselves. Avoidance of sensitive topics surrounding issues of sexuality was explained as appropriate behavior, given the level of intimacy ascribed to a friendship versus an intimate sexual relationship. Sex in an abstract sense may be the topic of discussion or jokes, but men with spouses or intimate others indicate they will not discuss certain sensitive topics with their female friends: "personal [sexual] preferences," their "sex life," "the intimate side of sex," "sexual gratification." Only one of the four unattached men indicated he would avoid these topics, and he had previously been married.

Behavior that might threaten the exclusivity of an intimate relationship includes verbal exchanges with a female friend. One married man was sure that his behavior toward his platonic friend must be clearly distinguishable from that toward his wife:

[I]f I tease her more than I tease my wife, it affects the relationship. My relationships with other women have to be lesser than with my wife.

It appears important that his wife observe his behavior, since she must perceive the distinction if he is to avoid unpleasant consequences:

[S]he'll go from the good attitude to the bad attitude. [What's the good attitude like?] Oh, smile, talkative, some laughter. [And a bad attitude is?] It's the opposite. She frowns, don't talk much, looks mean. (laugh) No, looks mad. (laugh) . . . We discuss our relationships and so sometimes there is a jealousy involved there.

Single men were less declarative in their statements regarding these norms, but they have, nevertheless, begun to internalize them:

I don't know if it's subconscious or not but I feel a little bit guilty sometimes if I become too close to [female friend], especially like I've said before, I've talked a lot about my work with her, a lot more and I think my girlfriend kind of senses this a lot.

They were the most verbal about the negative reactions and questions they received from their intimate other with regard to their "talking" relations with women friends:

My current lover doesn't particularly understand why I want to go out and see a woman. Not that she's lacking in understanding but it's just that she questions it; why I have to do that. . . . She says it's not jealousy or anything. I don't know . . . she has no platonic friends. I imagine just not knowing where my mind's at.

[My girlfriend]'s always been a little apprehensive about the friendship. I think she kind of feels like I talk to [female friend] about things on a man-to-woman basis that I should be talking to her about exclusively. For some reason [my girlfriend] doesn't feel comfortable about the fact that I talk to [female friend] in a very close way, about things that are very personal. . . . she has always been apprehensive.

Single men were more explicit about the threatening aspects of disclosure if they found their friend sexually attractive. They were much more conscious and deliberate about avoiding highly personal topics.

I think that's getting into some dangerous ground if you're going to complain about your intimate other to the person who would be next on your list. That's a dangerous area.

One single man was also conscious of jealousy on the part of his friend's spouse. Her husband had teased him about the friendship but he felt it "went deeper than that, he really did think something was going on. And he was losing touch with his wife, 'cause she was talking to me about problems instead of talking to her husband." During the times in their friendship when either one was experiencing a break-up or a separation in their intimate relationship, they would not see each other. When she was separated he felt he would "be in the way" while they were trying to "patch up their lives."

In order to meet the normative expectations of exclusivity in intimate relationships, attached males may disclose less to women. But single men may disclose more in order to enhance, encourage, or expedite intimacy.

Other Limits to Cross-Gender Talk

Avoiding discussions of "pick-up" behavior was cited by some men because it is a topic that would insult the sensibilities of their female friends or would otherwise cast themselves in an unattractive light. A bartender relates his own experience and that which he has observed in the course of his work:

> There's things that, there's just things that I wouldn't talk about or say to [female friend] and I probably know her better than some of my male friends, like if she and I were out to lunch and a nice-looking girl walked by or something, I wouldn't make a comment, whereas if I were with my male friends I might say something. I don't know why . . . maybe I just think it's dirty, and I wouldn't want to say it . . . you still see men that, when a woman goes away to go to the bathroom, or something like that, they make some comment among themselves, and even if it isn't about her, when she leaves they are going to talk about something they think she shouldn't hear, even women they work with and I'm sure they know real well. . . . they might mention something about another woman that was in the office or maybe something about another guy at work that they didn't want her to hear about, you know. More than likely it's something to do with, not so much sexual . . . something about another woman, and like that.

Some men are concerned about managing their friend's impression of them, and would therefore avoid discussing some of these matters:

> I wouldn't discuss picking up a girl in a bar 'cause I knew that she'd think I was just another one of them jerks walking down the road, another one of them jerks in the bar.

This reported behavior is contrary to the behavior observed by one of the authors in male-dominated work settings (Fine, 1987). Women in the minority of the work force in restaurants were expected to tolerate or participate in off-color humor and sexual innuendo. The dyadic friendship relation imposes a set of norms different from those when men are at work in groups that incorporate women.

Conclusion

Because of the variation in disclosure among men in different relationships, we suggest self-disclosure is, in part, a "role" phenomenon. However, claims of a "gender role" norm in operation should be carefully tested with rigorous distinctions for relational configurations that take into account the accessibility of others and normative constraints imposed by intimate relations. The characteristic of interest is whether the men have an intimate other whose expectations must be met and if they have access to an intimate other with whom they can share themselves to the relative exclusion of others.

Friendship is like a lightning rod, attracting attention and normative pressure to define the relationship. Where norms are not clearly codified or specified and participants in a friendship have no contractual or institutional obligations, each dyad must determine interpersonal boundaries. For men, the homophobia of our society requires carefully choreographed behaviors when with other men—togetherness is acceptable if in the context of sports, business, or family groups, but getting together just to be together or just to talk raises discomfiting feelings on the part of the man or questions from others. Competitive forces require him to avoid the appearance of vulnerability; inadequate strategies of self-presentation may produce the "inexpressive male." These characteristics of the traditional male role may be most relevant for men whose relationships conform to that tradition. Relational indicators of the "traditional male role" are lacking for men who are unattached, and may be less constraining for men in intimate relationships outside the institution of marriage.

A married male must manage the impressions that others have of him in order not to appear publicly interested in females other than his spouse. He must not give the cross-gender friend the impression that he might welcome intimacy leading to sexual expression of the relationship, nor can he appear to threaten her boundaries for intimacy. Managing his spouse's view may be more important than managing the impressions given to the target of disclosure. He must not appear to threaten the intimacy of the marital bond by disclosing to anyone outside of it, including his same-gender friends. This holds for single men in intimate relationships, as well. The unattached male, on the other hand, since he does not have a mate, is expected to get one, and greater disclosure to women holds promise for greater intimacy. But he does not have a spouse with whom to share the intimate aspects of self, and therefore will disclose more to his same-gender friends than will an attached male.

The definition of generic principles regarding friendship and disclosure is desirable for the purpose of revealing patterns across diverse population subgroups. Although this study involves only heterosexual individuals, both the maintenance of intimate relationships through norms of exclusivity and the accessibility of an intimate partner with whom to concentrate disclosures could be expected to affect disclosure within nonsexual friendships, regardless of sexual orientation. The relational structure of the social context and associated normative expectations need not depend on gender or sexual orientation. The application of refined relational categories in future research may hold promise for defining sociological principles governing self-disclosure that go beyond gender.

Notes

1. Hill and Stull (1987) suggest that the life cycle be taken into consideration by controlling for age. In related analyses, we found that disclosure to platonic female friends and to male friends is unaffected by the age of the man. However, in disclosures to a spouse or intimate other, older men reveal less in the aspects of work and body than younger men, and in matters of taste, disclosure by married men decreases with age, but increases with age among single men. Hacker (1981) found age effects for women, but not men and concluded that marital status, not age, was the relevant factor.

2. From Jourard's original 60-item questionnaire (Jourard, 1971b, pp. 189-191) we chose half of the items in each category as follows: Attitudes and Opinions (Views)—2, 5, 7, 8, 9; Tastes and Interests—1, 6, 7, 9, 10; Work (or studies)—2, 4, 5, 7, 10; Money—1, 3, 5, 7, 9; Personality—1, 3, 4, 9, 10; Body—1, 2, 4, 5, 6. Subjects were asked to rate items for each of three target persons. Each item was scored 0, 1, or 2 for depth of disclosure; a score of 2 represented the greatest amount of disclosure per item, and 0 the lowest. Responses were summed within each of the aspects of self to produce six disclosure scores for each of the target persons. The SDQ has received criticism on several fronts, including the assumption of unidimensionality for self-disclosure (see Hill & Stull, 1987, for a review).

3. Tables will be made available upon request from the first author.

4. Length of friendship also does not explain differences in disclosure. The mean years of the platonic friendship for single men in the sample is 9.63, for married men it is 6.50; for married and single men with intimate others it is 8.75 years, for unattached single men it is 7.83 years. F-tests from ANOVA were insignificant for all gender, marital, and relational status contrasts.

References

Allan, G. (1989). *Friendship: Developing a sociological perspective.* Boulder, CO: Westview.

Aries, E. J., & Johnson, F. L. (1983). Close friendship in adulthood: Conversational content between same-sex friends. *Sex Roles, 9,* 1183-1196.

Aukett, R., Ritchie, J., & Mill, K. (1988). Gender differences in friendship patterns. *Sex Roles, 19,* 57-66.

Booth, A., & Hess, E. (1974). Cross-sex friendship. *Journal of Marriage and the Family, 36,* 38-47.

Chelune, G. J. (Ed). (1979). *Self-disclosure: Origins, patterns, and implications of openness in interpersonal relationships.* San Francisco: Jossey-Bass.

Crawford, M. (1977). What is a friend? *New Society, 20* 116-117.

Davidson, L. R., & Duberman, L. (1982). Friendship: Communication and interactional patterns in same-sex dyads. *Sex Roles, 8*(8), 809-822.

Derlega, V. J., & Berg, J. H. (Eds). (1987). *Self-disclosure: Theory, research, and therapy.* New York: Plenum.

Derlega, V. J., & Chaikin, A. L. (1977). Privacy and self-disclosure in social relationships. *Journal of Social Issues, 33,* 102-115.

Derlega, V. J., & Grzelak, J. (1979). Appropriateness of self-disclosure. In G. Chelune (Ed.), *Self-Disclosure: Origins, patterns, and implications of openness in interpersonal relationships* (pp. 151-176). San Francisco: Jossey-Bass.

Fine, G. A. (1987). One of the boys: Women in male-dominated settings. In M. S. Kimmel (Ed.), *Changing men: New directions in research on men and masculinity* (pp. 131-147). Newbury Park, CA: Sage.

Fischer, C. S., & Oliker, S. J. (1983). A research note on friendship, gender, and the life cycle. *Social Forces, 62,* 124-133.

Haas, A., & Sherman, M. A. (1982). Reported topics of conversation among same-sex adults. *Communication Quarterly, 30,* 332-342.

Hacker, H. M. (1981). Blabbermouths and clams: Sex differences in self-disclosure in same-sex and cross-sex friendship dyads. *Psychology of Women Quarterly, 5,* 385-401.

Hill, C. T., & Stull, D. E. (1982). Disclosure reciprocity: Conceptual and measurement issues. *Social Psychology Quarterly, 45,* 238-244.

Hill, C. T., & Stull, D. E. (1987). Gender and self-disclosure: Strategies for exploring the issues. In V. J. Derlega & J. H. Berg (Eds.), *Self-disclosure: Theory, research, and therapy* (pp. 81-100). New York: Plenum.

Jourard, S. M. (1971a). *The transparent self.* New York: Van Nostrand.

Jourard, S. M. (1971b). *Self-disclosure: An experimental analysis of the transparent self.* New York: Wiley-Interscience.

Jourard, S. M., & Lasakow, P. (1958). Some factors in self-disclosure. *Journal of Abnormal and Social Psychology, 59,* 91-98.

Komarovsky, M. (1974). Patterns of self-disclosure of male undergraduates. *Journal of Marriage and the Family, 36,* 677-686.

Lewis, R. A. (1978). Emotional intimacy among men. *Journal of Social Issues, 34,* 108-121.

Miller, S. (1983). *Men and friendship.* Boston: Houghton Mifflin.

Myers, H. (1984). Just friends: Definition and maintenance of platonic cross-sex friendships. Unpublished manuscript, University of Minnesota.

O'Meara, J. D. (1989). Cross-sex friendship: Four basic challenges of an ignored relationship. *Sex Roles, 21,* 525-543.

Pogrebin, L. C. (1987). *Among Friends*. New York: McGraw-Hill Book Company.

Rubin, L. (1985). *Just friends: The role of friendship in our lives*. New York: Harper & Row.

Sattel, J. W. (1976). The inexpressive male: Tragedy or sexual politics? *Social Problems, 23*, 469-477.

Sherrod, D. (1987). The bonds of men: Problems and possibilities in close male relationships. In H. Brod (Ed.), *The making of masculinities: The new men's studies* (pp. 213-239). Boston: Allen & Unwin.

Tiger, L. (1970). *Men in groups*. New York: Vintage.

Won-Doornink, M. J. (1985). Self-disclosure and reciprocity in conversation: A cross-national study. *Social Psychology Quarterly, 48*, 97-107.

Wright, P. H. (1982). Men's friendships, women's friendships and the alleged inferiority of the latter. *Sex Roles, 8*, 1-20.

8

Men's Friendships with Women

Intimacy, Sexual Boundaries, and the Informant Role

SCOTT O. SWAIN

Cross-sex friendship is a relatively unexamined research topic and it has received minimal attention in both anthropological (Bell, 1981) and socio-logical inquiries (Allan, 1989). The limited sociological research on cross-sex friendship reflects the lack of societal expectations of, and value attributed to, such friendships (O'Meara, 1989). Cross-sex friendship is a recent social phenomenon in Western culture that has emerged as an aspect of the twentieth-century trend from homosociality to heterosociality (Gagnon & Simon, 1973). In the nineteenth century friendships were almost exclusively limited to same-sex friendships as men's and women's spheres were more rigidly defined and segregated (Smith-Rosenberg, 1985). The present study investigates men's styles of interaction and intimacy in these friendships and documents the reasons that men value their friend-ships with women.

The Nature and Conditions of Cross-Sex Friendship

Cross-sex friendship is a social anomaly that is overshadowed by cul-tural emphases on same-sex friendships, and heterosexual love and sexual relationships. Despite recent changes in sex-role behavior, the cultural

AUTHOR'S NOTE: Portions of the analysis and the writing of this paper were supported by NIMH training grant MH 17058, Center for Research on Women, Wellesley College.

importance of homosocial behavior remains evident in such gender-segregated organizations as the Boy Scouts (Hantover, 1978), sports programs (Coleman, 1976; Stein & Hoffman, 1978), and combat aspects of the military (Arkin & Dobrofsky, 1978). Although women have gained access to certain activities, such as competitive sports and non-combat positions in the military, this access is still often sex-segregated.

Since cross-sex friendship is not a clearly defined or expected social relationship, it is often interpreted in terms of heterosexual coupling or sexual relationships. For example, many heterosexual love relationships begin as platonic friendships, thus promoting a view of cross-sex friendship as a stage of development in the coupling process, rather than as a legitimate relationship in and of itself. When an adolescent develops a friendship with a cross-sex friend, family members and same-sex friends often tease, hint at, or praise the person for establishing a possible heterosexual dating, sexual, or love relationship. Claims that "we're just good friends" are often viewed as withholding information, or as an indication of embarrassment or bashfulness about the sexual content of the relationship.

The cross-sex relationship contains elements of same-sex friendships (a voluntary association that does not explicitly connote a sexual relationship) and heterosexual coupling relationships (an association that involves the "otherness" of men and women, and does not exclude the possibility of a future love or marital relationship). This ambiguity can threaten both heterosexual relationships and same-sex friendships. Same-sex friends are threatened by the feeling of competition with the "otherness" that a male-female relationship offers, the possibility of an emerging heterosexual love relationship, and the resulting realignment of time spent with same-sex friends. For similar reasons, cross-sex friendship may also threaten the socially valued heterosexual love relationship. Since there are few expectations of enduring cross-sex friendships throughout a person's life, couples may sacrifice them in order to eliminate such a threat (Brenton, 1966).

Previous research has explored the structural characteristics of cross-sex friendships and the conditions that determine access to such friendships (Bell, 1981; Booth & Hess, 1974; Powers & Bultena, 1976; Weiss & Lowenthal, 1975). Close cross-sex friendship occurs less frequently than close same-sex friendship (Babchuk & Bates, 1963) and has a shorter longevity. Also, cross-sex friends tend to be less homogeneous in their interests and attitudes than same-sex friends (Booth & Hess, 1974). Marriage often inhibits cross-sex friendship (Bell, 1981), and life stage is reported to influence both the number and quality of cross-sex friendships. Specifically, as men grow older they experience a decline in friendships, while women experience an increase in friendships (Powers & Bultena, 1976; Weiss & Lowenthal, 1975).

Cross-sex friendship is also likely to be characterized by a power differential between friends in terms of the older age, higher education, and greater job status that typifies many males in such relationships (Booth & Hess, 1974). Employed women are more likely to have a greater number of cross-sex friends than homemakers, and highly educated women are more likely to attribute a greater value to cross-sex friendship than do less educated women (Bell, 1981).

O'Meara (1989) has reviewed research on cross-sex friendship and has distinguished four issues that challenge research on cross-sex friendship. *First*, what is the process of defining sexuality in a relationship that is assumed by definition to be platonic? Also, how does sexuality impact such relationships even when they are platonic? *Second*, what are the types of emotional bonds established between cross-sex friends, and how do these bonds compare to those of same-sex friends? *Third*, how does the cultural environment of pervasive gender inequality affect the formation of cross-sex friendships? And *fourth*, how are these "subversive" friendships portrayed to relevant audiences, and how do these portrayals affect the cross-sex friendship itself?

Generally, intimate cross-sex friendship appears to be more difficult to establish and sustain than intimate same-sex friendship for both women and men. Several factors contribute to this difficulty. Despite the movement from homosocial to heterosocial interaction, men's and women's spheres are still distinctive and are shaped by a different set of social experiences, which involve learning different rules that govern interaction in friendships. From these experiences evolve sex-specific styles of expressing care and intimacy. Men's style tends to depend on shared activities and is more limited in verbal expressiveness. These differences in masculine styles clearly make establishing a cross-sex friendship a more challenging and difficult task.

The Relationship Between Gender and Intimacy

During the past 30 years there has been a large body of sociological and psychological literature that addresses the interpersonal styles of women and men. Although research has substantiated more similarities than differences between men and women (Maccoby & Jacklin, 1974;

Tavris & Wade, 1984; Tresemer, 1975), the prevailing view is characterized by a deficit approach to men's intimate capabilities and by variations of Komarovsky's theme of men's "trained incapacity to share"
(Balswick, 1976, 1988; Booth, 1972; David & Brannon, 1976; Jourard,
1964; Komarovsky, 1964; Pleck, 1981). Despite a majority of studies
that reveal nonsignificant differences in male and female disclosure
(Cozby, 1973; Maccoby & Jacklin, 1974), the dominant view assumes
greater self-disclosure among women and that self-disclosure is the prime
determinant of intimacy.

Cancian (1987) claims that research on intimacy and love is biased
by reliance on feminine styles of intimacy for the measurement and
interpretation of closeness and intimacy for both men and women. Further
studies suggest than men and women have different ways of assessing
intimacy (Caldwell & Peplau, 1982), with women utilizing self-disclosure
and men utilizing joint activities. Men are reported to express intimacy
covertly through reciprocal assistance, initiating contact, doing things
together, joking behavior, and nonverbal cues (Swain, 1988). Despite these
recent findings, however, men's styles of expressing intimacy and closeness in friendship are still largely defined as an inhibited capacity to show
care verbally (Balswick, 1988; Rubin, 1983).

Despite the great overlap in men's and women's interpersonal styles,
differences have been demonstrated that are particularly salient to the
study of cross-sex friendship. Men tend to prefer shared activities and doing something together, while women prefer talking and sharing disclosures about emotional matters (Caldwell & Peplau, 1982; Cancian, 1984;
Swain, 1988). Furthermore, specific contexts and types of interpersonal
behavior appear to connote different meanings to women and men. For
example, married men express intimacy primarily through sexual relations and doing tasks around the home, while women express affection
through verbal compliments and self-disclosing about feelings (Cancian,
1984).

For the purposes of this chapter, it is recognized that there is a varied
array of avenues and pathways that can lead to intimacy within a friendship. Self-disclosure is one possible format for intimacy. However, a
high level of self-disclosure does not guarantee intimacy. A mutuality
of give-and-take must exist for self-disclosure to be an effective way to
express intimacy. Intimacy is defined as interaction between friends that
connotes a mutual sense of closeness and interdependence. Shared activities and mutual problem solving can also be an avenue to shared intimacy
and are more typical of masculine-typed styles.

In cross-sex friendship the convergence of men's and women's worlds provides a setting to study the behaviors that characterize feminine- and masculine-typed intimate styles of care. This study compared men's friendships with other men to their friendships with women. This chapter focuses primarily on two of O'Meara's challenges: first, the need to define and maintain sexual boundaries in friendship relations, and second, the way that closeness and intimacy are expressed between men and women friends who come to the relationship with contrasting codes of conduct.

Method

This study is based on in-depth interviews with 15 men and 6 women that included questions concerning cross-sex and same-sex friendships. Using the same open-ended protocol, the men were interviewed by a male interviewer and the women were interviewed by a female interviewer. The sample was drawn from public university undergraduates and was young and white with a mean age of 22.5. The university population is particularly suited for this study since it provides a structure that is conducive to the formation of cross-sex friendship. The interview protocol drew from two questionnaire surveys ($N = 232$ and $N = 140$) that demonstrated differences in the relative importance and meanings that men and women attributed to both verbal and active behaviors with their same-sex friends (Swain, 1984).

Interviews lasted an average of 90 minutes and were transcribed and organized by question and content area for analysis. This focused sample may not generalize across age groups or represent this particular subgroup since the college sample was in a structural setting that promoted the opportunity to establish cross-sex friendships while the men and women pursued similar goals.

The Separate Worlds of Men and Women: Structural Barriers to Cross-Sex Friendship

Men and women grow up in overlapping yet distinctively different worlds. Styles of relating are shaped by the often sex-specific contexts and situations that young boys and girls and adolescents experience while growing up. Jim commented on this early division in his friendships:

Up to the sixth or seventh grade, . . . [you have to] stay away from the girls. So during that whole time you only associate with the guys, and you have all these guy friends. And after that, the first time you go out, you're kind of shy with the girls, and you don't get to know them too well. I didn't get over being shy with girls until my senior year [in high school].

Jim's first relationships with girls consisted of dating activities that are suggestive of heterosexual courtship and sexual coupling. This early segregation fosters the development of friendships with people of the same sex. Several men related the quality of their interaction with men friends and women friends to the differences in past interaction. As Gary noted:

It's something that's beat into you; society beats it into you. So it's more of a natural thing for me to talk with men. I don't have to constantly work at it. Maybe I've had more practice at it.

Communicating with men is familiar enough to Gary that it has become "a natural thing." He has had more "practice" interpreting the meanings of sex-specific language and gestures that are rooted in segregated male experiences. Using a similar style eases communication so that Gary doesn't "have to constantly work at it" like he does when with women friends. His description is similar to a person who contrasts the difficulty when speaking in a foreign language, while traveling in another country, with how easy it feels to communicate in one's native tongue on returning home. Jill commented on the differences in what she shares with her women friends and her men friends:

You probably don't share most of the everyday confidential things with guys that you do with the girls. Maybe it's because I live with three girls, and day-to-day things that are really strange can come up and you can talk about them and have a great time. I'm not as confidential with those guy friends.

When asked about their friends in general, men and women both mentioned more same-sex friends than cross-sex friends during the course of the interview. Despite the collegiate social context that promotes cross-sex contact, same-sex friendship continues to be the primary type of friendship for these women and men in their early twenties. Clearly these cross-sex friendships are subversive in terms of the lack of cultural expectations and support for them.

Self-Disclosing and Self-Censoring

The early segregation and separate contexts in which boys and girls develop their first friendships appear to influence the styles of intimacy that men and women prefer and feel most comfortable with. Contrary to previous reports of men's friendships (Komarovsky, 1976; Rubin, 1983), a majority of both men and women in this study valued confiding in a same-sex friend concerning personal problems and sexual matters. Laura responded to the question "Does the feeling of friendship feel the same for your men and for your women friends?"

> No, I think that might be different. I think I feel a closer bonding and intimacy with women, whereas with the men I feel a bond, but, I think it's just not as intimate. It could be more of a distance . . . but there are certain fears you don't tell the men friends as much: career decisions.

And Richard responded:

> I haven't had as many good girlfriends as guy friends, but I think for the most part it's harder for me to get to know a girl on the personal level.

It may, for Richard, be "harder to get to know a girl" because there are limited structural opportunities where young men and women can meet casually in a context that is not necessarily geared toward heterosexual coupling. Also, communication with two different styles of intimate expression requires monitoring and censoring behaviors that may not make sense or, worse, may be offensive. This requires the translation of behaviors that may carry different meanings. For example, in men's friendships the comment "not bad" can be a supportive complement to the friend's performance. However, in women's friendships this same phrase may appear as an aggressive understatement. Mike describes how he changes his behavior and feels different while around his women friends, as compared to his men friends:

> Around girls you act more of a gentleman. You don't cuss. You watch what you say because you don't want to say anything that'll offend them or anything . . . I'm more relaxed around guys. You don't have to watch what you say, I wouldn't [have to] be careful I shouldn't say something like this, or I shouldn't do this. That's because with the guys, they're just like you.

Mike goes on to say that his women friends refer to him as a "gentle-man." As a "gentleman," Mike censors his aggressive, rough, and re-laxed form of behaving in favor of a polite, more subdued style that is patterned after and more sensitive to women's styles of interaction. A man who is labeled a "gentleman" is rewarded for his knowledge of feminine styles of behavior. The "gentle" man smooths over the rough edges of masculine behavior when in the company of women. Similarly, a woman who is labeled "just like one of the guys" is rewarded for a knowledge and sensitivity to masculine styles of friendship behavior. Cen-soring part of oneself when in the company of a cross-sex friend reduces the possibility of misunderstandings and conflict, yet also affirms the boundaries of separation between women and men. Greg alluded to a "barrier" that distinguished his cross-sex and same-sex friends:

> There's still a barrier when I talk to girls, you know. I'm Mary's best friend, and there are certain things she doesn't talk to me about that she talks to her girlfriends about. I know that, I've been in the car [with Mary and her girlfriends] and I've heard her talking.

Through his close friendship with Mary, Greg describes a glimpse of women's style of interaction as an outsider in an all-women's group. When Jill was asked if she felt the same way toward her platonic men friends as she did toward her women friends, she responded:

> Oh, no—I think I probably hold my women friends closer than I do my men friends.

A majority of men said that they were more comfortable disclosing personal problems to close men friends. Jerry responded:

> I'm more at ease talking about my personal problems with men, with guys. It takes a lot to know a girl, to tell her, "You know, my dad and I are getting along terrible."

The separate worlds of men and women both encourage and discour-age different parts of individuals to emerge. Interacting with same-sex friends using similar styles of intimacy can be a supportive and comfort-able experience. However, the very predictability that is gained from communicating with someone who is "just like you" also inflicts a cost: Set patterns and expectations may limit a person when one must live up to whatever implicit rules accompany a style of intimacy by restraining behaviors that may threaten the common style of showing care.

Limitations of the Masculine Style

When asked to explain how his close friendships with men and women differed, Matt describes the unique part of his male friendships, then he hints at some of its restrictions:

> With men it's like a different part of you. One part for me comes out of the stuff I do with my men friends, like sports. You do things together, have a good time, drink beer, and just do whatever. And with the girls you just talk about whatever. There's some things that you could just talk to the girls about.

These restrictions in male friendships become more prominent in Matt's response to the question, "What do you tend to do with a male friend who has been helpful and you want him to know that you appreciate it?"

> Probably just come out and tell him. With my guy friends I just say "Hey, this might sound stupid, but I really appreciate you helping me out. I can't do it and I need your help."

He was questioned further: "Okay, when you said 'this might sound stupid', why would you say that?"

> It's just that whole masculine thing. Friends don't talk to you like that. I guess it's just something that's been that way, they probably wouldn't care if I said that or not. You have to bring up [some things] in a different way because of the people. You [just say] here it comes, [I] don't want to make this sound too dramatic, but—thanks for your help, I had a problem. It's like you almost have to clarify it before you say it.

"Okay, that's an interesting point, think of it this way, how wouldn't you want him to take it?"

> I wouldn't want him to take it like "You're such a loser. Thank you for helping me out of another jam. I'm just so weak a person that I need help for everything. Please stay there." Make it sound overdrawn. I just say "Hey, I need some help. Can you help me? Thanks a lot." I don't want it to sound overly dramatic.

The phrase "this might sound stupid" was used to "bring it up in a different way" to warn his friend of a statement that communicated vulnerability and dependence. Men's closeness is more restricted than women's in that weaknesses and fears that may be construed as dependency may be more difficult to express to other men. The discomfort experienced with dependency is summed up by Jack:

> I don't think anybody wants to be that person who's dragging [others down] and no one really wants a person to be dragging on them. You don't need to have too much of a burden. I mean you don't mind, but you'd rather not have it.

If people are worried about being "that person who's dragging" and presenting a friend with a burden, they will most likely restrict the range of problems they share and the emotions they express. Men tend to be more limited than women to certain formats in which they communicate closeness and affection to their men friends. Men's intimacy with men friends may be tempered by the balancing and bartering of dependency to reach an equilibrium whereby neither feels that he is *inordinately* dependent. Men are able to let down this guard when in the company of women friends who may not be suspicious or awkward when faced with dependency in a friend.

Feminine Style Limitations

Women's same-sex friendships also had some limitations. Gail discusses some of the drawbacks of her women friends:

> I have some female friends that I feel are a real drain on me. They take advantage of me being patient and listening to their problems, and it bothers me a great deal. So I don't consider them as close friends, and I'm trying, now that I'm in the History program, to draw away and only retain those friends that there's some kind of mutual give-and-take.

The dependency of certain friends becomes a "drain" or "burden" and limits the "give-and-take" and how close the friends can get. Gail was asked: "If there was one thing you could do to improve your friendships with women, what would it be?"

> I don't know how to say this without sounding really bitchy, [but] it would be for my friends who have a lot of problems, and I don't know if that's because I am some kind of compulsive person that attracts neurotic people or

what. But I wish they would try to solve their own problems or take action. It seems like everybody wants to talk about it, but they don't want to do anything about it and it makes me angry.

Gail framed her statement about how her friendships could be improved by saying, "I don't know how to say this without sounding really bitchy." Her discomfort and hesitation stem from her questioning one of the tenets of feminine-typed styles of intimacy, that is, that women should be unconditionally supportive and open to the self-disclosure of a friend. Gail's framing testifies to the difficulty women may have in limiting self-disclosure when it is one-sided and becomes a repetitive pattern rather than growth through self-revelation and a friend's feedback.

Women's friendships are open to the point where an unbalanced dependency can inhibit the "mutual give-and-take" of intimacy. Men are implicitly obligated not to ask "too much" of their friends; women are implicitly obligated to listen to all that a friend may ask for. Close cross-sex friendships promote the clarifying and balancing of these masculine and feminine styles of intimacy.

Thus, despite the familiarity and intimacy offered by same-sex friendships, they are restricted in certain aspects. Several men and women stated that they were more comfortable talking with cross-sex friends. In essence, men's friendships with women provide access to, and the interplay of, two varying formats of conveying and receiving affection and intimacy. Each person in the friendship must contend with these different formats since romance and sexuality are not the prime motives for interaction.

Frank describes the part of himself he can share with a woman friend but not with men friends. He was asked: "Can you think of any differences in what you would talk about or what you would do with men and women friends in terms of expressing feelings or, as you said earlier, inner secrets that you normally wouldn't share with friends?"

In this specific instance with her I feel I can relate just about anything. There are some things I would hold back from her, but of course I would hold them back from my men friends too, and my wife, and my psychologist, from anybody. With her, especially, I feel like I could tell her anything because she's so bright and I love talking to her. She knows how to respond to me. My other men friends, I don't think they would accept it as well as she would. Because I might be talking about some emotions I have, and emotions is not a word that men have. I would be more apt to talk about some of my more feminine

qualities, whatever you can call them. Some of my more feminine qualities
that everybody has, your emotionality and stuff like that.

Frank was less guarded with women than with men when speaking
about his emotions. Frank segregates himself much as the separate worlds
of men and women do, by referring to his emotions as "my more feminine
qualities." Friendships with women provided Frank with the opportunity to explore his "emotionality" and express his "feminine side" more
freely, without worrying and anticipating discomfort and fear of losing
a friend's respect.

Women commented on certain aspects of their friendships with men
that were meaningful. Gail responds to the question: "Can you think of
any meaningful occasions that you have spent with men friends?"

I like arguing with my men friends because I love smart men. I mean they
really turn me on, I love it, and I probably had the biggest fight with a man.
It was the biggest man/woman fight for two people who aren't married, but
it was just like a marriage. It was about what he was going to do with his
son . . . I care a lot about this person's kid, and we got close enough, intellec-
tually, that we were honest. It finally got down to that decision that he really
wanted the kid out of his life. . . . And it was just the two of us because everybody else had known that we were going to get into a heated discussion.
It was neat.

The assertive confrontation was challenging to Gail, and she enjoyed
the intensity of the honest, yet heated discussion. Women may find it
easier to express more competitive and confrontive behaviors with
close men friends than with women friends.

Confusion Over Sexual Boundaries

An added difficulty for these successful cross-sex friendships to
overcome is coping with ambiguous sexual boundaries. Since cross-sex
friendship is a relatively recent social phenomenon, there are fewer
guides and models for working out these conflicts. An important difference between cross-sex friendships and same-sex friendships was the
maintenance of sexual boundaries. Women and men questioned the reality
of the "platonic" friendship. Men's and women's platonic friends could
develop into a romance, and cross-sex friendship could emerge from
past love relationships. Often the issue of sexuality remained an ambiguous and undefined element of the friendship that, although sensed, was

not verbalized. A sexual relationship can be a threatening issue between friends, especially when either of the friends becomes involved in a coupling relationship. Richard answered the question: "What do you see as the main differences in what you do or feel around your men friends, as compared to your women friends?":

> Well, I work harder with women at not, I don't know how to say this. Its funny because I've had women friends that turned into girlfriends, and then went back to friendships. I work harder at something, I work harder at convincing myself and convincing her. I work harder with women convincing themselves that this is purely platonic. And so what I think I do is that I tend to talk about their relationships more intensely. It's kind of hard to put my finger on it. I work harder at convincing myself that this is truly platonic. Because there have been situations where there's a girl I wanted to be dating, not platonically, that the only way I could see her would be platonically. And I guess I was trying to convince myself that I didn't want this person physically, but I did.

The sexual dynamic has to be constantly defined and "worked at" because of the flux and ambiguity of a platonic cross-sex friendship. Men and women "work harder" perceiving and defining sexual boundaries because dominant cultural images associate sexual interest or contact when women and men get together. Sexual interest and a platonic interest in a friend are not easily separated. Several men mentioned flirting as an activity they do with platonic women friends. John describes the development of his friendship with Kate:

> There's my friend Kate. She's great, she's got a boyfriend, and she kind of helped me deal with problems of my girlfriend being away. We talked about just about anything. It started out with her essentially trying to seduce me, and then we both laughed about that and nothing ever worked out. And we both decided that it was best that she not do that. So we became the best of friends. She showed me her poetry and had me critique it.

Joan commented on the sexual confusion in platonic cross-sex friendship:

> In the back of my mind I think maybe that it is true that there is no such thing as the platonic relationship. That one or the other of the friends is going to have some sexual feelings. Because some of my friends, I know that I'm very much sexually attracted to them. But you never cross that barrier. I know that in some cases that I have men friends that are sexually attracted to me, but we just don't ever talk about that.

The awareness and maintenance of that "barrier" takes time and effort. Gender differences in sexual agendas add tension to the delicate balance of a voluntary friendship relation. Jack's response chronicles the difficulty in not crossing "that barrier," yet establishing an open friendship that bridges the gap between men's and women's worlds: "What's different about your close men friends and your close women friends?"

> The biggest difference is that when you get really close to your guy friends, you can tell them stuff. Like what you do on dates or when you're talking about the girls and stuff like that. And [men friends] just accept it at face value. You tell them all different types of stuff. Where if you're with your girlfriends, you can't really tell them, they'll go "Oh, what's this supposed to be?"

> Well, with Margaret I can. I can tell her the stuff that I did and she'll be like my good part of me, the angel part. And great . . . the devil part. But we'll start talking and we talk about dating so that I can see the women's view and she can see the men's view. But that's just a special case, that's the only girl that I can probably talk to like that. Also it's going to be more than platonic with the girls, and with guys it won't happen. That's the big thing where I've been friends with a girl a couple of years, and all of a sudden I go "I like her," more than just a friend. Then you kind of go "wait a minute." This happened with Margaret where I was on the indecision line. I mean I was so undecided. I mean it was so weird, I don't know, I can't really describe it.

Communication was established between the two friends in a "special case." The nature of the dialogue was based on informing each other of their respective worlds and perspectives. Jack mentions his woman friend (Margaret) as speaking for the "angel part of me," while the other "devil part" appears to be affiliated with masculine-typed sexual motives. The gap between men's and women's sexual motives and values is couched in this angel/devil metaphor that indicates severe separation of their respective agendas. The merging of feelings of friendship and sexual attraction causes anxiety and appears to be difficult for Jack to resolve. He later revealed that he never approached Margaret sexually and, because they were friends, never spoke about the sexual attraction until a year had passed, along with their passionate feelings. Jack's description of being "on the indecision line" and "so undecided" when he realized that he "liked her more than just a friend" chronicles the confusion experienced when using arbitrary culturally defined categories of friendship and love relationships to interpret the diverse and changing feelings he felt toward Margaret.

Cross-sex friendships are both enriched and plagued by fluctuating and unclear sexual boundaries. Such friendships offer a unique relationship by providing a situation that fosters the sharing and exploration of the similarities and differences of masculinity and femininity without the pressure that accompanies the role of a lover. However, the ambiguity between a platonic friendship and a sexual relationship can cause misunderstanding and may limit the relationship when either of the two cross-sex friends either becomes romantically attracted to the other or becomes involved in a separate heterosexual coupling relationship. Despite these difficulties, cross-sex friendships occasionally survive. What do men and women gain from these friendships that causes them to wade through these structural, sexual, and communication barriers?

The Informant Role and Androgyny

The ambiguity that characterizes platonic friendships pressures cross-sex friends to be sensitive to both men's and women's styles of intimacy in their efforts to communicate without the traditional expectations of a coupling relationship. This is similar to a traveler in a foreign country whose awareness must be heightened by the different nuances that accompany a different culture's style of communication. Several men and women referred to a "man's view" or a "man's perspective," as opposed to a "woman's view", or a "woman's perspective." The sexes are referred to as having different worldviews, similar to the differing agendas of opposing political parties. Cross-sex friends often have the role of a tutor or informant who translates the women's or men's perspective for their cross-sex friend.

Cross-sex friendship may enhance a person's capabilities for reacting to situations using both men's and women's styles of behavior, or what could be loosely referred to as androgynous behavior. Mike describes the differences in his relationship with an intimate woman friend [Ellen] in contrast to his other women friends:

> They [other women] weren't really honest, exactly. They had stuff that they'd keep to themselves. But they felt it and you could sense they felt it. There was something wrong but they wouldn't say it. But Ellen on the other hand, she would just flat out say it. She wasn't like the common girl . . . if she had something on her mind, she'd say it.

Mike describes the relationship he has with Ellen as "we're not lying to each other" and "we both know each other is telling the truth." His description of lying and truth-telling may be a way of describing the censoring of behavior between less intimate cross-sex friends when there exists a gap in understanding each other's style of intimacy. In such relationships, there is a reliance on stereotyped flirting behaviors more typical of coupling behavior. Mike gives more detail to these differences when questioned how his friendships with men and women differ:

> If Ellen wasn't so open or outgoing, then I could say that around girls you act more of a gentleman. You don't cuss; you watch what you say because you don't want to say anything that'll offend them. But Ellen is like me, a female version [of me], I can say anything.

The comfort and identification that Mike has with Ellen is described in terms of her outgoing and aggressive style that is integral to male styles of behavior. She is outgoing, aggressive, and speaks her mind. Mike suggests that she is aware of his world and his style of behavior by stating that Ellen is "just like a guy." He sums up this unique friendship: "We have a lot in common. If I was a female, I'd be her."

Ellen is described as "like me" because she reacts in the same ways Mike does, has a similar worldview, and has behaviors that are more commonly found in men than in women, such as "flipping someone off." The androgynous behavior of Ellen is defined in terms of the categories of male and female: "Ellen could be practically classified as a guy." "If I was a girl, I'd be Ellen." Mike uses traditional gender roles to classify the ambiguous and androgynous behavior of Ellen. The "sameness" associated with sharing the same styles of behavior and similar ways of interpreting behavior is defined in terms of the concrete category of sex. Mike's difficulty in describing Ellen's behavior in terms other than sex-role categories testifies to the recency of cross-sex friendship, and the difficulty in grasping a clear and tangible conception of androgyny.

Conclusion

In view of the social support that promotes same-sex friendship and heterosexual coupling, cross-sex friendship can be considered a subversive activity that can act as a catalyst for social change when it does not lead to a coupling relationship. Cross-sex friends had difficulty in both defining their feelings of sexual attraction and in dealing with the flux and ambiguity of sexual boundaries. These confusing boundaries appeared to be exacerbated by the lack of societal expectations of men's friendships with women and by the resulting attempts by outside audiences to interpret them in terms of heterosexual coupling relationships.

Men and women both had more close same-sex friends than cross-sex friends, which is to be expected when considering their structural opportunities and certain advantages that accompany a relationship where both friends use the same style of expressing affection. What is significant is that the men and women of this study have established close cross-sex friendships with little social support. Men's close friendships with women testify to the ability for both men and women to explore and learn new styles of communication. A person who has experience and understanding of a varied array of avenues to express affection and closeness may be able to respond to a friend in a style that is appropriate to a precise context specific. Future research should address the variation within men's friendships, women's friendships, and cross-sex friendships, and to specify the context-specific ways that people express closeness.

Men's close friendships with women testify to the flux and change in gender-based behavior. These rare close cross-sex friends had an unusual knowledge of both masculine and feminine styles of intimacy. These relationships tended to ameliorate masculine-typed restrictions on the variety of alternatives for expressing affection and intimacy. Often the relationship was based on problem solving and disclosing about heterosexual love relationships. The cross-sex friends took on the role of an informant by sharing and sensitizing each other to the meanings of the other sex's style of intimacy.

Intimate cross-sex friendship provides the setting for men to expand the limits of rigid conceptions of masculinity and explore areas of emotionality and the fear of dependency. The informant role that so often characterizes these friendships can foster a more intimate communication that breaks through the censoring and monitoring of behavior that men and women often engage in, and can also have a significant impact on men's heterosexual coupling relationship. Each cross-sex friend has a tutor to translate and explain gender-based styles of intimacy and closeness. Such friendships are an important arena for increased understanding between men and women and offer men the opportunity to explore and build a larger repertoire of expressive styles that may be differentially advantageous, depending on the given circumstances and context of intimacy. The maturation of cross-sex friendship as a socially accepted and expected relationship is integral to the continued development of more loosely defined and multifaceted roles for men.

References

Allan, G. F. (1989). *Friendship: Developing a sociological perspective.* Boulder, CO: Westview.

Arkin, W., & Dobrofsky, L. (1978). Military socialization and masculinity. *Journal of Social Issues, 34*, 151-168.

Babchuk, N., & Bates, A. (1963). The primary relations of middle class couples: A study in male dominance. *American Sociological Review, 28*, 377-384.

Balswick, J. (1976). The inexpressive male: A tragedy of American society. In D. David & R. Brannon (Eds.), *The forty-nine percent majority: The male sex role.* Reading, MA: Addison-Wesley.

Balswick, J. (1988). *The inexpressive male.* Lexington, MA: Lexington Books.

Bell, R. R. (1981). *Worlds of friendship.* Beverly Hills, CA: Sage.

Booth, A. (1972). Sex and social participation. *American Sociological Review, 37*, 183-192.

Booth, A., & Hess, E. (1974). Cross-sex friendship. *Journal of Marriage and the Family, 36*, 38-46.

Brenton, M. (1966). *Friendship.* New York: Stein & Day.

Caldwell, M. A., & Peplau, L. A. (1982). Sex differences in same-sex friendship. *Sex Roles, 7*, 721-732.

Cancian, F. M. (1984). Gender Politics. In A. Rossi (Ed.), *Gender and the life course* (pp. 253-264). Hawthorne, NY: Aldine.

Cancian, F. M. (1987). *Love in America.* New York: Cambridge University Press.

Coleman, J. (1976). Athletics in high school. In D. David & R. Brannon (Eds.), *The forty-nine percent majority: The male sex role.* Reading, MA: Addison-Wesley.

Cozby, R. (1973). Self-disclosure: A literature review. *Psychological Bulletin, 79*, 73-91.

David, D., & Brannon, R. (Eds.). (1976). *The forty-nine percent majority: The male sex role.* Reading, MA: Addison-Wesley.

Gagnon, J., & Simon, W. (1973). *Sexual conduct.* Chicago: Aldine.

Hantover, J. (1978). The Boy Scouts and the validation of masculinity. *Journal of Social Issues, 34*, 184-195.

Jourard, S. (1964). *The transparent self.* Princeton, NJ: Van Nostrand.

Komarovsky, M. (1964). *Blue collar marriage.* New York: Vintage.

Komarovsky, M. (1976). *Dilemmas of masculinity: A study of college youth.* New York: Norton.

Maccoby, E., & Jacklin, C. (1974). *The psychology of sex differences.* Palo Alto, CA: Stanford University Press.

Pleck, J. (1981). *The myth of masculinity.* Cambridge: MIT Press.

Powers, E., & Bultena, G. (1976). Sex differences in intimate friendships of old age. *Journal of Marriage and the Family, 11*, 739-747.

O'Meara, D. (1989). Cross-sex friendship: Four basic challenges of an ignored relationship. *Sex Roles, 21*, 525-543.

Rubin, L. (1983). *Intimate strangers.* San Francisco: Harper & Row.

Smith-Rosenberg, C. (1985). *Disorderly conduct: Visions of gender in Victorian America.* New York: Knopf.

Stein, P., & Hoffman, S. (1978). Sports and male role strain. *Journal of Social Issues, 34,* 136-150.

Swain, S. O. (1984). *Male intimacy in same-sex friendships: The influence of gender-validating activities.* Presented at the annual meetings of the American Sociological Association, San Antonio.

Swain, S. O. (1988). Covert Intimacy: Closeness in the same-sex friendships of men. In B. Risman & P. Schwartz (Eds.), *Gender in intimate relations: A microstructural approach.* Belmont, CA: Wadsworth.

Tresemer, D. (1975). Assumptions made about gender roles. In M. Millman & R. Kantor (Eds.), *Another voice* (pp. 308-339). New York: Anchor.

Weiss, L., & Lowenthal, M. (1975). Life course perspectives on friendship. In M. Lowenthal et al., (Eds.), *Four stages of life* (pp. 48-61). San Francisco: Jossey-Bass.

Tavris, C., & Wade, C. (1984). *The longest war.* New York: Harcourt Brace Jovanovich.

9

Sex, Friendship, and Gender Roles Among Gay Men

PETER M. NARDI

The connection between sexual orientation and gender roles has been confused by many people. Too often, assumptions about homosexuality or heterosexuality have led to assumptions about masculinity or femininity. Altman (1982, p. 55) states it succinctly:

> [T]he belief that homosexuality is somehow a reflection of a blurred sense of masculinity/femininity remains central to the Western imagination, and to the extent that our concepts of gender have implied a heterosexual norm, this is important in understanding the development of homosexual identity.

Understanding the differences between sexual identity and gender roles is enhanced when focusing on the issues of friendship and sex among gay men. For many people, being gay has been interpreted in terms of not being masculine or, more specifically, being seen as feminine. In fact, this attribution is arguably at the core of why homosexuality in men is feared by many and why many men fear expressions of intimacy and emotional closeness (Segal, 1990). Not only does a culture ascribe certain traits to men and women and then label those traits in terms of masculine or feminine social roles, but those roles are also attributed to sexual desire, especially among homosexuals (Altman, 1982).

AUTHOR'S NOTE: Many of the ideas discussed in this paper came from conversations, collaboration, and friendship with Drury Sherrod, who helped design the questionnaire and collect the original data used in this article.

What results, then, is a belief that gay men can act in some areas in traditionally masculine ways (primarily in the sexual arena) and in other areas in traditionally feminine ways (such as emotional relationships, temperament, or sometimes body language). Over the past several decades, this belief has evolved as American society experienced the transformation of much of gay subculture from feminine to masculine to androgynous images.

Throughout the 1970s, as the contemporary gay movement developed, a new style of homosexual manliness was constructed (Humphreys, 1971). Partly in compensatory reaction to the stigma of femininity and passivity imposed on gay men, a macho and hypermasculine look evolved (Levine, 1988). But it was also partly an expression of traditional male gender roles that existed all along for most gay men who had been socialized into masculinity and lived in gender conformity as children. In fact, one could interpret the changes dialectically: Pre-Stonewall imagery of gay men was primarily feminine; post-Stonewall and pre-AIDS semiotics of gay men were primarily masculine; and the AIDS years have synthesized these images into an androgynous look, on one hand eschewing the iconography of masculine gay clones (no facial hair, less macho clothing), and on the other hand adopting a combination of both masculine and feminine images (earrings, ponytails, for some, and masculine but stylish clothes).

The distinctions between such concepts as *masculinity* and *gay* are highlighted when discussing the role of friendship in gay men's lives. While evidence exists that many gay men relate to their friends in gender non-conforming ways that are not typical of the ways heterosexual men interact with their friends (Sherrod & Nardi, 1988), other data about the role of sex in their friendships support how much traditional male roles persist. In some ways, gay men's friendships are a good example of a combination of traditionally defined masculine and feminine gender roles that appear to characterize some of contemporary gay male subcultures. And by focusing attention on the role of sex in friendship, many of these issues are highlighted.

Sex and Friendship

Perhaps the least studied area in the friendship literature is the role sex and sexual attraction play in the development of friendship, and when it is discussed, it is primarily about heterosexual opposite-sex friendships. Seiden and Bart (1975, p. 220) speculate that "There is probably an erotic component in most close friendships. . . . but this appears to be disturbing to many people and is denied or repressed." Rubin (1985, p. 179) similarly argues:

> More than others, best friends are drawn together in much the same way as lovers—by something ineffable, something to which, most people say, it is almost impossible to give words. . . . [P]eople often talk as if something happened to them in the same way they "happened" to fall in love and marry.

Although Rubin (p. 180) also says that in friendship "the explicitly sexual is muted, if not fully out of consciousness," she does acknowledge the "appeal of the physical" in the process of friendship initiation and development. She feels that "most friends come together out of some combination of attraction to the other and their internal psychological needs and desires."

The sexual component in friendships typically emerges when discussing cross-sex friendships among heterosexuals. O'Meara (1989, p. 530) concludes:

> [C]ross-sex friendship is an ambiguous relationship in American culture in the sense that it has a deviant status reflected in a lack of instructive role models and appropriate terminology to capture its unique qualities, lacks coherent cultural scripts for guiding everyday interaction, and is influenced by gender-based schematic processing. . . . [C]ross-sex friends must continuously negotiate the private rules that guide their everyday behavior in a context that treats their existence as deviant and even threatening.

However, the more the social environment provides a context for initiating and maintaining cross-gender friendships while minimizing the relevance of the sexual dimension, the more likely such friendships can occur (Allan, 1989). So, when work situations are no longer dependent on a gender division of labor, when the age and marital status of the people involved are young and single, and when the potential friends are not constrained by traditional gender-role proscriptions, then the possibilities for a nonsexual cross-gender friendship increase.

When a sexual friendship does occur, "the basis of the solidarity of the friendship is altered and usually it is difficult to revert to the previous state once the sexual relationship ends" (Allan, p. 83). O'Meara (p. 534) similarly reports that for many men sex in friendship with women often destroys the friendship and, thus, passion and sexual attraction must be "continually monitored, contended with, and regulated through negotiation."

An interesting test case of the role of sex, gender roles, and sexual attraction in friendship is available when studying the friendships among gay men. O'Meara (p. 529) boldly states (without data to support it) that "this factor of sexual attraction appears nonexistent in friendships among gays." But given the sociological argument that "different 'boundaries' are constructed around friendships" in part due to personal choice and the sociocultural context (Allan, p. 15), the friendships of gay men might have a very different sexual component to them than cross-gender heterosexual friendships.

Sonenschein (1968), in an early ethnography of a gay male community, develops a typology of relationships based on duration and level of sexuality. Essentially, he argues that first order friendships (best and really close friends) and second order friendships (good friends but not permanent) were entirely nonsexual. Extended encounters (sexual affairs) were often unstable and not characterized by strongly committed social support, while brief encounters were typically nonpermanent sexual relationships. Permanent partners (lovers) are sociosexual relationships akin to heterosexual marriages in terms of commitment and stability. For the most part, Sonenschein concludes, gay men tend to separate those individuals who serve their social needs from those who serve their sexual needs.

A similar argument was made in an interview with a gay man in his twenties:

> I will not and have never had sex with any friend. I've either dated the person or became friends with them. Once I went out with this guy for 2 months and there was no physical relationship yet. We had agreed to take it slowly. But one day I realized I didn't want to sleep with him, so we talked about it. He's now my closest friend in the city.

On the other hand, sex and friendship may be more connected for other gay men. White (1983, p. 16) discusses the role of sex and friendship in his essay about gay men in the 1980s by comparing it to Japanese court life of the tenth century:

> Friendship . . . intertwines with sexual adventure and almost always outlasts it; a casual encounter can lead to a lifelong, romantic but sexless friend-

ship. . . . [S]ex, love and friendship may overlap but are by no means wholly congruent. In this society, moreover, it is friendship that provides the emotional and social continuity, whereas sexuality is not more and no less than an occasion for gallantry.

In some cases, gay men are acquaintances first and then become sexual partners; in general, though, people seem to be clearly distinguished as sexual partners or social partners, but rarely both simultaneously. Sonenschein (p. 72) speculates as to whether the category of "friends" is "really a residual category of individuals who did not work out as sexual partners or whether there are differential expectations through which individuals are initially screened to become either 'friends' or 'partners.' " The evidence from his observations and from our own data indicates that both processes operate: Many gay men have had sex with their best friends, but many have been sexually attracted without sex taking place.

One 34-year-old male we interviewed said:

> The best close friends I had were from when I was sexually active. . . . I would date for a few weeks and when they got too "amorous," I was very good at stopping the sex and turning it into a friendship. . . . It upsets me to realize that I cannot make new friends unless I work with them or have sex with them.

Given the dearth of studies on gay friendship, rather than develop research to test specific hypotheses, we designed an exploratory study to assess the relationship between sex and friendship among gay men. What follows, then, is both a speculative essay on the possibilities of sex and friendship among gay men and also a presentation of data from a survey of 161 gay men that explores these issues.

What guides this exploratory research is an attempt to understand the role masculinity plays in contributing to the relationship between sex and friendship among men. While a study of white, middle-class gay men does not directly answer such questions about heterosexual men or men in various ethnic and racial subcultures, it does introduce some insights and research questions about the interaction of gender, sexual orientation, and the structure of friendships.

Speculations and Possibilities

While there is evidence that some gay men recollect playing gender non-conforming roles and games as children (see Harry, 1982), there is no reason to conclude that all gay men were socialized without the traditional and normative values and roles of what the culture defines as masculine. Those traditional norms typically include the expectation that men be sexually assertive in relationships and initiate sexual activity. Furthermore, evidence from research on teenage sexuality often indicates that boys are sexual before intimacy is achieved with a partner (in fact, they try to gain intimacy through the sexual act), while girls more often seek intimacy prior to a sexual act.

Whether such patterns hold among homosexual boys and girls is rarely studied. But if one assumes a typical male socialization pattern, then we might conclude that gay men—being true to their gender roles— are likely to have sexual experiences with friends, perhaps as a way of achieving friendship. On the other hand, if we assume that gay men as boys were different in the enactment of traditional gender roles, then friendship might precede sexuality as a pattern in their lives.

Another avenue of research might concern the topic of attraction and friendship, independent of sexual behavior. If indeed attraction plays a part in the formation of all friendships, attraction (and the willingness to admit it) may emerge as an even more salient factor in gay men's friendships, since the potentiality for sexual interaction is much more likely.

In addition, the notion of falling in love with a friend can also be explored more directly with a gay male sample. Unlike any reluctance to discuss this subject among heterosexual cross-sex and same-sex friendships, gay friendships can address this topic clearly. In short, by using a sample of gay men, the issues of sexual attraction, being in love, and sexual behavior among friends can be investigated. In so doing, we can get a sharper understanding of the contextual nature of friendship and gender roles and the variations that exist among different subgroups of men.

Methodology

Subjects

One hundred and sixty-one gay men and 122 lesbians responded to a questionnaire survey, representing a response rate of 48% of the 620 subjects who were contacted through gay and lesbian organizations in the greater Los Angeles metropolitan area. For the purposes of this article, only the data from the gay men are discussed, except where information about gay men's friendships is clarified by comparison with the lesbians. (For further details about this study and additional data from the questionnaires, see Sherrod & Nardi, 1988.)

Because of the topic of this research, snowball sampling techniques —typically used in studies of stigmatized and hard-to-locate subjects where random sampling is impossible—was not used to obtain respondents. The built-in bias of sampling friends of friends with snowball methods might have produced a distorted picture of friendship patterns. Therefore, respondents were obtained by contacting gay and lesbian organizations, including political, social, religious, and professional organizations. Admittedly, the sample we obtained through this "social outcropping" technique may also be a biased sample of the population, but given the choices, we decided that the biases associated with the social outcropping technique would be less than those associated with the snowball method. As a result, the current study focuses on friendship among a sample of white, educated, middle- and upper-middle-class, urban gay men and lesbians who are open and attending gay-identified organizations. Consequently, the results may not be generalizable to nonurban, nonwhite, working-class, closeted gay men and lesbians who are not affiliated with gay-identified political and social organizations.

Questionnaire

A 19-page questionnaire was developed and pilot-tested on a small sample of gay men and lesbians. A revised form took approximately 30 minutes to complete. Questionnaires were preaddressed and stamped for easy return. The questionnaire asked respondents to provide information about three types of friendship: *casual friends*, *close friends*, and a *best friend*. These three categories of friendship were selected because previous research had demonstrated that people typically employ such categories when describing their friends (Caldwell & Peplau, 1982; Wright, 1982). The questionnaire included the following definitions of each type of friendship: A *casual friend* is "someone who is more than an acquaintance, but not a close friend; your commitment to the friendship would probably not extend beyond the circumstances that bring you together; for example, a work friend or neighbor." A *close friend* is "someone to whom you feel a sense of mutual commitment and continuing closeness; a person with whom you talk fairly openly and feel comfortable spending time." A *best friend* is "the friend to whom you feel the greatest commitment and closeness; the one who accepts you 'as you are,' with whom you talk the most openly and feel the most comfortable spending time." A question was also asked to determine whether the best friend was a current lover or partner of the respondents; if so, respondents were instructed to select another best friend for this section of the questionnaire, someone other than the lover/partner, if one existed. If someone had more than one best friend, respondents were instructed to select only one when answering this section of the questionnaire.

Respondents were asked to report whether they (a) had ever been sexually attracted to their best friend, (b) were sexually involved with their best friend, and (c) were ever in love with their best friend both "in the past" and "currently." We also asked them if they had sex with their casual friends and with their close friends (using a 5-point scale from "None" to "Most.")

In addition, respondents were asked to indicate (using a 5-point Likert scale where 1 = lowest and 5 = highest): (a) how much they have *actually* discussed their own sexual behavior with their casual, close, and best friends, and (b) how *important* it is to talk about sexual issues or concerns with their casual, close, and best friends.

Results

When we asked respondents to rate how important it was to have friends who they can talk with about sex, the percentage who answered "very important" or "extremely important" (4 and 5 on the scale) increased as they referred to casual, close, and best friends. As Table 9.1 (A) illustrates, 18.6% of the gay men said they felt it was either very important or extremely important to talk to their casual friends about sex; 56% said so about their close friends; and 76.2% said that about their best friend. Conversely, the percentage of those who feel it is not at all important (1 on the scale), decreased across the three categories of friendship from 32% to 4% to 2%. In brief, gay men expect to be able to talk about sex with their friends, especially their best friend and close friends.

Likewise (see Table 9.1, B), we find that 71.2% of the gay men have discussed with their best friend all or almost all details about sex; 53.4% have with their close friends; and fewer than 18% have with their casual friends. Fewer than 1% responded that they never discussed anything about sex with their best friend, around 10% said that about their close friends, and 36% of the gay men did not discuss sex at all with their casual friends. In short, one of the characteristics about best and close friends is that they are the people gay men talk to about sex.

Table 9.1 Discussing Sex with Friends (*N* = 161)

A. How important is it for you to talk about sex with your friends?

	Casual	Close	Best
Not at all important	31.7%	3.8%	2.2%
Very important	14.3%	38.4%	39.6%
Extremely important	4.3%	17.6%	36.6%
Mean (scale of 1 to 5)	2.29	3.57	4.05

B. How much have you discussed sex with your friends?

	Casual	Close	Best
Not discussed at all	36.1%	9.4%	0.8%
Discussed almost all	10.8%	35.2%	28.0%
Discussed all	7.0%	18.2%	43.2%
Mean (scale of 1 to 5)	2.28	3.37	3.97

C. With how many of your casual and close same-sex friends have you had sex?

	Casual	Close
None	37.5%	24.2%
One or two	28.8%	42.2%
Some	26.9%	24.2%
Many	5.6%	5.6%
Most	1.3%	3.7%

When respondents were asked to indicate with how many of their casual and close same-sex friends they actually had sex over the years, 37.5% said with none of their casual friends, and 24.2% said with none of their close friends (see Table 9.1, C). In comparison to lesbians, gay men were much more likely to have had sex with their casual friends (66.4% of the lesbians said they did not have sex with any of their casual friends) and to have had sex with their close friends (41.3% of the lesbians said with none of their close friends).

Despite some popular literature that suggests that gay men have many straight female friends, about 82% of our sample said their best friend was a gay or bisexual male, and fewer than 10% said their best friend was a straight female. This lends support to Altman's (1982, p. 60) observation that the gay male proclamation that "all my friends are women" is more likely today to be " '*None* of my friends are not gay': the new identity/community/culture is producing a separatism that tends to isolate gay men from straight men, from women, and from children."

With this in mind, the following responses for the questions about best friend are tabulated only for those whose best friend was a gay or bisexual male. Recall, also, that subjects in relationships were asked to select a person other than their lover.

As Table 9.2 shows, almost 80% of the gay men said they were attracted to their best friend in the past, and 52% continue to be attracted to him. Around 60% said they had sex with their best friend in the past, and 20% continue to do so. About 57% were in love with their best friend in the past, and 48% still are. Thus, in this particular sample, attraction clearly plays an important role in selection of a friend, and sex was once a part of that early friendship, as were feelings of love. Over time attraction and love have diminished for many, but almost half still maintain those emotions. However, few remain sexually involved any longer with their best friend. Approximately 20% of the gay men also said their current best friend is an ex-lover (in contrast to 45% of the lesbians).

Discussion

Since this was an exploratory project, it is difficult to answer specific questions about the reasons why these findings exist. What does emerge, however, illustrates that sexual attraction and sexual involvement are salient components in the early stages of friendship for most gay men in this sample. This should not be too surprising since many gay men meet their potential friends in situations where sexual attraction is a relevant factor for initiating interactions. Furthermore, sexual involvement is often the next step for men in getting to know someone, in contrast to a model, especially for women, where sex follows a period of getting to know a person. As the men get to know each other, decisions are made to continue in a romantic manner or to "let's just be friends"—a statement that signifies the end of a sexual relationship and the start of a nonsexual friendship relationship.

While attraction and feelings of love may still persist, sexual involvement ceases, suggesting the emergence of an "incest taboo" among the "family" of friends (see Nardi, 1992; Weston, 1991). If the men continue to see each other, a friendship may develop, evolving from a casual one to a close one and, perhaps, into a best friendship. This would explain the higher percentage of men (in comparison to women who, in general, tend not to initiate interactions sexually) who said they had sex with casual friends. One might argue (given the percentage of lesbians whose best friends are ex-lovers and the fewer number who had sex with casual friends) that gay men are more likely to have had sex first and then

Table 9.2 Sexual Behavior and Attraction with Same-Sex Best Friend
(N = 118) (percentage answering Yes)

	In the past	Currently
A. Sexually attracted to best friend	79.4%	51.5%
B. Sexually involved with best friend	58.8%	20.4%
C. In love with best friend	57.4%	47.6%
D. Best friend is an ex-lover	18.8%	

develop a social intimacy with their friends. As they become more intimate and disclosing, sexual involvement decreases. So that when the
sex ends, the friendship can continue if some degree of closeness and
sharing has been established. But if the relationship was based primarily
on sex, when that ends, the friendship does also. The fact that lesbians are
significantly more likely to continue to maintain friendship with an
ex-lover might suggest that their relationships were established first on
a basis of intimacy and sharing, rather than on one of sex.

Again, since the data don't address these questions directly, they are
provided as hypotheses for future research. What needs to be explored
further, then, is whether sexual orientation or traditional gender roles
prevail in explaining how gay men connect sex and friendship. As men,
they see sex as the way to intimacy. But as gay people, they develop a
strong emotional intimacy with other men, unlike what research shows
about how heterosexual men relate to other men (Sherrod & Nardi, 1988).

So while gay men are often seen as challengers to the hegemonic masculinity of white, heterosexual men (Segal, 1990), perhaps when it comes
to sexual behavior they are conforming to traditional masculine gender
roles. While same-sex friendships among gay men are not directly comparable to other-sex friendships among straight men, they do illustrate the
potential for both breaking down traditional gender roles and maintaining them. They show how men perpetuate the traditional masculine image
of sex as the means to intimacy while, at the same time, they subvert
the norm of masculinity by showing that men can be intimate with one
another at an emotional, sharing level.

This contradiction may not be all that unusual. An examination of extra-
ordinary social conditions and crises often allows men a wider range of
behaviors than regularly expressed. Segal (1990, p. 103), for example,
argues that, in the "constant pressure to confirm masculinity in its difference from femininity," when men are at their most powerfully masculine

selves, such as in combat, "they can embrace, weep, display what Western manhood depicts as more feminine feelings and behaviour."

With gay men, the social conditions of marginalization, oppression, and exclusion have contributed to this duality of traditional masculine roles and expressive, caring intimacy with friends. Or, in other words, sexual orientation and gender roles do not necessarily predict one another with consistency.

Thus, it is in the area of friendship and sex that one can seek some answers to how gender and sexual orientation are constructed in our culture and, in particular, how concepts of masculinity are shaped by concepts of homosexuality and heterosexuality. Owens (1987, p. 230) quotes Foucault, who said in an interview: "The disappearance of friendship as a social institution, and the declaration of homosexuality as a social/political/medical problem, are the same process." This is so, Segal (p. 139) agrees, because masculinity has been defined by its opposition to femininity and homosexuality: "The possible imputation of homosexual interest to any bonds between men ensured that men had constantly to be aware of and assert their difference from both women and homosexuals." And it is with the emergence of concepts of homosexuality in terms of a social identity and not just a sexual act that Rotundo (1989, p. 21) concludes that "Romantic male friendship is an artifact of the nineteenth century."

Thus, by understanding how gay men today organize their friendships and the role it plays in their lives, the tenuous connections between gender and sexual orientation grow even weaker and the various ways masculinity is constructed in a culture get uncovered. For it is in the area of sex and friendship among gay men that the issues of traditional masculine roles and traditional feminine roles are clarified for all people in contemporary American society.

References

Allan, G. (1989). *Friendship: Developing a sociological perspective*. Boulder, CO: Westview.

Altman, D. (1982). *The homosexualization of America*. Boston: Beacon.

Caldwell, M., & Peplau, L. (1982). Sex differences in same-sex friendships. *Sex Roles, 8*(7), 721-732.

Harry, J. (1982). *Gay children grown up: Gender culture and gender deviance*. New York: Praeger.

Humphreys, L. (1971, March/April). New styles in homosexual manliness. *Transaction*, 38-46, 64-65.

Levine, M. (1988). *Gay macho: Ethnography of the homosexual clone*. Doctoral dissertation, New York University.

Nardi, P. M. (1992). That's what friends are for: Friends as family in the gay and lesbian community. In K. Plummer (Ed.), *Modern homosexualities: Fragments of lesbian and gay experience*. London: Routledge.

O'Meara, J. D. (1989). Cross-sex friendship: Four basic challenges of an ignored relationship. *Sex Roles, 21*(7/8), 525-543.

Owens, C. (1987). Outlaws: Gay men in feminism. In A. Jardine & P. Smith (Eds.), *Men in feminism* (pp. 219-232). New York: Methuen.

Rotundo, A. (1989). Romantic friendships: Male intimacy and middle-class youth in the northern United States, 1800-1900. *Journal of Social History, 23*(1), 1-25.

Rubin, L. (1985). *Just friends: The role of friendship in our lives*. New York: Harper & Row.

Segal, L. (1990). *Slow motion: Changing masculinities, changing men*. New Brunswick, NJ: Rutgers University Press.

Seiden, A., & Bart, P. (1975). Woman to woman: Is sisterhood powerful? In N. Glazer-Malbin (Ed.), *Old family/new family* (pp. 189-228). New York: Van Nostrand.

Sherrod, D., & Nardi, P. M. (1988). *The nature and function of friendship in the lives of gay men and lesbians*. Paper presented at American Sociological Association, Atlanta.

Sonenschein, D. (1968). The ethnography of male homosexual relationships. *Journal of Sex Research, 4*(2), 69-83.

Weston, K. (1991). *Families we choose: Gays, lesbians, and kinship*. New York: Columbia University Press.

White, E. (1983, June). Paradise found: Gay men have discovered that there is friendship after sex. *Mother Jones*, pp. 10-16.

Wright, P. (1982). Men's friendships, women's friendships and the alleged inferiority of the latter. *Sex Roles, 8*(1), 1-20.

10

The Relationship Between Male-Male Friendship and Male-Female Marriage

American Indian and Asian Comparisons

WALTER L. WILLIAMS

Very often popular critics complain about problems of alienation result-ing from men's inability to develop intimate friendships. Humans, like other social animals, need and want intimacy, yet many men feel an in-ability to express that part of their being freely. This lack of close friend-ships is decried by many (see, for example, Brod, 1987; Franklin, 1984; Kilgore, 1984; Kimmel & Messner, 1989; Miller, 1983; Pleck & Pleck, 1980). Yet suggestions for change are inevitably greeted with a chorus of disbelievers who dismiss such relationships among men as being uto-pian, unrealistic, or even "unnatural." Given our observation of the way most American men act, we tend to think that this is the only way men *can* behave and still be "men." We might acknowledge, and even admire, the intense friendships that often exist among gay men, but this intensity itself seems to suggest that such friendships are not part of the standard masculine pattern. If men wish to retain their sense of being masculine, if they wish to be successful, if they wish to keep from being "emascu-lated," then close friendship seems to be the inevitable casualty.

Such a viewpoint is understandable, given our ignorance of other real-istic alternatives. If the only point of reference is from within contem-porary American culture, this viewpoint is easy to accept because so few "successful" white heterosexual men seem to challenge it. When examining men's friendships from the perspective of other cultures, however, it is the American style that seems strange.

Not enough research has been done on this subject to draw valid generalizations, but what investigation has been done on male friendships shows a quite different pattern from one culture to another. And within any particular culture, there is variation based on class, ethnic background, sexuality, and other differences. Masculinity, no less than other aspects of personality, is a socially constructed achieved status (Gilmore, 1990). The lack of intimacy and demonstrated affection among American men is quite unlike the situation in many other cultures. Many Americans may be aware, from newspaper photographs, that the acceptable style of formal greeting for men in France, Russia, and other European cultures is to embrace and kiss each other. Some of us may even be aware that Arab leaders often are seen walking arm in arm, or holding hands as they talk. Yet most of us are so ignorant of men's daily behavior in much of the non-Western world that we do not realize the peculiarity of men's interactions in the United States. In short, contemporary American mainstream masculinity is rather unique in its suppression of displays of affection, and of close and intimate friendships, between adult men.

Most of human history has occurred in small-scale societies where people know one another much more closely than in modern cities. For about 99% of our history as a species, humans existed in small hunter-gatherer bands. In more recent epochs, pastoral herdsmen or settled agricultural villages emerged. Only within the last century, and only in certain areas of the world, have urban populations surpassed rural ones. Perhaps it is time for us to examine the ways of life of these various social patterns and to see what lessons we might learn about how better to conduct our own social relations. This chapter focuses on male friendship patterns in other cultures, using select examples as a means of demonstrating not only that intimate relationships among men are realistic and possible but also that these kinds of relationships have indeed existed in many other times and places.

Friendship Across Cultures

To understand the differences between friendship in other cultures and friendship in contemporary America, it is necessary to look at some diverse examples; however, very little ethnographic data exist. While marriage patterns have been analyzed exhaustively by ethnographers, hardly any anthropological attention has been devoted to friendship—even though friendship is universal behavior. Friendships are often unstructured and spontaneous, thus fitting poorly with anthropologists' theories about the structures of society (Leyton, 1974). Gilmore (1990) has recently written the first cross-cultural study of manhood as an institutionalized social category; but despite the importance of his work, there is still a lack of cross-cultural focus on men's friendships.

The most extensive anthropological study of friendship remains *Friends and Lovers*, by Robert Brain (1976). Based largely on his fieldwork in Africa, Brain's book provides numerous examples where friendships are encouraged by being ceremonialized and formalized in society. In southern Ghana, for example, same-sex best friends go through a marriage ceremony similar to that performed for husbands and wives. This same-sex marriage, for members of the noble class as well as commoners, includes the payment of "brideprice" to the parents of the younger friend. Among the Bangwa of Cameroon, where Brain did most of his research, social pressure is directed to every child to encourage him to pair up with a best friend, much in the same way that other societies pressure everyone to find a spouse. Cautionary myths are told about the misfortunes falling to a self-centered person who neglects to make a friend. A major theme of popular songs is the celebration of friendships, in contrast to Western pop music, which emphasizes heterosexual romance and sex. In fact, Bangway same-sex friendships are even more durable than male-female marriages. These friendships typically last from adolescence through old age, while marriages commonly split up when children reach adulthood.

Once a year, in the major Bangwa ceremony at the king's palace, men exchange gifts and formally proclaim their friendships as continuing for another year. When a man dies, his funeral ceremony is paid for by his best friend rather than his family. The friend's public mourning is treated even more seriously than the lament of the deceased's widow and children. Throughout the life course, friendship is publicly recognized and ceremonialized among the Bangwa in multiple ways that are not even verbalized among most American men (Brain, 1976).

The institution of "godparenthood," so often commented upon by anthropologists as a form of "fictive kinship" to give a child the advantage of an extra set of parents, is also often a means of formally recognizing friendships. Godparenthood institutionalizes the relationship between the parents of the child and their best friend. In some areas of Latin America, two men will perform a rite of baptism that makes them "godbrothers"

(Brain, 1976). Such ceremonies formalize and give social and religious respect to friendship in a way that modern American society does not. Even though the mythic basis for such a ceremony in Judeo-Christian cultures exists in the Biblical story of Jonathan and David, there is a noticeable lack of ritual in Protestant Christian churches that celebrates close friendships. The Catholic Church even warns its priests and seminary students against forming "particular friendships," thus depriving its unmarried clergy of *any* form of intimate relationship. On the sports field, probably the place most encouraging of same-sex camaraderie in modern America, the emphasis is on team loyalty, competition, and success—rather than on particular friendships.

North American Indian Friendships

How do other cultures manage to encourage these intense friendships among men? In order to understand the important role of such friendships, I turn to my own research with North American Indians. As with many other cultures, same-sex friendships among aboriginal North Americans were emotionally intense because marriages were not the center of a person's emotional life. Marriage was primarily an economic arrangement between women and men to produce offspring and gather food. This arrangement had its basis in a division of labor by gender. Although wide ranges of activities were open for both women and men, in most pre-Columbian American societies there existed a basic division between masculine tasks and feminine tasks. While some individual males or females had the option of doing the tasks usually associated with the other sex, by taking on a highly respected *berdache* gender role that mixed the masculine and feminine aspects together, most people limited their skills to either masculine or feminine ones (Williams, 1986).

By dividing the necessary tasks of each family into "men's work" and "women's work," people only had to learn half of the necessary skills, and gained the expertise of their spouse in tasks that were different from their own skills. Because many Native American societies did not have social taboos against homosexual behavior, same-sex marriages were also recognized, just as long as one of the spouses took on a berdache role and agreed to do the labor of the other sex. The emphasis of the culture was to encourage marriage and parenthood (either by procreation or adoption), not to try to dictate what kind of sexual behavior a person should engage in. As a result, homosexually inclined individuals were not alienated, and family ties were quite strong. By marrying, a person could gain the assistance and support of the spouse's kin group, and thus could double the number of relatives to whom one could turn for support in time of need.

For American Indian societies, as with most societies in all of human history, marriage has primarily been an economic arrangement. Marriage partners in many of these situations might or might not be sexually attracted to each other, but they did expect to be able to depend on each other and their kinsmen for economic support. They had little expectation that they would be each other's best friend. Other than when they were engaging in sex, husbands and wives kept a certain respectful emotional distance from each other. They would bring their resources home to provide food for their spouse and children; they would eat at home and sleep there (at least some of the time). But American Indian men, like those in many other cultures, would not spend much of their leisure time at home. In some native societies husbands and wives did not even sleep together. Among groups as disparate as the Cherokees in the Southeast and the Yupik Eskimos of Alaska, males above age 10 regularly slept in the village "men's house," a sort of community center for males that doubled as the men's sleeping quarters, while the women and small children slept in their own individual houses.

Friendships in such sex-segregated societies followed the same pattern. For friendship, men's primary psychological needs would be met by their long-term friends from childhood. And those friendships were, of course, with persons of the same gender. Men usually had deep feelings of love for their mothers, aunts, grandmothers, and sisters, based on their intimacy in early childhood, but the only adult male who would experience continued close friendships with women was the androgynous berdache, who moved back and forth between the separated gender worlds of men and women. Because of their in-between gender status, berdaches (or their masculined female counterpart) often served as a go-between to negotiate agreements or settle disputes between men and women. In some groups, like the Cheyenne Indians of the Plains, men were so shy around women that they would often ask berdaches to negotiate proposals of marriage.

In such a situation, where each sex felt such shyness in dealing with the other, they each turned to same-sex friends for primary intimacy needs. Early Western explorers often commented upon the especially warm friendships that existed between an Indian man and his "blood brother." A nineteenth-century United States Army officer, for example, reported about "brothers by adoption" that he observed from his years on the frontier. Speaking of Indian male pairs, he pointed out the contrast with more reserved friendships among white men. He said that Arapaho males "really seem to 'fall in love' with men; and I have known this affectionate interest to live for years." The union of two men was often publicly recognized in a Friendship Dance that they would do together (Trumbull, 1894, pp. 71-72, 165-166).

One of these friendships among Lakotas was described by Francis Parkman, who met the two men during his journey on the Oregon Trail in 1846. They were, he wrote:

> [I]nseparable; they ate, slept, and hunted together, and shared with one another almost all that they possessed. If there be anything that deserves to be called romantic in the Indian character, it is to be sought for in friendships such as this, which are common among many of the prairie tribes. (Parkman, 1969, pp. 280-283)

This is not to suggest that these special friendships should be equated with homosexuality. The emphasis for the Indian men was a close emotional bond, which might well be nonsexual in many or maybe most of these friendships. If two close friends engaged in sexual activity, that would be considered their own private business, which would not be publicly mentioned. Even if they were known to be sexual with each other, they would not be labeled as a distinct category like "homosexual." As long as they continued to follow a masculine lifestyle, they would not be socially defined as a berdache. And they certainly would not be stigmatized for their erotic acts. The socially recognized part of their relationship was their deep friendship; native communities honored that. What this meant is that Native American men were allowed to develop intense friendships, and even to be able to express their love for their blood brother friend, without worry that they would be stigmatized. Except for the berdache, any concept like "homosexual" was foreign to the thinking and social world of American Indians.

Friendship and Marriage: Andalusia and Java

The pattern of friendship that traditionally existed among Native Americans, where a man gets his intimate needs met more by his male friends than by his wife, is quite common in various areas of the world.

When Brandes (1987) did his field research in rural areas of Andalusia, Spain, he found that both men and women feel more comfortable revealing their deeper thoughts to a same-sex friend than to their spouse. Brandes was told by his male informants that the home is basically women's space; for men it is "only for eating and sleeping." Men in Andalusia spend most of their leisure time with their male friends at the local tavern. When their teenaged sons become old enough to be brought into the men's friendship sphere, then the men take over the raising of the adolescent males; otherwise men are not much involved in the rearing of younger children. Except for harvest season, when adults are busy working long hours, a man is expected to spend several hours each day with his best friend. He goes home only in the evening for a late dinner just before bedtime. Since any association between an unrelated woman and man would arouse suspicion of adultery, men and women avoid close social interaction with the other sex.

It should be noted that these intense male-male friendships in Andalusia are not seen as a threat to the family in any way. Marriage is strong, but is kept within its bounds of economic co-dependence, food consumption, sex, and sleeping. Marriage relationships between husbands and wives are close, but are not expected to answer one's personal intimacy needs, which are met by one's same-sex friends. As a result of this system, people have two types of close bonds: the structured mixed-sex marriage-kinship system, and the unstructured same-sex friendships networks. These two bonds strengthen and complement each other, providing supportive allegiances and psychological outlets from the pressures of life. Rather than threaten each other, each of these two bonds has its restricted area and does not try to impose on the other. The two together work better than either marriage or friendship would by itself (Brandes, 1987).

My thinking on the complementary relationship between close friendships and marriage partnerships has also been influenced by my fieldwork on the island of Java, which is the most populous island in the archipelago of Indonesia. In 1987 and 1988 I lived in the classical court city of Yogyakarta, where Javanese culture remains strong. Javanese people show a strong sense of reserve in terms of public interaction between women and men, even when they are married. A scandal would ensue if a husband and wife kissed in public, and except for younger urbanites, who have been influenced by American movies and television shows to adopt more Westernized lifestyles, it is rare even to see a Javanese man and woman holding hands in public. This reserve is part of a larger pattern of the limits placed on male-female intimacy. One reason that such reserve exists has to do with arranged marriages. Traditionally, there was no such thing as dating between proper young women and men in Java. Marriages were arranged by parents, with the bride and groom often meeting each other for the first time at their wedding ceremony. Before marriage, people spend most of their time with same-sex friends rather than in heterosexual dating.

Many Americans are shocked to hear of such a custom as arranged marriages, yet our shock is no greater than the shock felt by Javanese who observe American patterns of relationships. I have had several fascinating conversations with Indonesians on this topic. While they admire the material wealth of the United States, Indonesians often wonder "why Americans seem so intent on making themselves miserable." After watching American movies together, I noticed how often they expressed puzzlement about the way Americans experience so much stress by falling in and out of love. "Why," they asked me, "do Americans experience such fragile personal relationships?" One Indonesian spoke for many when he told me that he had the impression that "Americans don't seem to have a hold on anything. They don't seem committed—to their relationships, their friends, or to anything else." It is obvious to them that Western romanticism and traditional forms of family life are not working for many Americans.

In the United States, various groups have called for a "return to the traditional family" as a cure for society's ills. Yet, the nuclear family seems to be less and less able to deal with the realities of the stresses facing people in modern America. Progressive voices have not really articulated a vision for the future, beyond merely accepting the fact that divorce and singlehood are becoming more and more common. The question is, are there other alternatives to the patriarchal nuclear family that will help to prevent an increasing sense of alienation in the lifestyle of the twenty-first century? The extended family is long gone from the American scene, and the nuclear family seems likewise destined. One-to-one relationships continue to be made and broken in fairly similar patterns among both heterosexual couples and homosexual couples. Can people live comfortably with the uncertainty of not knowing how long their partnership will last? These are questions that terrify many, and people are pulled between their desires for the adventure of love and the security of a long-term relationship. Magazines are filled with articles telling worried spouses "how to keep your husband/wife in love with you."

No one seems to be asking the question that maybe it is precisely the romantic ideal of "being in love" that is itself the problem with contemporary marriages. It is in this regard that we might be able to learn something from Indonesian patterns. It became quite evident to me, during my time in Java, that Indonesian husbands and wives do not seem to feel the necessity of "being in love" all the time. In their view, such romantic ideals only lead to grief, because they promote so much longing that families are broken apart.

In Indonesia, under the influence of Westernization, younger people are beginning to choose their marriage partner by "falling in love," but the older generation questions the ideal of romantic love as the primary basis for one's emotional life. I interviewed elderly husbands and wives whose marriages had been arranged by their parents, asking them how they could have adjusted to life together without getting to know each other and falling in love beforehand. They told me it was precisely *because* of their nonromantic approach that their marriage worked. They pointed out that even if two young people know each other intimately for several years, and think that they are completely right for each other, they are so inexperienced in human relationships that they cannot possibly know anything definite about the other person. Plus, individuals change so much over the life course that it does not matter much what kind of person the other one was at that moment. The important advantage of an arranged marriage, in the Javanese view, is that the two young people are *not* "in love," and therefore they are not disillusioned later when they fall out of love. (For interviews with elderly Javanese, where they detail their thoughts about arranged marriages and friendship patterns, see Williams, 1991).

Such nonemotional marriages work because they are complemented by people's emotional needs being met by same-sex friendships. The strong balance between marriage and friendship is most strikingly presented in the context of wedding ceremonies that I observed in Java. The most obvious difference from an American wedding was that all the men sat on one side of the room while the women sat together on the other side of the room. The seating pattern was consciously designed to reflect the separateness of women and men. Weddings are a big event in the villages, reflecting the importance of the family in Javanese culture.

In contrast to an American wedding, which focuses on the love between the bride and groom, a Javanese wedding ceremony emphasizes the economic and social obligations of the new couple to each other, to their future children, to their parents and other relatives, and to the community as a whole. The couple sits down together on the wedding seat, the bride on the women's side, and the groom on the men's, indicating that they retain their closeness to their same-sex friends, even while becoming husband and wife.

Throughout the ceremony, the major emphasis is the economic obligation of the bride and groom. Nowhere does "love," or any expression of emotion between the two partners, put in an appearance. After thinking about the meaning of this ceremony, and talking with Javanese people about the role of marriage, love, and friendship in their lives, I think that perhaps this deliberate deemphasis on love in a marriage is—ironically, to us—one of the reasons for its stability. Instead of an ideal of romantic love, Indonesians seem to have more realistic expectations for a marriage, keeping it more or less restricted to its economic and procreative functions. (For further elaboration of the Javanese wedding ceremony, see Williams, 1991).

In the Javanese view, marriage should not be too intimate. To them, a person's intimacies are best kept where they were already located before two people got married: with their same-sex friends. A man continues to have his relatives and male age-mates as his most intimate friends, and a woman does likewise with her female friends and relatives. They do not expect that their spouse will be either some knight in shining armor or a princess in perpetual beauty, and so they are not disappointed later. As in Andalusia, friendship is not antipathetic to the marriage bond, but they are complementary to each other. One's sexual partner is not expected to also be one's best friend. Given the economic importance of marriage in Javanese village life, the exaltation of friendship among one's same-sex friends serves as a balancing point.

As their separated seating at the Javanese wedding ceremony makes clear, women are not expected to separate themselves from other women and give all their emotional support to their husbands. Both they and their husbands are getting many of their emotional needs met by their same-sex friends. If husbands and wives do not sit together at a ceremony as symbolic as a wedding, why should it be expected for them to be together otherwise? In their workday, men and women are likewise often separated. Women spend much of their time at the market, selling their family's food produce to other women. Markets for food sales are primarily women's spaces, with men seldom involved. At their domestic work, women are either in the kitchen or at the riverbank, washing their clothes in company with other women. Men are off plowing with the oxen, or working in all-male labor gangs in the fields or the irrigation canals.

During the evening hours in a typical Javanese village, after the day's work is completed, husbands and wives will each go their separate ways. Women will visit and chat with other women, while the men will gather among themselves. They may be involved with an arts organization or a dance group, and each of these groups is either all-male or all-female. Men may play musical instruments, or women may join a singing group, but there is little overlap between the sexes in many of their leisure activities.

The Future of Friendship

Strong extended family kinship networks have often not been able to survive the extensive geographical mobility characteristic of modern America. Relatives are separated as the capitalist job market has forced many people to migrate to other locations. Under these pressures, "the family" has been reduced from its original extended form (the most common type of family among humans) to a mere nuclear remnant of parents and children. In modern America, a person's "significant other" has now become practically the sole person with whom he or she can be intimate. For many couples, this is too much to ask of their relationships, as the significant other is expected simultaneously to be sexual playmate, economic partner, kinship system, best friend, and everything else. Because of the dictatorship of the romantic ideal, many Americans expect their spouse to meet all their emotional needs. That is doubly difficult to do while both partners are also holding down full-time employment outside the home.

As more American marriages become households where both spouses have jobs outside the home, there is less energy left for being emotionally supportive of one's partner. Even these rump nuclear family marriages are, therefore, in increasing numbers of cases, falling apart. The flip side of the American ideal of individual freedom and progress is thus often a legacy of individual alienation and loneliness.

In contrast, by not expecting the marriage relationship to fulfill all of a person's needs, many other cultures allow people more emotional closeness to same-sex friends. To take one example, in some cultures, families are not often broken up over the issue of homosexuality. In such a situation, in fact, there is not as much emotional need for homosexually inclined individuals to construct a separate homosexual identity. There will, of course, still be a certain percentage of people who erotically prefer a same-sex partner, but that inclination may be fulfilled within the friendship bond. There is no social pressure for persons to leave their marriage just because they desire same-sex erotic contacts. Sexual desires may have little to do with family bonding, because the marriage is not assumed to be sexually exclusive.

Same-sex friendships need not, of course, include a sexual component, but as far as the society is concerned, the important factor is the friendship rather than the sexual behavior. The person might be sexually involved with a same-sex friend while also being heterosexually married. Both forms of bonding occur, and a person does not have to choose one over the other. This flexibility resolves to the advantage of society and the individual. There is a looseness and an adaptiveness that allow for close intimate interaction with both sexes within the dual bonds of marriage and friendship.

In cultures that do not stigmatize same-sex eroticism, and do not divide up people into "homosexuals" and "heterosexuals," there is remarkable freedom from worry among males that others will perceive them to be members of a distinct "homosexual" category. This freedom from worry demonstrates that much of the inhibition that contemporary American men feel about their friendships is due to the fear that others might categorize them as homosexual. This can most clearly be seen by contrasting the behavior of late twentieth-century Indian men with their non-homophobic ancestors. As contemporary Indian people have absorbed more and more mainstream white American values, through Christian missionaries, government schools, off-reservation residence, and television, they have become more homophobic. On reservations today, friendships are not as intense as among past generations. American Indian men's alienation from each other is a "miner's canary" to warn us of the even more extreme alienation going on among mainstream Americans. Friendships among heterosexual men are one of the main casualties of homophobia.

Given all these pressures, which restrict men's expressions of their feelings and increase their stress levels, it will be valuable to get some concrete ideas as to how we can get beyond some of these dilemmas facing American men. A cross-cultural analysis is one possible source of knowledge regarding how men can conceptualize their intimacy needs.

First, it is necessary to move beyond the view that every person is either exclusively heterosexual or exclusively homosexual. Two facts emerge from the anthropological literature: (a) There is a diversity in individual sexual inclinations, with some persons clearly preferring the other sex and some clearly preferring the same sex, but many (probably a majority) having a mixture of erotic feelings for both sexes; and (b) for most people, healthy human operation requires the spreading around of intimacy to a wider circle of people. This is the most common pattern, in the extended family networks and the close friendships, of probably the majority of cultures, yet this is precisely what twentieth-century American culture has failed to do. Since our geographical mobility precludes the reestablishment of extended family kinship systems for most Americans, it behooves us to reexamine the cross-cultural data on friendships and to try to start building alternative forms of relationships on this basis.

Perhaps it is time for us to begin a more fundamental public discourse questioning the primacy of the male-female romantic ideal (i.e., "the traditional family") as sufficient for meeting human intimacy needs by itself. Many Americans know that something is wrong with their lives, but the only solution they hear is popular music's refrain that they should fall in love, and the allied heterosexist "pro-family" rhetoric. Perhaps a new rhetoric of friendship needs to be emphasized. It is not an exaggeration to say that there has been a denigration of friendship in the United States. The pro-heterosexual, pro-marriage discourse has almost obliterated intense same-sex friendships. This is not to suggest that people should abandon their sexual partners, but that they should expect less of such a partner than his or her total emotional support.

In the 1970s, radical feminist separatists' and gay men's friendship networks emerged as never before. New possibilities seemed to be emerging. By the 1980s, however, as a drive for social respectability set in, fueled by the AIDS crisis, gay men and lesbians tended to settle into same-sex couplehoods that mirror the American heterosexual marriage rather than the more widespread intimacy patterns of many other cultures.

As we prepare for a new century, a revitalization of the psychological and social importance of friendship should become a high priority. Ironically, the AIDS crisis has brought out the importance of friendship "buddy" networks, as well as domestic partners, as caregivers within the gay and lesbian community. In the non-gay community as well, more attention must be given to ceremonializing and ritualizing friendship relationships in the same way that romantic relationships and marriages have been. More serious respect can be given, from one's partner as well as by society at large, for the importance of friends. Since sexual attractions are often subject to change over the years, maybe more people will be living the slogan that "lovers come and go, but friends remain."

Certainly, these suggestions do not imply that all people will evolve new kinds of relationships, but it does imply the need for equal social respect being given for a variety of friendship types. It suggests that, rather than regretting the passing of a traditional form of marriage that has already disappeared for many people, Americans will be better served by paying more attention to our needs for close intimate friendships. The problem is not the breakdown of marriage as much as it is the need to develop wider distributions of individuals to whom we can express our intimacy. In this society, women are doing this much more successfully than are men. Before American men dismiss the possibility of anything different, they might educate themselves to the necessity of getting over barriers to intimacy with friends, whether this is due to homophobia or to a competitive ethos at the workplace. We already have, in the examples from other cultures, many functioning models that have well served the emotional needs of men for centuries. These models bear further investigation. Those who have highly developed friendships can recognize the power of these relationships to carry us forward into the future. For at least some of us, maybe this is a better place to focus our intimacies, rather than placing all our hopes on some romantic love that might later turn sour and then become so disruptive in our lives.

If our society is to survive, when traditional family patterns are evolving and geographical mobility strains the limits of intergenerational connections, it is up to innovative individuals to search out new forms for intimate relationships beyond sexual partnerships. We need to analyze and nurture our long-term close friendship networks as the best possible base on which to build an emotionally satisfying future.

References

Brain, R. (1976). *Friends and lovers*. New York: Basic Books.

Brandes, S. (1987). Sex roles and anthropological research in rural Andalusia. *Women's Studies, 13*, 357-372.

Brod, H. (Ed.). (1987). *The making of masculinities: The new men's studies*. Boston: Allen & Unwin.

Franklin, C. (1984). *The changing definition of masculinity.*. New York: Plenum.

Gilmore, D. (1990). *Manhood in the making: Cultural concepts of masculinity*. New Haven, CT: Yale University Press.

Kilgore, J. (1984). *The intimate man: Intimacy and masculinity in the 80s*. Nashville, TN: Abingdon.

Kimmel, M., & Messner, M. (Eds.). (1989). *Men's lives*. New York: Macmillan.

Leyton, E. (Ed.). (1974). *The compact: Selected dimensions of friendship* (Newfoundland Social and Economic Papers No. 3). Toronto: University of Toronto Press and Memorial University of Newfoundland.

Miller, S. (1983). *Men and friendship*. Boston: Houghton Mifflin.

Parkman, F. (1969). *The Oregon Trail*. Madison: University of Wisconsin Press.

Pleck, E. H., & Pleck, J. H. (1980). *The American man*. Englewood Cliffs, NJ: Prentice-Hall.

Trumbull, H. C. (1894). *Friendship the master passion*. Philadelphia: Wattles.

Williams, W. L. (1986). *The spirit and the flesh: Sexual diversity in American Indian culture*. Boston: Beacon.

Williams, W. L. (1991). *Javanese lives: Women and men in modern Indonesian society*. New Brunswick, NJ: Rutgers University Press.

11

"Hey, Home—Yo, Bro"

Friendship Among Black Men

CLYDE W. FRANKLIN II

Despite the fact that black men are visible figures on the American landscape, their lives and their masculinities are the least understood. Staples (1986, p. 57) recognizes this fact and suggests that black men in America are enigmas because "they are the least studied of all sex-race groups." Certainly, cultural images of black men as deviants are ubiquitous in our society. In fact, there is no dearth of media portrayals of black men as sexual superstuds, athletes, and rapacious criminals (e.g. rapists, pimps, thieves, drug pushers, drug addicts, and so on). Rarely, however, do we get glimpses of black men in their everyday roles as fathers, workers, husbands, friends, and American citizens (Staples, 1986). Who are black men qua men? What are their masculinities all about?

Among multiple reasons why few studies have been devoted to the lives and masculinities of black men are three major ones: (a) the reluctant recognition by many persons in American society that black males can be potential occupants of masculine roles; (b) societal blockage of black males' efforts to assume hegemonic masculine roles; and (c) the failure by society to recognize black male sex roles as "masculine."

General ideas in America suggesting that black males primarily are "sexual," "physical," "deviant," and "socially disorganized" seem to be couched in a genetic inferiority perspective that disregards the role of systematic racial discrimination in determining their plight (Oliver, 1989). Just as important, however, is that such a perspective runs counter to perceptions of black males as "masculine" sex-role occupants.

Not only are others' perceptions of black men's masculinities affected by societal stereotypes of black men, but black men's perceptions of their own masculinities are also affected. For example, in the 1960s Nathan Hare wrote of the frustrated masculinity many Negro males experienced because they were denied access to hegemonic masculine roles, such as attempts to assume head of household roles. Especially important, according to Hare (1971), was the fact that black men felt they were prevented from assuming the provider-protector role in black families by blocked opportunities. Still, many black males did develop alternative masculine roles, which included nurturing their wives and children, holding menial jobs, and assuming low-profile positions within the home. Needless to say, many in society did not recognize these roles as masculine.

The black male sex roles that have developed over the years are extremely complex social constructions. The signing of the Emancipation Proclamation on January 1, 1863, formally ended slavery, but it did not mean that black males could begin to construct their masculinities without interference from the legacy of a patriarchal slave/master system.

Not only have black men been denied opportunities to construct masculinities congruent with societal expectations for adult males, but also they have been encouraged to develop dysfunctional alternatives to traditional definitions of masculinity. Oliver (1989, p. 120) points out that successful enactment of the traditional male role is generally dependent on a male's access to educational and employment opportunities. Due to what some writers call an inferiorization process and institutional racism, numerous lower-socioeconomic-status black males have redefined masculinities in terms of violence, toughness, sexual conquest, and thrill seeking (Karenga, 1977; Madhubuti, 1990; Oliver, 1989; Perkins, 1975; Staples, 1982). Instead of internalizing societally endorsed male values of self-reliance, economic success, political power, family protection, and family provision, many of these black males have developed "tough-guy" and "player of women" orientations (Oliver, 1989).

Black men's conceptions of themselves, regardless of class, are critical variables related to their friendship formations. Values endorsed and orientations developed by black men influence greatly their self-concepts, which in turn affect the nature of their same-sex friendships. The precise manner in which black men's self-concepts affect their friendships can be seen in the relationships between *self, role identities, identity salience,* and *commitment.*

According to Stryker (1980), the *self* is a structure consisting of self-knowledge and self-feelings. These self-conceptions and feelings are termed *role identities* and Stryker believes that they are "ordered and hierarchical" in nature. This means that some of the identities are more likely to be involved in social situations than others. Direct and indirect socialization determines *role identities* as well as the *salience* of these identities. Basic institutions in American society (e.g., family, educational, political, economic, religious) are agencies of socialization. However, because black males typically participate minimally in such institutions (with the exception of the black family), either they are not influenced or they are influenced negatively by them. The literature is replete with examples of how societal institutions influence males to internalize rigid sex-role prescriptions and proscriptions inimical to male same-sex friendships (Farrell, 1986). Because working-class black males experience greater isolation from mainstream society than upwardly mobile black men, they may not internalize the same taboos against male same-sex friendships, which result in non-self-disclosure, competitiveness, and nonvulnerability.

Just as important as identities and identity salience to black men's friendship formations is *commitment,* which is conceptualized by Stryker (1980, p. 61) as allowing greater precision in specifying linkages between society and the individual. "To the degree that one's relationships to specified sets of other persons depend on being a particular kind of person, one is committed to being that kind of person," says Stryker (p. 61). Actually, commitment may be the key variable in working-class black men's friendships and may influence positively their same-sex friendships.

On the other hand, lower commitment to friendships by upwardly mobile black men may influence negatively their same-sex friendships. It is not difficult to understand why upwardly mobile black men would experience less commitment in their same-sex friendships. Frequently such men have relatively high rates of participation in those mainstream societal institutions, such as the political, the economic, and the governmental, which discourage same-sex friendships. Indeed, participation in these institutions may actually support and encourage emotional inexpressiveness, independence, competitiveness, homophobia, and the pursuit of power. In other words, as black men become upwardly mobile they increase their participation in society's mainstream institutions. As black male participation in such institutions increases, however, there may be an accompanying decrease in the degrees and amounts of affection, intimate talks, nurturance, and holism characterizing their same-sex friendships. Black males struggling to be a part of mainstream society are quite likely to become committed to being societally approved males.

According to many, societally approved males appear to construct same-sex friendships lacking in social support, self-disclosure, intimacy, affection, nurturance, and holism (Garfinkel, 1985; Lewis, 1978; Pogrebin, 1987; Vittitow, 1981). In the remaining sections of this chapter, black male friendships are explored and discussed.

Studying Black Men's Friendships

Obtaining personal accounts, using short, unstructured interviews from 30 black males ranging in age from 18 to 63, was the chief research technique used in this exploration of black males' same-sex friendships. The men were asked to give subjective accounts of their same-sex friendships or lack of friendships. Personal accounts included reports of the number of such friendships, characteristics of the relationships, depth of the friendships, meanings of the friendships, extensiveness of the friendships, and so forth. Respondents roughly represented three social strata in a midwestern city with a population of more than 100,000 black people: 12 men were working-class (earning $18,000 or less in unskilled blue-collar positions); 12 men were professional, white-collar (earning between $25,000 and $50,000); and 6 were corporate, upper-middle-class (earning $50,000+).

The "personal accounts" method was used to understand black men's subjective interpretations of their intimacy or lack of intimacy with other black men because it is the most appropriate when information is "sought about another's personal life in the world" (Schwartz & Jacobs, 1979, p. 62). Individual respondents came from two churches, a fraternal organization, a barbershop, and a university. The personal accounts were given over a 3-month period in 1990.

Data also were produced from casual conversations with approximately 18 men, in groups of two and three, who attended the inaugural meeting of the National Council of African American Men held in Kansas City, Missouri, during the summer of 1990. Following each conversation, notes were written and filed. The men attending this conference were mostly professional, white-collar men and some were corporate, upper-middle-class.

Black Men's Friendships

> For Black men in this society, the world is a hostile dangerous place—a jungle. It is uncompromising territory where a man is either the hunter or the hunted; he either seizes the power or loses it; he either rises to the never-ending tests of his manhood or falls a victim. Since Black Men's relationship to power and sense of manhood has always been challenged in this land we must always be on the move, always wary, always careful, always thinking and always on guard. He must walk that fine line between paranoia and prudence. It helps if we have a main man to walk with. In fact, I think it's critical. (Simmons, 1981)

Research on black men's same-sex friendships in the United States is practically nonexistent. Actually this is to be expected since there is a dearth of information about black men and about male friendships in general. One of the few articles about black male same-sex friendships appeared in *Essence* magazine in 1981. Simmons (1981, p. 37) feels that black men do not become "cut buddies" (close friends) "unless they have in common a basic and instinctive understanding of each other's psychological and emotional needs, as well as the forces they must confront and share a willingness to meet those needs and forces." Shared experiences, according to Simmons, are the basic underpinnings of this instinctive understanding. It is, perhaps, due to the importance of shared experiences that class emerged as a significant factor to consider in black men's friendships in the study reported here. For this reason, findings on black men's friendships are given in two sections: (a) working-class black men and friendship, and (b) upwardly mobile black men and friendship.

The literature is relatively consistent. Men's friendships generally are centered around activities and specific tasks and are lacking in social support and self-disclosure (Caldwell & Peplau, 1982; Pleck, 1976). But are these findings generalizable to all male aggregates regardless of race, ethnicity, or social class? More specifically, are black men's same-sex friendships similar to the male same-sex friendships studied and reported in the literature? Who are some of these men who shout "hey, home" and respond "yo, bro"? The following sections shed some light on black men's same-sex friendships.

Working-Class Black Men and Friendships

There have been numerous discussions about the amount of social pathology existing among lower-socioeconomic-status black males in recent years (Gibbs, 1988; Strickland, 1989; Wilson, 1987). Little information exists, however, on the extent to which some black males construct meaningful and functional lives for themselves. Intense, emotional, and extremely close friendships may be examples of socially constructed environments that facilitate and nurture such lives. These environments seem to serve as buffers against a society generally hostile to black males (Madhubuti, 1990). In other words, a type of "consciousness of kind" seems to develop among some black working-class men, as evidenced by their interpretations of their gestures and conversations with their friends. Overwhelmingly, the men pointed out that their responses and behaviors with their friends symbolized, in some way, shared oppression and victimization in American society. Even the greeting and response —"yo, bro," "hey, home"—tell a friend that "I share your daily experiences of prejudice and discrimination; I, too, feel reviled because of my color; I, too, experience daily condescension; but I, too, feel enormous pride in being a black man; and I, too, feel that I have certain inviolable rights as a man in America." These are powerful utterances black men make to each other. They are more than greetings and responses; they are political statements connoting survival, togetherness, and commonality.

Because the greetings, responses, and interpretations of both were made within the context of black male same-sex friendship relations, it is reasonable to assume that they are significant for understanding working-class black men's same-sex friendships. "When I talk with my friends, they know what I'm saying, you know. I can make a statement and they pick up everything about it, you know . . . the feelings, what I'm talking about, what I like, don't like. White guys can't do that . . . and bourgie black guys either," Lawrence replied when questioned about the manner in which he conversed with his friends. He also went on to say that all of the black guys he knew had friends with whom they related in the same way.

I am convinced, because of numerous conversations I have had with black men on street corners and in parks, barbershops, and other gathering places, that these men's friendships are warmer and more intimate than the ones reported by upwardly mobile black men and those reported in the literature (e.g., Pogrebin, 1987). I contend that the sources of warmth and intimacy may lie in their shared political ideology.

Supporting a characterization of working-class black men's friendships as warm, intimate, self-disclosing, holistic, and political were descriptions of their activities and conversations with each other. As Aaron said, when asked to describe his relationship with his male friends: "My homey is a part of my life, man. He is my main dude. He would do anything for me and I will do anything for him. It's just the way I was brought up." He stated further that he had another friend he was just as close to but he was in the army. Tim described his friendship with Gene and Joe in even more political terms, stating that "We spend most of our time together, helping each other out because you know, the white man will get you, if you don't stick together—you have to scheme to make it in this country, man."

"We just chill out together, man. After work, we just hang out and be real cool together. We don't even have to be scoping the ladies—of course we do that, too," Max laughs. "But, mostly we just hang tight," he continues. "What do we talk about? Robert, Jack or Bill, with any one of them guys, I can talk about anything I want and they won't tell a soul. I feel so close to them, man. Don't you have dudes like that? Dudes you can trust! Wow, man, these are some heavy questions."

Certainly one can understand how shared oppression and victimization can lead to shared political ideology. This is precisely what occurred for many black males in America during the late 1960s. Shared political ideology increases the need for affiliations with like-minded persons. Research shows that persons high in friendship motivations and/or need for affiliation are more motivated to form warm, friendly, and stable interpersonal relations than those persons low in need for friendship motivation/affiliation (McAdams & Losoff, 1984). Sharing racial/political ideology may very well affect individuals' perceptions of similarity between themselves and others. Perceived similarity may, in turn, directly affect one's friendship motivation or need to affiliate. Need for affiliation is related to warmth and intimacy in affiliations. Axiomatically, then, shared political ideology may lead to warmer and more intimate affiliations. Talking with working-class black men about their social relationships, one gets the distinct impression that there is no paucity of friendship motivation, need for affiliation, or warmth in their friendships.

According to interview responses with working-class black men and informal conversations about their same-sex friendships, expectations of loyalty, altruism, and closeness are essential features of their friendship associations. Often these men speak quite seriously about their friends, some almost to the point of crying, thus reflecting the intensity of their feelings for their friends. Perhaps it is precisely because these friendships are holistic, intense, and empathic that some of these men turn unexpectedly violent when one of the parties perceives a violation of trust, loyalty, or closeness. Some proportion of black-on-black male violence today certainly is associated with accelerated use and selling of drugs. However, a relatively large proportion of black male same-sex violence, I contend, may be related to violations of friendship expectations. Such violations may include being perceived as disloyal, untrustworthy, unhelpful, lying, and cheating, to mention a few. When these friendship violations were mentioned during the interviews, all of the working-class men's responses indicated that they would be revulsed, disappointed, and enraged if their friends violated their friendships. Many even felt that such violations called for some type of severe punishment. When respondents were probed further regarding reasons for their feelings, some indicated that disloyalty and untrustworthiness discovered in a friend would be like some type of invalidation of their own self-worth or their own identity. "It would be like he had made a fool of me, my supposedly best friend," most of them replied. Noteworthy about the responses of these men also was their intensity when they considered the possibility of friends being disloyal, violating their trust, and lying to them. Nine of the men showed visible signs of agitation and/or revulsion as they mulled over the possibility that their friends would interact with them in such a manner.

Succinctly, some working-class black men's friendships appear to be quite intimate, to the point where they interact with their friends as though they are family members. Moreover, frequently families of black men interact with black men's male friends as though the men are family members. Certainly this reflects extremely close relationships between working-class black men. These reports, suggest, like Simmons (1981), that they can and do talk about everything in their lives with their friends. Unlike the male friendships described by Pogrebin (1987) as non-self-disclosing and lacking holism, working-class black men's same-sex friendships appear to be high in self-disclosure, intimacy, and holism.

Working-class black men "hanging out" in public places frequently indicated that criteria for friends are "guys that stick by you through thick and thin," "someone who will not let you down," "someone you tell everything to," and "a dude you can do a lot of stuff with."

As stated earlier, black men's lives and friendships are just as diverse as other men's lives and friendships. Thus, it is axiomatic that a sizable and growing number of black men are responding to rigid male proscriptions and prescriptions in decidedly different ways from their brothers of lower socioeconomic status. Whereas black men of lower socioeconomic status, because of previously described necessity, often have constructed a brand of masculinity that has nurtured warm, close, empathic, and holistic friendships between men, their more upwardly mobile brothers seem to be constructing different kinds of relationships. Black men entering mainstream society often find that in order to be successful, they have to actively play out roles similar to those played out by other "successful" men. Frequently this means, according to these men, maintaining a certain amount of distance from their male "competitors," or "acting white," as three upwardly mobile black men cynically responded to my query about their friendships with other black men.

Upward mobility for black men in America is a slow, tedious, and precarious process. For purposes of this study, men falling into the upper-level incomes were defined as upwardly mobile, and it was assumed that they were on the rise. Because none of those interviewed indicated that retirement was in their near future and all had aspirations of "better things to come," I felt comfortable labeling them "upwardly mobile black males."

Upwardly Mobile Black Men and Friendship

A striking feature of upwardly mobile black men's socialization that is directly relevant for black men's same-sex friendships is the commonality between the socialization messages they received and the ones received by working-class black men. Both received messages emphasizing the need for trust, empathy, warmth, and altruism between black males, simultaneously with messages telling them of threats to black men from the larger society and warnings of how attempts would be made to block their efforts to succeed. For upwardly mobile black men, blocked opportunities and discriminating policies are perceived as lesser impediments to their own successes and constructions of a hegemonic masculine identity. In discussions with these men about such impediments to their own successes and about their male friendships, generally the talk centered around "being the best" in spite of prejudice, "being helpful to others," "being competent," and "playing the game." Most of the upwardly mobile black men did not talk extensively about their friends, and when three of them did talk, their discussions revolved around the time spent with their friends watching sports and talking about the business ventures they were individually interested in embarking upon.

Unfortunately, when black men accept and begin to display societal definitions of masculinity, many of the traits thought to be essential for the development of close friendships are lost. Basically what happens is that expectations for these males begin to change. Empathy, compassion, trust, cooperation, and other such traits are eschewed in favor of ones such as aggression, competitiveness, stoicism, rational thinking, and independence. Not only do these traits become role expectations for upwardly mobile black men held by significant others and society in general, but they also become role expectations the men hold for themselves. The result of such alterations in role expectations is diminutions in male-male friendships, both quantitatively and qualitatively.

Upwardly mobile black men seem quite similar to males in general in their same-sex friendship relationships. Many of the upwardly mobile black men I interviewed stated that they "really did not have time to cultivate deep relationships" because they spent most of their time "trying to get ahead." Some other upwardly mobile black men questioned whether "it is necessary for there to be deep relationships between men." Still, a relatively small number of other black men moving up the social ladder indicated that they "do experience a feeling of commonality with other black men." These men said that "simple glances," conversational consensual validation, "brief acknowledgments," and the like, all serve to give them "a feeling of unity when around other black men."

Still, these men did not discuss whether they were involved in intimate friendships with other black men. In contrast to the interviews and conversations with working-class black men, those held with upwardly mobile black men revealed few "deep" friendships. "Striving for success" was indicated by many as the chief obstacle to such relationships. Whether "class" affects male friendship patterns similarly in other racial and ethnic aggregates is an empirical question that cannot be answered in this chapter. However, based on what we know presently about male friendships, qualities such as closeness, empathy, and caring are associated with female friendships rather than male friendships (Allan, 1989). The fact that numerous working-class black men and relatively fewer numbers of upwardly mobile black men indicated closeness, empathy, and caring in their same-sex friendships certainly is worthy of further investigation.

Discovering that upwardly mobile black men report fewer friendships and these are less empathic, less compassionate, and less caring should not be surprising. Males moving up the social ladder generally in the United States frequently are expected to portray a masculine style characterized by competitiveness, aggressiveness, instrumentality, coolness, and rationality. In fact, not assuming a role that embodies such traits can very well mean that a black male does not move up the social ladder. One upwardly mobile black man, who works for a nationally known, non-profit volunteer organization and has daily contact with upwardly mobile black men, states: "A lot of guys I meet who are new in the area don't appear concerned about developing friendships. Instead, they want to know how they can 'network' with a minimum amount of involvement. In other words, they ask, how can I get maximum exposure with minimal involvement in interpersonal relationships?"

"Upwardly mobile black men form relationships with others on the basis of the financial profitability of those relationships, and then they say they do not understand why they don't have many close friends," another upwardly mobile black male related. Two others conversing about upwardly mobile black men's friendships and/or lack of such relationships, agreed that "many substitute their involvement in voluntary associations and organizations where they can experience male comaraderie for close male friendships."

"Upwardly mobile black men seem to be seekers of friends rather than actual participants in friendship relationships," voiced another black corporate executive. These and similar revelations by upwardly mobile black men about their views on same-sex friendships and participation in them seem much more similar to their white male social-class counterparts than their divergent social-class black male counterparts. Close friendships appear not to assume the same prominence in the lives and masculinities of upwardly mobile black men as they do in the lives and masculinities of working-class black men. When a black bank vice-president was asked why this seems to characterize upwardly mobile black men's same-sex relationships, he suggested: "Maybe that is the price we have to pay for making it in America—actually it is not such a horrible price, because this is what it's all about today."

Conclusion

According to Scheff (1990, p. 4), there is nothing more significant in human social relations than emotion: "Maintenance of bonds is the most crucial human motive." From this perspective, friendship bonds between males are natural occurrences. Yet, as discussed earlier, research on male same-sex friendships indicates that frequently such associations either are truncated ones or occur with much difficulty. As noted, male sex-role socialization agencies frequently teach men to be non-intimate, non-self-disclosing, homophobic, non-nurturing, and competitive (Allan, 1989). These agencies produce many men who do very little to maintain social bonds with other men. In essence, male sex-role socialization in the United States traditionally has meant teaching males to internalize traits that distort and often inhibit male same-sex friendships. In my study of black men's same-sex friendships, black men's conceptions of themselves, their identities, and their commitments all were critical variables related to friendship formation. The precise manner in which the variables related to friendship formation was through both social class and race. For working-class black males, race appeared to be a positive factor supporting the social construction of warm, holistic, nurturant, and intimate same-sex friendships. For upwardly mobile black males, class emerged as a salient negative factor thwarting the social construction of warm, holistic, nurturant, and intimate same-sex friendships. Altering their core selves in the direction of hegemonic masculinity, upwardly-mobile black males become less marginalized to the American mainstream but simultaneously less comfortable assuming close same-sex friendships. "Homeys" and "bros," characteristically black working-class men, develop and maintain same-sex friendships qualitatively different from those of upwardly mobile black men, whose same-sex friendships mirror those discussed in the literature. While working-class black men's same-sex friendships are warm, intimate, and holistic, upwardly mobile black men's same-sex friendships are cool, non-intimate, and segmented. Black men's friendships appear to change as they move up the social ladder. Despite the fact that few, if any, black men ever extricate themselves from their master status, color, they do gain the dubious right to be similar to other American men discussed throughout the literature—the right to rarely experience a close friendship with a man or a woman and the right not to have an intimate "homey" or be an intimate "bro."

Only relatively recently has a black scholar (Madhubuti, 1990) begun to outline a male socialization process, which involves rites of passage into manhood and steps for internalizing a sociopolitical ideology that can produce black men able to form productive, warm, and intimate relationships with each other.

As Madhubuti (1990) states, socializing African-American male youth is a very difficult task often left to ineffective agencies and agents. Such forces, according to Madhubuti, place these young males in the hands of socializing agents and agencies incapable of dealing effectively with their bio-sexual energies. Because often young black males resist their mothers' primarily single socializing efforts, many of them develop their masculinities according to their own and their peer groups' inventiveness and ingenuity.

Searching for a solution to male socialization problems, which threaten to make "black men obsolete, single and dangerous," Madhubuti (pp. 16-17) first outlines a working definition of black masculinity that involves, among many traits, perceiving emotions as strength; valuing love for self, children, and family; cooperating and sharing resources; being sensitive to the needs of others (both women and men); being soft, strong, understanding, patient, creative, and always in a process of growth. The definition, itself, is seen as only a starting point for Madhubuti, who proposes that it should be incorporated into all the rites of passage defining black males, such as birth namings, birthdays, formal schooling, graduation, age groupings, sexual activity, high school education, military and/or college, marriage, and other cultural forces that are seen as crucial for stabilizing and giving direction to black youth. A solution to black male socialization problems involving a redefinition of black masculinities and incorporating them into rites of passage toward manhood is quite inventive. I believe that many of the traits emphasized in Madhubuti's redefinition of black masculinity, such as love, cooperation, sharing, and sensitivity, are essential for the social construction of friendship relationships and thus should greatly benefit black male friendships.

References

Allan, G. (1989). *Friendship: Developing a sociological perspective*. New York: Harvester Wheatsheaf.

Caldwell, M. A., & Peplau, L. A. (1982). Sex differences in same-sex friendships. *Sex Roles, 8*, 721-732.

Farrell, W. (1986). *Why men are the way they are*. New York: McGraw-Hill.

Garfinkel, P. (1985). *In a man's world: Father, son, brother, friend, and other roles men play*. New York: New American Library.

Gibbs, J. T. (1988). *Young, black and male in America: An endangered species*. New York: Auburn House.

Hare, N. (1971). The frustrated masculinity of the Negro male. In R. Staples (Ed.), *The black family*. Belmont, CA: Wadsworth.

Karenga, R. (1977). *Kwanzaa: Origin, concepts, practice*. Los Angeles: Kawaida.

Lewis, R. A. (1978). Emotional intimacy among men. *Journal of Social Issues, 34*, 108-121.

Madhubuti, H. R. (1990). *Black men: Obsolete, single, dangerous?* Chicago: Third World Press.

McAdams, D. P., & Losoff, M. (1984). Friendship maturation in fourth and sixth grades: A thematic analysis. *Journal of Social and Personal Relationships*, 11-27.

Oliver, W. (1989). Black males and social problems: Prevention through Afrocentric social-ization. *Journal of Black Studies, 20*, 15-39.

Perkins, U. E. (1975). *Home is a dirty street: The social oppression of black children.* Chicago: Third World Press.

Pleck, J. H. (1976). Man to man: Is brotherhood possible? In N. Glazer-Malbin (Ed.), *Old family/new family: Interpersonal relationships* (pp. 229-244). New York: Van Nostrand.

Pogrebin, L. C. (1987). *Among friends: Who we like, why we like them, and what we do with them.* New York: McGraw-Hill.

Scheff, T. J. (1990). *Microsociology: Discourse, emotion and social structure.* Chicago: University of Chicago Press.

Schwartz, H., & Jacobs, J. (1979). *Qualitative sociology: A method to the madness.* New York: Free Press.

Simmons, M. (1981, November). *Essence*, pp. 35-38.

Staples, R. (1982). *Black masculinity: The black male role in American society.* San Fran-cisco: The Black Scholar Press.

Staples, R. (1986). *The black family: Essays and studies.* Belmont, CA: Wadsworth.

Strickland, W. (1989, November). Our men in crisis. *Essence*, pp. 49-52, 109-115.

Stryker, S. (1980). *Symbolic interactionism: A social structural version.* Menlo Park, CA: Benjamin/Cummings.

Vittitow, D. (1981). Changing men and their movement toward intimacy. In I. A. Lewis (Ed.), *Men in difficult times* (pp. 290-296). Englewood Cliffs, NJ: Prentice-Hall.

Wilson, W. J. (1987). *The truly disadvantaged: The inner city, the underclass, and public policy.* Chicago: University of Chicago Press.

12

Like Family

Power, Intimacy, and Sexuality in Male Athletes' Friendships[1]

MICHAEL A. MESSNER

> The locker room had become a kind of home to me . . . I often enter tense and uneasy, disturbed by some event of the day. Slowly my worries fade as I see their unimportance to my male peers. I relax, my concerns lost among relationships that are warm and real, but never intimate, lost among the constants of an athlete's life. Athletes may be crude and immature, but they are genuine when it comes to loyalty. The lines of communication are clear and simple . . . We are at ease in the setting of satin uniforms and shower nozzles.
>
> —Bill Bradley (1977)

Introduction

Throughout most of this century, it was commonly believed that men who worked together, fought together, and played together within public institutions such as the workplace, the military, and sport tended to form deep and lasting friendships. Men, it was believed, enjoyed the Truly Great Friendships, while women's friendships with each other were characterized by shallow cattiness and gossip. Moreover, social commentators such as Lionel Tiger (1969) and George Gilder (1973) argued that civilization itself rests on the foundation of men's "natural" tendency to bond together in public life. This highly romanticized view of men's friendships was turned on its head in the mid-1970s by a new perspective, which was inspired by a revived feminist movement. Men's liberationists began to examine the quality of men's friendships with other men, and found them wanting. Men's friendships, it was argued, tend to be destructively competitive, homophobic, and emotionally impoverished (Balswick, 1976; Farrell, 1975; Fasteau, 1974; Morin & Garfinkel, 1978; Pleck & Sawyer, 1974).

By the mid-1980s, the social-scientific literature tended to echo this emphasis on the "emotional limits" and "impoverishment" of men's friendships, especially when compared categorically with women's friendships. In the forefront of this perspective were adherents of feminist psychoanalytic theory, who argued that early developmental differences, grounded in the social structure of mothering, created deeply rooted (unconscious) differences between women and men (Chodorow, 1978; Dinnerstein, 1976). As a result of these internalized gender identity differences, males develop more "positional" identities (with fears of intimacy), while females develop more "relational" identities (with fears of separation) (Gilligan, 1982; Rubin, 1983). One result of these differences, according to Rubin (1985), is that women tend to enjoy deep, intimate, meaningful, and lasting friendships, while men have a number of shallow, superficial, and unsatisfying "acquaintances." Rubin characterizes the dominant form of men's friendships with other men as "bonding without intimacy."

By the late 1980s, this negative characterization of men's friendship had itself been called into question. Following Cancian's (1987) observation that since the Industrial Revolution, social conceptions of love and intimacy have become "feminized," Swain (1989) argues that Rubin and others have been guilty of judging men's friendships against the standard of the type of intimate relationships that women tend to construct. Women tend to place a very high value on *talk*—and indeed, for a relationship to be "intimate," there must be a willingness and ability to verbally and mutually share one's inner life with another (Rubin, 1983, 1985). Since men friends tend to *do things* with each other, rather than spending their time talking about their inner lives, they are engaged in "bonding without intimacy." Swain asserts that if we instead examine men's friendships from the point of view of men, rather than through a "feminine model," we see that men's friendships are in fact characterized by a "covert style of intimacy" (p. 71). Men already have an "active style of intimacy," and should not be forced to learn "feminine-typed skills to foster intimacy in their relationships" (p. 85). In short, women and men tend to experience and define intimate friendship in different ways, and neither should be judged by the standard of the other.

This chapter aims to shed light on this ongoing debate through an examination of men's friendships within a specific social institution— organized sports. At issue in this debate, I will argue, is the question: From whose standpoint should we examine men's friendships? If we judge men's friendships through an idealized feminine standard, men's friend- ships will appear impoverished. It is valuable and important to understand how men experience and define their own friendships. But in analyzing gender difference in friendship patterns, it is crucial to move beyond the "separate but equal" stance, where women's friendships are evaluated through a feminine standpoint, and men's friendships through a mascu- line standpoint. As we ask what men's friendships mean to men, we also need to ask the femin*ist* (not femin*ine*) question: How do these male friend- ship patterns fit into an overall system of power? This means examining both the quality of men's friendships with each other and the ways that male friendships and peer groups construct men's attitudes and relation- ships toward women. This is the task of this chapter. Through a concrete examination of men's friendships within the institution of sport, I hope to shed light on the complexity of men's friendships—both in terms of individual men's experience of friendships, and in terms of the role of men's friendships in constructing the larger gender order. Through an analysis of in-depth interviews with 30 male former athletes of diverse age, race, and socioeconomic status,[2] I will describe and analyze male athletes' friendships with each other. Then I will examine the ways that men's friendships and peer groups serve to construct their relationships with—and attitudes about—women.

The Paradox of Men's Friendships in Sport

Years after the end of an athletic career, it is not uncommon to hear men talk almost reverently of their friendships with former teammates. For instance, Gene,[3] a former professional football player, said:

> The guys I played with, I had the utmost respect for. Because once you've been through training camp together, and those hard times together, you learn

to know and feel things about 'em that can't anyone else ever feel if they haven't been in those situations with 'em. The most important persons are your teammates, and to be loved and respected by them means more than anything—more than the money aspect, if a guy would tell the truth about it.

These kinds of statements were not reserved for former professional athletes. Jim, who played football, basketball, and baseball through high school, spoke of his relationships with teammates with similar reverence:

I'd say that most of my meaningful relationships have started through sports and have been maintained through sports. There's nothing so strong, to form that bond, as sports. Just like in war, too—there are no closer friends than guys who are in the same foxhole together trying to stay alive. You know, hardship breeds friendship, breeds intense familiarity . . . You have to commonly endure something together—sweat together, bleed together, cry together. Sports provide that.

This (often highly romanticized) sense that close friendships between men are forged in "adversity," through "enduring hardship" together, was a common theme in former athletes' discussions of their friendships with teammates. But despite almost universal agreement that sports provided a context in which this kind of mutual respect, closeness, even love among men did develop, there was usually a downside to men's descriptions of their relationships with teammates. For instance, Brent, a former high school basketball player said that in his early teens, his relationship with this best friend was a "sports rivalry." He described this friendship as:

[A] sort of love-hate relationship. There were times when we . . . I remember fighting him. I remember getting into fights, but at the same time I remember going to his house and having good times. It was never a real deep relationship.

It is this sort of ambiguity that was most characteristic of men's descriptions of their relationships with teammates. "Forged in battle," these are often the closest relationships that these men ever have; yet athletic battles as often take place among teammates as they do with other teams. This ambiguity can be examined as a manifestation of the development of masculine identities within the competitive, hierarchical world of athletic careers.

The Team Structure:
Antagonistic Cooperation

The public face that a team attempts to present to the rest of the world is that of a "family," whose shared goal of winning games and championships bonds its individual members together. But the structure of athletic careers is such that individuals on teams are constantly competing against each other—first for a place on the team, then for playing time, for public recognition and star status, and eventually, just to stay on the team. Rather than being purely cooperative enterprises, then, athletic teams are characterized by what Riesman (1953) calls "antagonistic cooperation." In sport, just as in the modern bureaucratic corporation, "a cult of teamwork conceals the struggle for survival" (Lasch, 1979, p. 209).

Coaches attempt to mitigate the potentially negative consequences of this individual struggle for survival by emphasizing the importance of "team play." In fact, several men said that having learned to "play a role" on a team, rather than needing to be the star, was a valuable lesson they learned through sports. For them, teamwork was an exciting and satisfying experience. As Jon, a former high school basketball player, put it:

I like the feeling of getting on a team where you might not have the best individuals, but with teamwork and somehow a sense of togetherness, you can knock somebody off that's better than you.

This sort of satisfaction, though, appeared to be more common among young males like Jon who knew that they were not stars, who knew that their futures did not lie in athletic careers. As he put it:

I would never have gotten my name in the newspaper—maybe if I had been a better scorer, but I never was. The way I would make my niche in basketball was obviously by being a good passer—I always got a thrill out of it.

For those who did see themselves as stars (or potential stars), who were committed to athletic careers, the competition with teammates was very real and often very intense. Athletes have developed their own ways of dealing with the structured reality that one teammate's success might mean one's own demotion. For instance, the fact that new players on a team often pose a threat to the veterans is dealt with through ritualized testing and hazing of rookies. A former pro football player, Billy, said that as a rookie on his college football team, he had to "earn the respect" of the older players before being accepted as a teammate. He did this by "getting knocked on my butt by them," and then in turn, "knocking them on their butts. After that, they respected me." Nathan, another former pro football player, agreed that "you get your respect, but you have to earn it. . . . They won't just give it to you right off." Part of the ritual involves showing the proper deference to the veteran players, not appearing so "cocky." One year, Nathan said:

> A rookie came in, and the veterans hadn't even come to camp yet, and this guy was talking about what he was going to do to [the team's veteran defensive stars], how he was gonna be the leading pass receiver. He lasted about 2 days. They hurt him, and I think he stayed in the training room about 2 weeks. Came out, lasted another day, and they sent him back. Finally he had to be cut from the team. People were popping him, right, just because he had a loud mouth.

Once a team is formed, a coach does his best to channel these sorts of internal antagonisms toward an external "enemy" (Sabo & Panepinto, 1990). As Gene explained:

> No matter what you hear about teams—they don't get along, they fight each other—you just try to let some outsider come in and come up fightin' one of 'em. It'd be like two brothers who fight like cats and dogs, but you let *somebody else* mess with one of them and he's gotta be ready to deal with both of them at one time. Same thing: A team *is* a family. It *has* to be.

Lurking just below the surface of this "family" rhetoric, though, lies intense, often cutthroat competition. Several men told me of difficult, even destructive relationships that developed between themselves and teammates as a result of competition for individual rewards and recognition. This was especially true in cases where two players were vying to be seen as the star of the team. Jim told of a high school basketball game in which his teammate/rival was "basket-hanging," and had gotten 26 easy points by halftime, which put him within 5 points of the school record.

> I must have fed Tim [the ball] eight times in the first half. At halftime, our center says to me, "Hey, this is bullshit. I'm getting all the rebounds, and I haven't gotten a shot. Why can't Tim get a few rebounds instead of all the [easy baskets] at the other end?" So I said, "Oh, I'll take care of that," 'cause I was the one throwing him the ball all the time. So I'd get the outlet pass and I'd just bring it up. Tim ended up with 28 points. I'm sure he still begrudges

that—I mean, he could have broken every record in the book, but anybody who could make a layup could have done that.

The intensity of this kind of competition between teammates can actually increase as one moves up the ladder of athletic careers, where the stakes are higher. Chris told me that through college, friendships with basketball teammates were important and meaningful to him, but when he got to the professional ranks, he found it was "all business," with little room for the development of close friendships:

[When you get] to pro ball, all of a sudden you got assholes out there. It's the money. The competition is greater. You're dealing with politics. I was drafted second round. They had a lot of draft picks and it was real cutthroat. So you see a lot of good players come and go. It was tight. You're dealing with money. You're dealing with jobs. It's a business, and that really turned me off. I had dreamed it would be *everything*, and I got there and it was a job. You know, a fuckin' job where a man screams at your ass.

At times, these sorts of antagonisms are racially oriented. Thomas, for instance, described his shock in his first year of pro football in finding that black players were second-class citizens on his team:

There was no togetherness on that team. Race had a lot to do with it. And money. They didn't want no brother making no money . . . You know, a white player would walk into the damn locker room and tell one of the brothers, "Turn off that damn nigger music! I don't want to hear that shit!" And the brother would go over and turn the music off! Boy, oh boy, when the guy turned off the music, that just about blew my mind! I said to myself, this cat ain't got no heart . . . And then they went after me, 'cause I'm the rookie, the number-one draft choice. They wanted me to sing. *I ain't singing: Fuck 'em. I'm a grown man. I ain't gonna sing.* Then they tried to get me on the football field and I ended up fuckin' around and hurtin' a couple of people 'cause I knew what they were gonna do. It didn't take me very long to get 'em quiet.

Few men described such overtly antagonistic racial conflicts on the team, yet most did say that informal friendship networks on teams tended to be organized along racial lines. For instance, Larry, a black man who had played college football recalled that: "For the most part, the white guys hung out with each other, and the brothers hung out with the brothers." Nevertheless, several white and black men told me that through sports they had their first real contact with people from different racial groups, and for a few of them, good friendships began. Unfortunately, most of these friendships were not strong enough to persist outside the context of the team situation, where social, cultural, peer, and familial pressures made it difficult to nurture and maintain cross-racial friendships.[4]

Masculine Identity and Friendship in Sport

How do we explain men's tendency to describe their friendships with teammates both in highly romanticized terms of "family" and as destructively competitive? First, the structured system of "antagonistic cooperation" clearly puts teammates into ambiguous relationships with each other. Yet the structure of the athletic context does not fully or adequately explain the experience of the participants. We also need to consider the gendered psychological and emotional tendencies that these males brought to their athletic experiences.[5]

As I outlined earlier, Rubin (1983; 1985) argues that men's early developmental experiences have left them with a deep fear of intimacy (which she defined as the ability and willingness to mutually share one's inner life with another person).[6] As a result, though men do want to spend time with other men, they tend to maintain emotional distance between themselves by organizing their time together around an activity that is external to themselves. As Jim stated above, "Sports provide that." Here men can enjoy the company of other men—even become close—without having to become intimate in ways that may threaten their "firm ego boundaries," and thus their fragile masculine gender identities.

We can now begin to make sense of former professional basketball player Bill Bradley's (1977) seemingly paradoxical description of his relationships with his teammates as "warm and real, but never intimate." Bradley seems most comforted here by the simultaneous existence of a certain kind of *closeness* with a clear sense of *boundaries and distance*. This seeming paradox is explained when we consider it in light of the interaction between masculine gender identity and the gendered structure of sport as a social institution: The hierarchical and rule-bound structure of athletic careers, and especially the structure of "antagonistic cooperation" on the team, dovetails with men's ambivalent need to develop closeness without intimacy with other men.[7] In short, competitive activities such as sports mediate men's relationships with each other in ways that allow them to develop a powerful bond together, while at the same time preventing the development of what Rubin calls "intimacy."

Beyond "Separate but Equal"

Thus far, I have argued that the depth of athletes' friendships with each other is limited by the affinity between the structure of sport and the structure of developing masculine gender identities. But to simply leave it that men's friendships constitute "bonding without intimacy" belies the depth of affection that so many of these men expressed for each other. In fact, my research suggests that male athletes do tend to develop what Swain (1989, p. 72) calls "covert intimacy," a "private, often nonverbal, context-specific form of communication." Whereas women's style of intimacy emphasizes the importance of talk, in men's covert intimacy, "closeness is in the 'doing,' " and "actions speak louder than words and carry greater interpersonal value" (p. 77).

Though it appears to be true that "men and women have different styles of intimacy that reflect the often-separate realms in which they express it" (Swain, p. 78), there is a danger in adopting a stance of simply viewing men's and women's friendships as "separate but equal." For instance, Swain discusses a man who told him that "a couple of girls picked up [him and his friend] and we got laid and everything . . . after, [he and his friend] went out and had a few beers and compared notes." Swain (p. 77) concludes that "though this sort of quote might imply sexual exploitation . . . the commonality gained from a shared life experience did provide meaningful interaction among the men." Clearly, this talk among men is "meaningful interaction" *when examined from the point of view of the men.* But rather than simply viewing male friends' sexual talk about women in terms of its functions for male friendships, it is also crucial to examine the ways that this kind of talk among men might contribute to the construction of a certain kind of attitudes toward and relationships with women. In other words, I am suggesting that we move away from examining men's friendships with each other from a *feminine* standpoint (Rubin), or from a *masculine* standpoint (Swain), and instead ask *feminist* questions: How are male athletes' friendships with each other affected by—and in turn affect—their attitudes toward and relationships with women? And how do these attitudes and relationships contribute to the construction of the larger gender order?

Sexuality and Sexual Attitudes

"Big Man on Campus." "Sexual Athlete." For many, these terms conjure up the dominant cultural image of the athlete on campus: He is extremely popular, self-assured, and (hetero)sexually active. Other boys and young men are envious of the ease with which he can "get women." My interviews at times revealed a grain of truth to this popular stereotype of the athlete. Chris, for instance, said that even as a second-string professional basketball player, it was:

> [J]ust the good life [laughs]—I mean, you could wave at one way up in the 15th row, and after the game, she's standin' right there by the locker room . . . that's what makes it fun, you know.

Similarly, when asked how he related to others when in school, Thomas said:

> I liked to be the big man on campus, and sports was a highlight because it gave me that opportunity. *Everybody* knew who I was. Big Tom. *Everybody* knew who I was.

On the surface, these two statements would seem to affirm the dominant stereotype of the athlete as a confident young man at ease with himself and with his sexuality among his peers. Interestingly though, when asked about their *specific* relationships with females, a very different picture emerged. "Big Tom," for instance, stated:

> Girls, in high school, were really not prime in my life [laughs]— . . . When I was in high school, I thought I was an ugly guy. You know, being under a lot of pressure, and being so much bigger than everybody, and everybody's always looking at you. In high school, you don't know what looks *mean*—it could be good, it could be bad. At one time I felt like I was a freak, so I was more or less into myself. I don't think I had one girlfriend.

This sense of awkwardness and insecurity with respect to girls and women seemed almost universal among the men I interviewed. David's shyness in high school was compounded by his low-class status, so for him, sports became an escape from dealing with girls:

> No doubt I was shy, and I think it had to do with the fact that if I did make a date with a girl, how was I gonna' go? What was I gonna spend? 'Cause I had none of it. So I just used sports as an escape.

Clarence, a high school football player, had similar problems with girls:

> In my senior year [of high school], I remember dating all these girls, [but] I wasn't sexually active. I hadn't had intercourse—I might have done a little petting, but never any genital stuff. I think I was popular, and was seen as an attractive boy, but I didn't have a sense of it. I just thought I was absolutely ugly as hell.

Several of the men I interviewed recalled hoping that being seen as an athlete would give them the confidence to overcome their insecurity with girls. Jon said that he had hoped that being on the high school basketball team would help him overcome his shyness "and make it easier to talk with girls. It didn't." But several of these men reported that they did eventually develop ways to "talk to girls," despite their shyness. For instance, Eldon, a black former college track and field competitor, said that in high school:

> I was lame, as they called it. So I didn't know how to do women so well. My stepmother threw a 16th birthday party for me and invited a lot of friends, and I remember that day, trying on a lot of the roles that I saw guys playing, and it kind of shocked me because the women took it seriously, you know. That was a big turning point for me. I didn't particularly like, especially, some of the black modes of relating to women, I thought were *stupid*—just *nonsense*—sweet nothings seemed silly to me. [But] anyway, I tried it, my version of it, and to my surprise some woman took it seriously. That meant it was possible [laughs] . . .

Calvin, a former college basketball player, described a similar transformation from tortured shyness with girls in high school to developing a "rap" with women in college:

> I was just scared, and bashful, and shy. I did not know what to say or what to do. It was very uncomfortable. This was a very bad time, 'cause you're always around a lot of girls at parties . . . very uncomfortable in groups and with individuals . . . Finally [I went] off to college and went to the extreme of trying to attract a lot of girls, [and was] semi-successful. You knew you had to have a date on Fridays, and knew you had to have one on Saturdays, and so you just walked through the student union, and you'd just have this rap you'd thought of, and you'd just put it on. It was peer pressure . . . I'm naturally a shy person . . . but somehow in college I was able to somehow fall into the right kinds of things to do and say.

We can see from these stories that developing a "rap" with women becomes an almost ritualized way that a young man helps himself overcome an otherwise paralyzing shyness, a sense of "lameness" when trying to relate to women. Developing a "rap" with women involves a certain dramaturgy, a conscious self-manipulation ("you'd just put it on"), and one result is that girls and women become the objects of men's verbal manipulation. And this specific form of verbal manipulation of women does not spring naturally or magically from men's shyness. Rather, it is socially learned through the male peer group. Notice that Eldon learned to "do women" by watching his male peers. And Calvin, though somewhat mystified as to how he was able "somehow" to overcome his shyness and "fall into the right things to say," also cites "peer pressure" as a motivating force. Clearly, an analysis of the development of men's sexual relationships with women must take into account the ways that male peer groups structure attitudes and feelings about sexuality and emotional commitment to women.

In his study of male college fraternities, Lyman (1987) argues that there is an erotic basis to the fraternal bond in male homosocial groups. In the past, the key to maintaining the male bond was the denial of the erotic. Organized sport, as it arose in the nineteenth and early twentieth centuries was based, in part, on a Victorian antisexual ethic. First, it was believed that homosocial institutions such as sport would "masculinize" young males in an otherwise "feminized" culture, thus preventing homosexuality.[8] And second, the popular (and "scientific") belief in the "spermatic economy" held that "the human male possessed a limited quantity of sperm that could be invested in various enterprises, ranging from business through sport to copulation and procreation. In this context, the careful regulation of the body was the only path to the conservation of energy" (Mrozek, 1983, p. 20). As Crosset (1990, p. 53) points out, in a social context which held that young men's precious energies would be drained off should they expend too much sperm, sport was elevated as the key "to regenerate the male body and thus make efficient use of male energy."

Some of the older men in my study went through adolescence and early adulthood when the remnants of the ideology of the "spermatic economy" were still alive. Eldon, for instance, said that as a young runner, from the late 1940s through the mid-1950s, he had been "a bit cautious about sex, because I still had some old-fashioned notions about sexual energy [being] competitive with athletic stuff." Most of these men, though, came of age during the sexual revolution of the 1960s and early 1970s, when the dominant credo became, "If it feels good, do it." As a result, the male peer group, within the athletic context, became a place where sexual activity and *talk* of sexual activity (real or imagined) were key components of the peer status-system.

But if the bond among men is erotic, and the culture is increasingly telling them "if it feels good, do it," what is to prevent the development of sexual relations among these young men who are playing, showering, dressing, and living together in such close quarters? The answer is that the erotic bond among male friends and teammates is neutralized through overt homophobia, and through the displacement of the erotic toward women as objects of sexually aggressive talk and practice in the male peer group. In boyhood, adolescent, and young adult male peer groups, "fag," "girl," and "woman" are insults that are used almost interchangeably. Through this practice, heterosexual masculinity is collectively constructed through the denigration of homosexuality and femininity as "not-male." For example, Bill, a former high school football and basketball player, described how his athletic male peer group helped to structure his own public presentation of his sexuality:

I was shy [with girls]—I hung out more with guys. I never dated. I never was real intimate with anyone. It was just kinda scary because I thought I'd get teased by my peers.

(For not being involved with women?)

For *being* involved! But you *gotta* be involved to the point where you get 'em into bed, you know, you *fuck 'em,* or something like that, yeah, that's real important [laughs]—but as far as being intimate, or close, I wasn't. And that wasn't real important. Just so I could prove my heterosexuality it was real important. But I always wanted to look good to females—'cause I didn't have the personality [laughs]—*to get 'em into bed!* So I wanted to be able to have the *body* and the, uh, the sort of friends around who, uh, who admired me in some sort of way, to have that pull.

This sort of use of women as objects of sexual conquest is important for gaining status in athletic male peer groups, but also tends to impoverish young males' relationships with females. As Neal, a former high school football player put it, he and his friends on the team used to:

[T]ell a lot of stories about girls. I guess it was a way to show our masculinity . . . [But] I never got emotionally involved with any of the girls I went out with. I never got close to any of them.

The link between young males' tendency to "tell [sexual] stories about girls" and their lack of intimacy with girls and young women is an important one. As Lyman points out, young males commonly use sexually aggressive stories and jokes as a means of "negotiating" the "latent tension and aggression they feel toward each other." And they also are using this joking relationship to "negotiate the tension they felt between sexual interest in the girls and fear of commitment to them . . . [they use] hostile joking to negotiate their fear of the 'loss of control' implied by intimacy" (Lyman, 1987, p. 156). Thus, while talk of sex with females bonds the males together, the specific forms of sexual talk (sexual objectification and conquest of women) help males deal with their terror of intimacy with women (which many of them described, above, as "shyness," "lameness," and such). Again, in the words of Lyman (p. 151): "In dealing with women, the group separated intimacy from sex, defining the male bond as intimate but not sexual (homosocial), and relationships with women as sexual but not intimate (heterosexual)."

In fact, male peer groups tend to police their own members in terms of intimacy with females. Though male peer groups routinely confer high status on one who is sexually active (or says he is), they also commonly respond to a friend who starts to spend a lot of time with a girlfriend by taunting him that he is "pussywhipped." The result of this kind of locker-room culture is that many young men end up suffering from a kind of " 'sexual schizophrenia.' Their minds lead them toward eroticism while their hearts pull them toward emotional intimacy" (Sabo, 1989, p. 39). Some young men deal with this split by keeping their emotional attachments with females a secret, while continuing to participate in locker-room discussions about sexuality with their male peers. Frank, a former high school basketball and tennis player, had one such relationship in high school:

> We started sneaking around and going out late at night and no one else knew. I didn't tell any of my friends . . . We got along great, sexually and emotionally, though she said I didn't express my feelings enough . . .

In a very real sense, these young males' relationships with girls and women—whether sexual or not—were *constructed through* (indeed, were often distorted by and subordinated to) their friendships with their male teammates.

At times, the male peer group's policing of its members' relationships with females took on a racial angle. Larry, for instance, said that when he was a college football player:

> [T]he biggest conflict we had was black males dating white girls. . . . The white males would call up the white females and call them whores, bitches, and prostitutes—you know, insulting language, like "if you ball him, you'll ball anybody, so come over here and ball me, too."

In this case, then, the peer group was not only policing intimacy with women, but also attempting to impose controls on interracial sexuality.

The need to prove one's manhood through sexual conquests of women was experienced as a burden by many young heterosexual males, and was sometimes complicated by racial tensions, but it was especially oppressive for gay men. In his youth, Mike had thrown himself into sports, rather than into dancing, largely because he was terrified that people might find out that he was gay. Sports allowed him to construct a masculine public image. Yet within sports, this meant that he had constantly to construct a heterosexual image:

> I hated high school. I mean, I just didn't know who I was. I think I had quite a bit of negative self-esteem at that time, 'cause I really felt different . . . I mean, I didn't drink, I didn't like to screw around, and this was what all my friends did, so I felt compelled to go along with this stuff, and all the time hating it . . . I dated some women, some that I loved because they were just really fine people—uh, physically, there was not a great deal of passion. *For males,* there was a passion . . . [But] homophobia was rampant, especially in athletics. You see, I think a lot of athletes go into athletics for the same reason I did. They need to prove their maleness. And I did, I readily admit it. I wanted to be viewed as a male. Otherwise I would be a dancer today. I wanted the male, macho image of an athlete . . . I felt I've gotta hide this thing—'cause I know what they were thinking: If I were gay, they would see me as less than a man, or *not a man.* So I'm gonna *be a man,* 'cause *that's what I am.* So I was protected by a very hard shell—and I was *clearly* aware of what I was doing . . . just as a lot of gay men are aware that they're living a lie . . . it's a terrible thing to live with.

Though his secret knowledge of his own homosexuality made this process a much more *conscious* one for Mike ("I was *clearly* aware of what I was doing"), his public construction of manhood-as-heterosexual was not all that different from what his straight counterparts were doing.

Whether gay or straight, the denial and denigration of gayness and femininity (in one's self and in others) were important keys to these young men's construction of masculine identities and status in their male peer group.[9] As Mike said:

> Go into any locker room and watch and listen, and you'll hear the same kind of garbage—I call it garbage now, and I thought it was garbage then, but I felt compelled to go along with it, because I wanted that image. . . . And I know others who did, too. I know a *lot* of athletes are gay. And I think a lot of athletes are attracted to athletics because they're fighting feelings of tenderness—not necessarily gay—but they're fighting feminine qualities. . . . I know a lot of football players who very quietly and very secretly like to paint, or play piano, and they do it quietly because this to them is threatening if it's known by others.

The pressure to be seen by one's peers as "a man"—indeed, the pressure to see one's *self* as "a man"—kept most young males in conformity (at least on the surface) with this homophobic and sexist locker-room "garbage." Conformity with sexist and homophobic locker-room culture was a way—for gay as well as for non-gay men—to publicly construct their gender identities. But gay athletes were far more likely to see this construction of identity *as a conscious strategy* than were heterosexual athletes (Pronger, 1990). As Brittan (1989, p. 41) explains, "In everyday life most heterosexuals do not have to do too much identity work because they tend to function in contexts in which heterosexuality is taken for granted."

For a few, though, conformity with what Mike called locker-room "garbage" led them to question—even reject—the jock culture and the specific form of masculinity and sexuality that predominated there. Brent, for instance, said that toward the end of high school:

> I really got turned off to the way the guys were relating to the girls. It was really ugly in certain ways, like just treating them like objects, totally judging them by their surface appearances, talking amongst themselves in really abusive language about girls, how they're gonna do this or that to them . . . I thought it was wrong. I thought that people shouldn't be treated that way. I started to realize that the way I related to women was *not* the way these guys were relating to them, and therefore I didn't want to relate with them on that level. So I started to distance myself from the same activities, and started to feel really alienated from my buddies.

This sort of realization about—and rejection of—the sexist treatment of women was a rare exception to the rule. And it is significant that this realization was made by a young athlete who several years earlier had come to realize that he was not a "career athlete." That he had already begun to disengage from his athletic career meant that he had less invested in the athletic male peer group. For young men who were fully committed to athletic careers, this sort of rejection of one of the key bonds of the male peer group would have amounted to career suicide. So whether they liked it or not, most went along with it. And when the "garbage" went beyond verbal sparring and bragging about sexual conquests to actual behavior, peer group values encouraged these young men to treat females as objects of conquest. Frank described a "night on the town" with his male friends. He was a virgin in high school and terrified at his own lack of sexual experience. But when they hit the town, he said, "We were like wolves hunting down prey. Dave told me, 'If a girl doesn't give it up in 60 seconds, drop her!' "

It is this sort of masculine peer group dynamic that is at the heart of the rape culture (Beneke, 1982; Herman, 1984). Kanin (1984) argues that college men who have experienced pressure from their current male friends to engage in sexual activity are more likely to commit acquaintance rape. Similarly, Koss and Dinero (1988, p. 144) find in their national study that "involvement in peer groups that reinforce highly sexualized views of women" is an important predictor of "sexually aggressive behavior" by college males. And Warshaw (1988, p. 112) concludes from her research on date and acquaintance rape that "Athletic teams are breeding grounds for rape [because they] are often populated by men who are steeped in sexist, rape-supportive beliefs." Indeed, sportswriter Rich Hoffman states in a story in the *Philadelphia Daily News* that between 1983 and 1986, a U.S. college athlete was reported for sexual assault an average of once every 18 days (cited in Warshaw, 1988, p. 113).

Only a fraction of male athletes actually rape women. The (mostly verbal) sexual objectification of women that is an important basis of male athletes' friendships with each other actually hurts young males by making intimacy with women more difficult to develop. But ultimately, it is women who pay the price for young men's tendency to use sexual talk of women to mediate their relations with other men. Johnson (1988, p. 119) argues:

> That the peer group's pressure to be heterosexual occurs in a context in which women are sex-objectified may well have the consequence of making it difficult

for males to become sexually aroused in a relationship in which they do not feel dominant over the female. If one learns about sexuality in the context of being rewarded by other males for "scoring," for "getting pussy" or just "getting *it*," then this does not augur well for egalitarian sex.

Conclusion

Feminist scholars argue that sport is an institution constructed largely through gender relations (Bryson, 1987; Hall, 1988; Messner, 1988; Theberge, 1981). The feminist critique of sport has revealed that within athletics, specific kinds of masculine identity, values, attitudes, and relationships are constructed (Kidd, 1987; Messner, 1987; Messner & Sabo, 1990; Sabo, 1985). Though an individual athlete may feel as though his athletic career is a lonely, individual quest for success, in fact, he is actively participating in a social process of masculine gender identity construction. And this identity construction is accomplished through relationships with others within institutional contexts (Connell, 1990).

When I asked former athletes to talk about the kinds of friendships that they had with teammates, most of them immediately dropped into the language of "family." This was not too surprising. Like family relations, friendships with teammates are often among the closest relationships that young men develop. But underneath the talk of respect, love, and closeness among teammates lies another reality: Athletic teams, like families, are also characterized by internal antagonisms rooted in hierarchy. And these socially structured competitive antagonisms among teammates are exacerbated by boys' and young men's tendency to fear certain kinds of closeness with others.

This is not to say that men do not develop intimate friendships among athletic teammates. The men I interviewed developed a kind of *covert intimacy*, an intimacy that is characterized by *doing* together, rather than by mutual talk about their inner lives. That the men whom I interviewed valued these friendships is beyond question. In fact, they often spoke reverently of the friendships they developed while involved in athletic careers. But I have suggested in this chapter that in evaluating men's friendships, it is desirable to move beyond either judging them (negatively) from a *feminine* standpoint, or observing that, from a *masculine* standpoint, men value the particular kinds of intimacy they have with male friends. Instead, I have argued that it is important to look at men's covert intimacy in the larger context of structured power relations between men and women, and between men and other men. When examined in this way, we can see that, though men often feel good about their athletic friendships, the fact that these kinds of friendships are often cemented by sexist and homophobic talk (and, at times, actions) suggests that men's covert intimacy within sports plays a part in the construction of a larger gender order in which men's power over women is reasserted (often through sexuality). Moreover, it is revealed that through these kinds of athletic friendships and peer-group dynamics, heterosexual men marginalize gay men, while policing and limiting any "feminine" tendencies in themselves. Homophobia discounts the possible existence of erotic desire among men, while aggressive sexuality expressed toward women displaces the erotic bond among men toward a devalued female object. As a result, the bond among males is cemented, while the ability to develop egalitarian relationships with either males or females is impoverished.

Overall, these sorts of relationships among men contribute to the construction of a gender order that is dominated by heterosexual males. But there are contradictions in this construction of masculinity that suggest potential avenues for change. First, individually, men's lives are emotionally impoverished by the limits of the kinds of relationships that they commonly develop in organized sports. It is possible that the recognition of these limits will lead some men to reject the promise of masculine power and status in favor of joining together with women in constructing a more humane world and more egalitarian relationships. Perhaps more important, concrete analyses of men's identities and relationships in sport reveal that, although their collective actions serve to construct men's overall power and privilege over women, men do not equally share the fruits of this privilege. What we observe in sport is the construction of a *dominant form* of masculinity—what Connell (1987) calls "hegemonic masculinity."

Outside of sport—and indeed, submerged within sport—there are clearly groups of marginalized and subordinated men who are oppressed by narrow constructions of hegemonic masculinity. The example of gay athletes, discussed above, is a case-in-point. And poor and ethnic minority male athletes, though they often see sport as an arena in which to construct a respected masculine identity, are far more often than not locked into their subordinate class and racial status because of their single-minded focus on sports success (Messner, 1989). If gay men, poor men, and minority men can reject these narrow conceptions of masculinity (which ultimately oppress them), there is the possibility that they might see in feminism a key to the development of an egalitarian society. For it is only within the context of egalitarianism that truly intimate friendships can develop and flourish.

Notes

1. This chapter is part of a larger study to be published as *Power at Play: Sports and the Problem of Masculinity* (Beacon Press, 1992). I thank Bob Blauner, Pierrette Hondagneu-Sotelo, Michael Kimmel, Peter Nardi, and Don Sabo for comments and suggestions on earlier drafts of this work.

2. My research aimed at exploring and interpreting the meanings that males themselves attribute to their participation in athletic careers. The tape-recorded interviews were semistructured, and took from $1\frac{1}{2}$ to 6 hours to conduct. I asked each man to talk about four broad eras in his life: (a) his earliest experiences with sports in boyhood; (b) his athletic career; (c) retirement or disengagement from the athletic career; and (d) life after the athletic career. In each era, I focused the interview on the meanings of "success and failure," and on the boy's/man's relationships with family, with other males, with women, and with his own body. Most of the men I interviewed had been involved in the (U.S.) "major sports"—football, basketball, baseball, track. All had at some time in their lives based their identities largely on their roles as athletes and could therefore be said to have had "athletic careers." Twelve had played organized sports through high school, 11 had played through college, and 7 had been professional athletes. At the time of the interviews, most had been retired from playing organized sports for at least 5 years. Their ages ranged from 21 to 48, with the median at 33. Fourteen were black, 14 were white, and 2 were Latino.

3. All names of interviewees used in this article are pseudonyms.

4. C.R.L. James' eloquent description of a painful reunion that he had with a former cricket teammate/friend seems to capture the essence of cross-racial friendships that develop in the athletic context: "We had nothing to say to each other, our social circles were too different, and he never came again. He went to Europe to study medicine and years afterwards, when we were grown men, I met him once or twice. We greeted each other warmly, but I was always embarrassed and I think he was too. There was a guilty feeling that something had gone wrong with us. Something had. The school-tie can be transplanted, but except on annual sporting occasions the old school-tie cannot be. *It is a bond of school only on the surface. The link is between family and friends, between members of the class or caste*" (James, 1983, p. 41, emphasis added).

5. Duquin (1984), in her comparison of male and female college athletes, found that female athletes are more likely to bring "an ethic of care" to their athletic experiences, while males are more likely to employ "the orientation of self-interest." This suggests that men's gendering identities are more consistent with the hierarchical structure and the value on individual competition that characterize the current sports world. Men would be more likely to be comfortable with the kinds of relationships that are developed in this world, while women would be more likely to attempt to find ways to develop more intimate relationships with teammates. This difference might also explain why female athletes are more likely to attribute the causes of their successes to factors "external" to themselves (coaches, teammates, family, luck), while males are more comfortable taking individual credit for their successes (see McHugh, Duquin, & Frieze, 1978).

6. Rubin's definition of "intimacy," while helpful in constructing her typology of gender differences in friendship patterns, is class biased. Her emphasis on *verbalization* of one's "inner life" is based on a very upper-middle-class, therapeutic definition of intimacy, which might ignore or devalue other, nonverbal forms of expression that might be more common in social groups who are not so immersed in the professional/therapeutic culture.

7. In the words of Ian Craib, the relationship between structure and personality is best viewed as an "elective affinity. The 'normal' structure and operation of institutions, as they have developed in modern capitalist society, makes use of, and perhaps routinely (though not necessarily) confirms the routine structure and processes of the male personality" (Craib, 1987, p. 737).

8. Here are some of the roots of the still-popular misconception that male homosexuality is connected to some essential "femininity," a confusion of *sexual identity* with *gender identity*. This confusion is clearly a cultural manifestation (see W. L. Williams, 1986).

9. C. L. Williams (1989) observes that homophobia and misogyny are a common part of basic training for male Marines.

References

Balswick, J. (1976). The inexpressive male: A tragedy of American society. In D. David & R. Brannon (Eds.), *The forty-nine percent majority* (pp. 55-67). Reading, MA: Addison-Wesley.
Beneke, T. (1982). *Men on rape.* New York: St. Martin's Press.
Bradley, B. (1977). *Life on the run.* New York: Bantam.
Brittan, A. (1989). *Masculinity and power.* Oxford & New York: Basil Blackwell.
Bryson, L. (1987). Sport and the maintenance of masculine hegemony. *Women's Studies International Forum, 10,* 349-360.
Cancian, F. M. (1987). *Love in America: Gender and self-development.* Cambridge: Cambridge University Press.
Chodorow, N. (1978). *The reproduction of mothering.* Berkeley: University of California Press.
Connell, R. W. (1987). *Gender and power.* Palo Alto, CA: Stanford University Press.
Connell, R. W. (1990). An iron man: The body and some contradictions of hegemonic masculinity. In M. A. Messner & D. F. Sabo (Eds.), *Sport, men and the gender order: Critical feminist perspectives* (pp. 83-96). Champaign, IL: Human Kinetics.
Craib, I. (1987). Masculinity and male dominance. *The Sociological Review, 38,* 721-743.
Crosset, T. (1990). Masculinity, sexuality, and the development of early modern sport. In M. A. Messner & D. F. Sabo (Eds.), *Sport, men and the gender order: Critical feminist perspectives* (pp. 45-54). Champaign, IL: Human Kinetics.
Dinnerstein, D. (1976). *The mermaid and the Minotaur: Sexual arrangements and human malaise.* New York: Harper Colophon.
Duquin, M. (1984). Power and authority: Moral consensus and conformity in sport. *International Review for Sociology of Sport, 19,* 295-304.
Farrell, W. (1975). *The liberated man.* New York: Bantam.
Fasteau, M-F. (1974). *The male machine.* New York: McGraw-Hill.
Gilder, G. (1973). *Sexual suicide.* New York: Bantam.

Gilligan, C. (1982). *In a different voice: Psychological theory and women's development.* Cambridge, MA: Harvard University Press.

Hall, M. A. (1988). The discourse on gender and sport: From femininity to feminism. *Sociology of Sport Journal, 5,* 330-340.

Herman, D. (1984). The rape culture. In J. Freeman (Ed.), *Women: A feminist perspective* (3rd ed.) (pp. 20-38). Mountain View, CA: Mayfield.

James, C.R.L. (1983). *Beyond a boundary.* New York: Pantheon.

Johnson, M. M. (1988). *Strong mothers, weak wives: The search for gender equality.* Berkeley: University of California Press.

Kanin, E. J. (1984). Date rape: Differential sexual socialization and relative deprivation. *Victimology, 9,* 95-108.

Kidd, B. (1987). Sports and masculinity. In M. Kaufman (Ed.), *Beyond patriarchy: Essays by men on pleasure, power, and change* (pp. 250-265). Toronto: Oxford University Press.

Koss, M. P., & Dinero, T. E. (1988). Predictors of sexual aggression among a national sample of male college students. In R. A. Prentky & V. Quinsey (Eds.), *Human Sexual Aggression: Current Perspectives. Annals of the New York Academy of Sciences, 528,* 133-146.

Lasch, C. (1979). *The culture of narcissism.* New York: Warner.

Lyman, P. (1987). The fraternal bond as a joking relationship: A case study of sexist jokes in male group bonding. In M. S. Kimmel (Ed.), *Changing men: New directions in research on men and masculinity* (pp. 148-163). Newbury Park, CA: Sage.

McHugh, M. C., Duquin, M. E., & Frieze, I. H. (1978). Beliefs about success and failure: Attribution and the female athlete. In C. A. Oglesby (Ed.), *Women and sport: From myth to reality* (pp. 173-191). Philadelphia: Lea & Farber.

Messner, M. (1987). The meaning of success: The athletic experience and the development of male identity. In H. Brod (Ed.), *The making of masculinities: The new men's studies* (pp. 193-210). Boston: Allen & Unwin.

Messner, M. (1988). Sports and male domination: The female athlete as contested ideological terrain. *Sociology of Sport Journal, 5,* 197-211.

Messner, M. (1989). Masculinities and athletic careers. *Gender & Society, 3,* 71-88.

Messner, M. A., & Sabo, D. F. (Eds.). (1990). *Sport, men and the gender order: Critical feminist perspectives.* Champaign, IL: Human Kinetics.

Morin, S. F., & Garfinkel, E. M. (1978). Male homophobia. *Journal of Social Issues, 34*(1).

Mrozek, D. J. (1983). *Sport and the American mentality: 1880-1910.* Knoxville: University of Tennessee Press.

Pleck, J., & Sawyer, J. (Eds.). (1974). *Men and masculinity.* Englewood Cliffs, NJ: Prentice-Hall.

Pronger, B. (1990). Gay jocks: A phenomenology of gay men in athletics. In M. A. Messner & D. F. Sabo (Eds.), *Sport, men and the gender order: Critical feminist perspectives* (pp. 141-152). Champaign, IL: Human Kinetics.

Riesman, D. (1953). *The lonely crowd: A study of the changing American character.* New Haven: Yale University Press.

Rubin, L. B. (1983). *Intimate strangers: Men and women together.* New York: Harper & Row.

Rubin, L. B. (1985). *Just friends: The role of relationship in our lives.* New York: Harper & Row.

Sabo, D. (1985). Sport, patriarchy and male identity: New questions about men and sport. *Arena Review, 9,* 1-30.

Sabo, D. (1989, Winter/Spring). The myth of the sexual athlete. *Changing Men: Issues in Gender, Sex, and Politics, 20*, 38-39.

Sabo, D. F., & Panepinto, J. (1990). Football ritual and the social reproduction of masculinity. In M. A. Messner & D. F. Sabo (Eds.), *Sport, men and the gender order: Critical feminist perspectives* (pp. 115-126). Champaign, IL: Human Kinetics.

Swain, S. (1989). Covert intimacy: Closeness in men's friendships. In B. J. Risman & P. Schwartz (Eds.), *Gender in intimate relationships: A microstructural approach* (pp. 71-86). Belmont, CA: Wadsworth.

Theberge, N. (1981). A critique of critiques: Radical and feminist writings on sport. *Social Forces, 60*, 2.

Tiger, L. (1969). *Men in groups.* London: Nelson.

Warshaw, R. (1988). *I never called it rape.* New York: Harper & Row.

Williams, C. L. (1989). *Gender differences at work: Women and men in nontraditional occupations.* Berkeley: University of California Press.

Williams, W. L. (1986). *The spirit and the flesh: Sexual diversity in American Indian culture.* Boston: Beacon.

Index

Africa, 188
African-Americans. *See* Blacks
Age, 128, 150. *See also* Youth
Aggression, 67, 160, 208, 228
AIDS, 174, 198
Allan, G., 5, 72, 117, 175
Andalusia, 192
Asian. *See* Java
Athletes. *See* Sports

Beal, J. F., 35, 46-49, 52, 55
Berdache, 189, 190, 191
Blacks, 201-213, 221, 229
Bonding, 61, 228, 233. *See also* Solidarity
Boundaries, 145-146, 222

Chodorow, N., 20, 24, 33, 102, 216
Class, 17, 18, 19, 29, 36, 38-39, 42, 43, 44,
    45-49, 52, 55, 76, 118, 128-129, 179,
    201-213, 233, 235
Community, 74-104
Companionship, 91-96

Competition, 17, 18-19, 138-139, 199, 210,
    218-222

Emotional (female) vs. rational (male) ap-
    proach, 17-18, 22-24, 26, 27, 52, 66,
    72, 95-96, 98-99, 102, 104, 115, 134,
    155, 164, 169, 205, 210, 216, 222

Family, 115-130, 193, 198, 232. *See also*
    Relatives
Fatherhood, 115-130
Feminist, 30, 38, 41, 55, 102, 216-217,
    223, 232
Fraternal organizations, 41, 52, 71-72
Friendship, 1-3, 5, 18, 22, 162-163
    couples, 92-95
    men vs. women, 5-6, 23, 30, 36, 41, 101,
        116, 130, 133-134, 150, 155-158, 215-
        217, 223. *See also* Gender, Women
    men with women, 18, 49-51, 54, 80, 92,
        132-150, 153-170, 175, 181, 192. *See also*
        Gender, Women

239

About the Contributors

Theodore F. Cohen is an Associate Professor in the Sociology-Anthropology Department at Ohio Wesleyan University where he teaches a variety of courses, including The Family, Gender in American Society, and Masculinity and Men's Roles. He has authored papers on the impact of marriage and fatherhood on men and on men's attachments to work and family. He is starting a new interview project comparing the work and family lives of women and men in three different occupations. He received his Ph.D. in sociology from Boston University in 1986.

Gary Alan Fine is Professor of Sociology and head of the department at the University of Georgia. He received his Ph.D. in Social Psychology from Harvard University in 1976. He has taught at Boston College, Indiana University, University of Chicago, University of Bremen, and the University of Minnesota. Professor Fine's research focuses on the sociology of culture, particularly as culture is expressed through interaction and social structure. He is the author of *With the Boys: Little League Baseball and Preadolescent Culture*; *Shared Fantasy: Role Playing Games and Social Worlds*; and *Talking Sociology* (second edition). He is currently working on research on the organizational structure of the restaurant industry, the relationship of human beings to their natural environment, and the technique that adolescents use to persuade others.

Clyde W. Franklin II is Professor of Sociology at The Ohio State University in Columbus. He specializes in Social Psychology and Gender and has published numerous articles in social psychology, racial and ethnic relations, and gender. His more recent work has centered on issues related to black male sex roles and black female–black male relationships. He has published *Minority Group Relations* (with James G. Martin); *Theoretical Perspectives in Social Psychology: The Changing Definition of Masculinity*; and *Men and Society*. He serves on several academic editorial boards and is the editor for the *Journal of African American Male Studies*.

Karen V. Hansen teaches sociology and feminist theory at Brandeis University. As a Mellon Faculty Fellow and a Bunting Institute Fellow at Harvard/Radcliffe, she is writing a manuscript investigating community life of working men and women in antebellum New England. She edited, with Ilene Philipson, *Women, Class, and the Feminist Imagination*.

Michael A. Messner is Assistant Professor in the Department of Sociology and the Program for the Study of Women and Men in Society at the University of Southern California. He has published numerous articles on men and masculinity and on gender and sport. His current research interests include men and feminist politics and gender in sports media. He has co-edited two books, *Men's Lives* (with Michael S. Kimmel); and *Sport, Men, and the Gender Order: Critical Feminist Perspectives* (with Donald F. Sabo). His book, *Power at Play: Sports and the Problem of Masculinity,* is forthcoming from Beacon Press in 1992.

Peter M. Nardi is Professor of Sociology at Pitzer College, one of the Claremont Colleges located near Los Angeles. He completed his doctorate at the University of Pennsylvania and his undergraduate degree at the University of Notre Dame. He has published articles on men's friendships, AIDS, anti-gay hate crimes and violence, magic and magicians, and alcoholism and families. He has recently served as co-president of the Los Angeles chapter of the Gay & Lesbian Alliance Against Defamation (GLAAD).

Helen M. Reid is a doctoral candidate at Columbia University. Her primary areas of interest are inequality and heterogeneity in social structures at the macro, micro, and network levels of analysis. Her other research interests include the study of educational interventions in high school populations and the study of HIV and suicide prevention in adolescent populations.

Victor J. Seidler is a Senior Lecturer in Social Theory and Philosophy in the Department of Sociology, Goldsmiths' College, University of London. He is the author of *Rediscovering Masculinity: Reason, Language, and Sexuality*; *Recreating Sexual Politics: Men, Feminism, & Politics*; and editor of *The Achilles Heel Reader: Men, Sexual Politics, and Socialism*. His most recent work is *The Moral Limits of Modernity: Love, Inequality, & Oppression*. He is the editor of Routledge's *Male Orders* series, exploring how dominant forms of masculinity have helped shape prevailing forms of knowledge, culture, and experience.

Daphne Spain is an Associate Professor of Urban and Environmental Planning and Associate Dean of the School of Architecture at the University of Virginia. Her most recent book, *Gendered Spaces*, examines the relationship between gender segregation and women's status. She is also pursuing earlier interests in gentrification by examining parallels between urban and rural communities undergoing rapid change.

Scott O. Swain counsels and teaches at Las Lomas High School in the San Francisco Bay Area, following a year of postdoctoral training at the Wellesley College Center for Research on Women. After completing his undergraduate work in social science at the University of California, Berkeley, he counseled and taught high school students on the Hoopa Indian Reservation in Northern California. He returned to graduate school at the University of California, Irvine, and completed doctoral research on intimacy in men's same-sex friendships. His current research interests include the impact of the masculine role on homeless men and cyclical changes in gender role ideation.

Barry Wellman, raised in the Bronx, learned to appreciate public communities in schoolyards and on street corners as a member of the Fordham Flames. He developed social network approaches to the study of community in the 1960s at the Harvard Department of Social Relations. Building upon this interest, he founded the International Network for Social Network Analysis in 1976 and headed it for more than a decade. He co- edited *Social Structures: A Network Approach* (1988). For the past 20 years he has been studying the community that does exist in cities. He is currently Professor of Sociology at the Centre for Urban and Community Studies, University of Toronto.

Walter L. Williams is Associate Professor of Anthropology and the Study of Women and Men in Society at the University of Southern California. He received his Ph.D. from the University of North Carolina and has taught at the University of Cincinnati and at UCLA. His books include *Black Americans and the Evangelization of Africa*; *Southwestern Indians Since the Removal Era*; *Indian Leadership*; and his study of the berdache, *The Spirit and the Flesh: Sexual Diversity in American Indian culture*. In 1987-1988, he was a Fulbright Professor of American Studies at Gadjah Mada University in Indonesia. His most recent book is *Javanese Lives: Women and Men in Modern Indonesian Society*.